Manifesting Magnificence

Manifesting Magnificence

Consciously Creating the Life You Choose to Live

Using the unlimited, natural energy which flows through the universe, you can manifest magnificence into every thing you do.

A guide for everyday life

by

Andrew Lutts

Library of Congress Control Number: 2008907936
ISBN: Hardcover   978-1-4363-6754-7
                 Softcover   978-1-4363-6753-0

This book was printed in the United States of America.

To order additional copies of this book, contact:
Xlibris Corporation
1-888-795-4274
www.Xlibris.com
Orders@Xlibris.com
52968

CONTENTS

Energy In Action

Group Manifestation

Mastering Manifestation

SECTION 3
Higher Dimensional Living—Application of Concepts

Higher Dimensional Living

INDEX OF IMAGES

This book is dedicated to everyone on the spiritual path.
May your answers come to you in the right way, at the right time,
in a most perfect way, with ease and grace.

PREFACE

Consciously Creating the Life
You Choose to Live

The knowledge contained within this book has the power to change your life. Now is the time to learn the truth about yourself as a human being and the real powers you have inside you. It is time that this knowledge is returned to you. This book will help you remember how to:

1) Make use of the eternal laws of the universe that we are all subject to. Learn what these powerful laws are, and how to make them work for you in a step-by-step way.

2) Release issues of fear, control and limitation that are holding you back and are no longer serving your highest good.

3) Tap into the unlimited flow of universal life force energy as it moves through you, *energizing* and *electrifying* you, creating positive changes all around you.

4) Apply concepts of free will, consciously changing and improving your life in the ways that you want to.

5) Find love in your life and all the happiness it brings, as you awaken to a new source of unlimited universal life force energy.

6) Harness the power of the spoken word, as you command and declare changes in your life with supercharged affirmations.

7) Become completely at peace with yourself, and the world around you.

8) Reawaken to your divinity, and become a clear, conscious balanced human being with increased abilities.

9) Attract wonderful new people, situations, and opportunities to you.

10) Discover and accelerate your personal growth path. Graduate to your next level of personal growth.

11) Reduce unwanted lack, illness, and disease in your life. Create vibrant health, prosperity, relationships, and whatever else it is you want to manifest in your life.

12) Find love in yourself, and in that love know that you are never alone or unsupported.

13) Become one with Source, and fully understand what it really means to be connected to All That Is.

14) Use these ever-present natural energies in an unforced flowing way, knowing that they are based on scientific theories of quantum physics.

DEFINITIONS

Manifesting—To bring to light. Clearly apparent to the sight or understanding; obvious. To show or demonstrate plainly; reveal. To be evidence of; prove. To make evident or certain by showing or displaying. Common definition: To make happen, to bring about.

Magnificence—the quality of being magnificent or splendid or grand, greatness or lavishness of surroundings; splendor, grand or imposing beauty. Common definition: something great, wonderful.

Become A Master of Your Own Life

This book shows you how to create your life the way you want to live it by using a clear, easy to follow, step-by-step method. You do not need to understand advanced concepts of philosophy, psychology, science, spirituality, physics, metaphysics, or religion. Everyone can do it. This information is now available for all to use.

As you begin to apply these simple concepts to your everyday life, you will witness first-hand positive changes transforming your life. In fact, even without your doing anything consciously, things will change as you read this book. Just by reading, knowing, understanding and remembering this information, you will be different, and others will view you differently. They will view you differently and interact with you differently, because they will subconsciously be aware that you *know*.

You will *know* the truth about how the universe works, and how energy flowing through it can be guided for positive change in your life. Not only will you know, but you will be powerful, with the knowledge and ability to create and manifest the things, situations and opportunities that you really want in your life, the things that you really want to do, and the relationships that you really want to have. You will be a master of your own life, with the ability to *manifest magnificence.*

INTRODUCTION

This book came to be for two main reasons:

1) As my life has progressed I have carefully studied and watched the process of manifestation, and observed how some people seem to struggle with it while others manifest naturally and easily. I asked myself, why is this? I have applied manifesting concepts and theories in my own ways, in my own life. I have watched family, friends and others manifest in different ways with different results. I learned about the immense power of a strong and clear intention, learned about affirmations and visioning, and how our own beliefs affect our experiences and our reality.

2) About fifteen years ago I had a series of remarkable personal, transformative events occur in my life. And of those, probably the most significant was when I *woke up*. It was a somewhat traumatic event.

For a brief moment in time, which was actually an eternity, I was fully aware. I was fully conscious. I was completely at one with All That Is. I was shown everything in the universe for what it truly is. I saw angels, spirit guides, things from the past, and the wonders of space and time. I experienced the splendor of it all. And I saw God. And then, by divine design, I forgot it all. Oh my!

Well, not all of it. As the years have passed, I remember more and more of it each day. And I am bringing that knowledge of the ages back into our third dimension, back to humanity. And this is what I share with you in this book. Like you, I am on the path. And I know that together, we can explore the realms of science and spirit, and nature and love, in an attempt to integrate the knowledge of the ages into our daily lives.

Andrew Lutts
July 2008

15

ACKNOWLEDGEMENT

I would like to acknowledge the following people who assisted me with the manifestation of this book: Chris Cross, Judy Copp, Anne Kay, Ellen Mogensen, John Cali and my fellow metaphysical book group members including: Ron Kafker, Janet Hever, Heidi Lutts, Tony Reis, Amy Chevoor, Rory and Rena Goff, and many others over the years. Also many thanks to my fellow North Shore Writing Group members for their support and encouragement. I also thank Margaret, Josiah, Hajeep, Bruce, and the Council of Twelve Ancient of Days, for their divine guidance and inspiration. In many ways this book has been a co-creative effort, among many, as these people came forward to assist me with this undertaking, by helping me better understand and convey the true nature of reality and our place in it.

Editor—Kathleen Victory Hannisian (www.bluepencilconsulting.com)

Illustrator—Lisa Greenleaf (www.lisagreenleaf.com)

Cover Graphic Design—Laurie McAdams (www.northernmindcreative.com)

Author Photograph—Bobbie Bush Photography (www.bobbiebush.com)

Author Web Site—Intention.net (www.intention.net)

Affirmations Included in this Book

Throughout this book are various affirmations. They can be easily identified by the small capitals typeface. You may speak, write, rewrite, transcribe, edit, share, personalize and otherwise use these affirmations in any way you like for your own personal situation and benefit.

Note: Words synonymous with God when used to describe God and God-type energy are capitalized. These include Source, All That Is, Universal Life Force Energy, Infinite Intelligence, Creator, Goddess, Unity Consciousness, Eternal Wisdom, Great Spirit, the Light of All Light, and others.

Religion and Spirituality

Please know that this book discusses topics of metaphysics, religion and spirituality. However, know that all the strategies of manifestation discussed in this book work equally well with or without any personal spiritual or religious beliefs. This book was not written to "win you over" to any way of thinking, but to help you discover ways to manifest wonderful things, opportunities, and possibilities in your world.

AFFIRMATION: I NOW DECLARE THAT THE KNOWLEDGE CONTAINED IN THIS BOOK IS PROVIDED FOR AND SHARED WITH THE INTENTION OF THE GOOD OF ALL AND HARM OF NONE. — THE AUTHOR

CHAPTER 1

Understanding

*What you believe is what you get. You are only limited by
what you can think, and believe.*—Richard W. Lutts, Sr.

UNDERSTANDING MANIFESTATION AND THE POWER IT HOLDS

Simply put, manifestation is the ability to create. We all live in the third dimension, with physical energy, forces and matter. In this physical world, energies flow through and around us. By recognizing these energies and understanding the flow of energy, we can create and manifest in our world.

Many people wish to obtain physical things in the world, such as money, cars and houses. Certainly these things can be manifested, and this book shows you how to do it. But there are other things you can manifest too. You can manifest positive relationships, happiness, success, accomplishment, vibrant health, good luck, understanding, healing, love and anything else you can dream of. In fact you can literally manifest things and situations into your life that are so wonderful, they are truly *magnificent*.

THE PHYSICAL AND NON-PHYSICAL

Many things in our world are just outside our physical third dimensional world. These things can be considered metaphysical, or simply *beyond the physical*.

A few examples of some of these things which are just beyond the physical are gravity, magnetism, and radio waves. And although we cannot "see" these things, we know they exist, and trust that they are what we believe them to be. Conventional science tells us it is so. Other examples of things beyond the physical are human thoughts, human perceptions, and strong feelings for another person.

Taking this concept further, studies in quantum physics now support the existence of and interaction of additional metaphysical elements in our universe. (More in Chapter

7, Science and Quantum Physics). Understanding how the universe works is important in the manifestation process. Once you understand how the universe really works, you can use these universal laws to your benefit and manifest greatness into your life.

A NEW WAY TO VIEW THE WORLD

You have probably been taught your whole life that to make things happen, you should take an action. Certainly in the third dimension this is one of the most common ways to achieve a result. But there is a far better, quicker, easier, more natural and more effective way to make things happen. You can make full use of metaphysical principles to create change in your world. Not only are metaphysical methods of creation superior for bringing about change, they also often:

-   work better
-   work much more quickly
-   involve much less conscious effort
-   make use of all resources available
-   work perfectly, in the perfect way, at the perfect time

In a way, the difference between creating with traditional third dimensional methods and manifesting with metaphysical methods can be described as the difference between *sleepwalking* (and walking into walls) and being fully *awake* (and clearly seeing which doorways are open to you).

Many people know that our thoughts are linked to energy and that our thoughts and beliefs determine which form this energy takes. People use thought for purposes such as creativity, positive thinking, goal-setting, faith, healing, meditation, and prayer.

However, this book shows how you can even more consciously create and manifest in your life. By using the proven tools, methods, steps and strategies in this book, you will be consciously creating with your intentions.

Quantum physicists theorize that *your thoughts literally shift the universe on a particle-by-particle basis to create your physical life.* Look around you. Everything you see started as an idea, an idea that grew as it was shared and expressed, until it grew enough into a physical object through any number of "manufacturing" or "growth" steps.

Sometimes we can physically "see" ourselves create right before our eyes, as we literally create something from nothing:

1) Plant a garden, and watch it grow
2) Organize a group
3) Buy a piece of land and build a house on it

4) Start a business

5) Start a family

These things are created from nothing, just an idea! In fact, you literally become what you think about most. Your life becomes what you imagine and believe in most. What you dwell upon becomes your reality. The world is literally your mirror, enabling you to experience in the physical plane what you hold as your truth, until you change it.

For example, if you say to yourself, "I could never be rich," then you are expressing that feeling and personal belief out into the world. And in dwelling on that expression of limitation, it becomes your reality.

> I NOW OPEN MY HEART AND MIND TO ALL THE POSSIBILITIES IN THE UNIVERSE. I AM NOW OPEN TO SEEING THE UNIVERSE IN A WHOLE NEW WAY.

COMMON PROBLEMS, CHALLENGES AND OPPORTUNITIES

Energies around us manifest in various ways. This is a result of the natural order of the universe. It is also because people are energy, and attract energy toward them. Depending on your energy, you will attract different people and things into your life. Some of these things are great and wonderful, other things are less desirable. People attract different things to themselves for different reasons, and often don't even realize what they are attracting.

For example, have you ever known anyone who liked to fight, and likes an argument? They will attract people to them who like a conflict, too. In fact, on a larger scale, they may find themselves fighting city hall, the legal system, schools, companies, and the federal government. This is the way they work, attracting the energy of conflict to them. The more they want to fight, the bigger the adversary they will find (or will find them). The universe will always find you a worthy opponent, if you really want one.

Conversely, other people will attract positive, harmonious things. Have you ever known someone who is always positive, and always feeling great? These types of people are attracting positive things and events to them.

When you are perfectly in balance and in right way with the world, things manifest effortlessly. Conversely, when things in your life are not occurring as they should, it may be because you are a bit out of balance.

Here is a long list of many of the issues, problems, concerns, and difficulties which many people encounter at some time in their lives. See if any of these challenges are creating an opportunity for you to put yourself back into balance, in order to help you better manifest in your world.

THE CHART OF EXPRESSIONS SEEKING BALANCE

EXPRESSION WHEN OUT OF BALANCE	EXPRESSION WHEN IN BALANCE
lack of abundance	abundance and prosperity
problems trusting others, distrust	complete trust and faith, understanding, openness
discordant, unhappy, incomplete relationships	harmonious, lively, active, dynamic relationships
low self-esteem	acceptance of self, love in action, understanding unconditional love
difficulty expressing feelings	speaking your truth, opening to truth, centered and balanced, expressive
fearful, anticipating the worst	trusting
lack of personal power, personally powerless	unlimited personal power, confidence in abilities
feelings of no control, fear of the future	free will choice, allowing perfection to unfold
victim mentality	personal responsibility
always putting oneself first, selfishness, greed, gluttony	sharing and co-creation, understanding unlimited resources in the universe
lack of safety	safe in self, at ease and safe in environment
inadequate personal boundaries	understanding and utilizing your boundaries
cultural diversity problems	acceptance and tolerance, honoring others for who they are
feelings of loneliness, not comfortable being alone	comfortable with oneself, experiencing unity, at one with Source
a sense of abandonment, left behind	one with the universe and oneself, love and self acceptance, connection to Source
feeling a lack of respect from others	self-worth, self love
attracting conflict, fighting	sharing, acceptance, loving
envy, jealousy	understanding that you can create for yourself
wanting something badly, impatience	allowing the universe to provide appropriately
fear of intimacy and bonding	community, one mind, group consciousness
unable to forgive, unable to release and let go	complete and unconditional forgiveness, unconditional love

BELIEVING IT CAN BE

You can be, do and create anything you want in your life. Has anyone ever told you this truth? Do you believe it, really? You are only limited by what you *believe* you can do. It is the law of the universe. All you need to do is read the first page, take the first step, or climb the first mountain. For once the momentum has begun, not even an army can stop it. Remember, you have the universe on your side!

Here's an example: My good friend Michael was looking to buy or build a house in the old neighborhood where we grew up. It was a fairly developed area, with not many vacant lots left to build on. However, one day we were out in a boat and spotted an empty lot of land adjacent to a former neighbor of his. It looked like it would make a great location for a new house. Not only that, but it was waterfront property. I asked him about it, because it seemed perfect for him.

"It's an un-buildable lot," Michael replied. "The lot is too small, plus there is something wrong with it. Not exactly sure what, but I know you just can't build a house there. It's un-buildable! That's why that lot has been empty for many years," he said with some measure of authority. Even further prodding by me could not convince Michael that the lot we were looking at was almost ideal for him for many reasons, and that it might be worth looking into.

Well, I think you can guess the rest of the story. Sure enough, the next summer, there was a beautiful, modern home built right on that house lot, just the kind of house Michael would have built if only he had believed it could be done.

Do you have any "beliefs" like my friend's that you just *know* to be true? Are they holding you back, and limiting the opportunities available to you? Do you have any beliefs like "I could never do that," or that something "just can't be done?"

> I NOW RELEASE ALL FEARS, DOUBTS AND LIMITATIONS. I NOW REMAIN
> OPEN TO ALL POSSIBILITIES. I TRUST IN THE DIVINE TO HELP ME SEE
> ALL THE OPPORTUNITIES AVAILABLE TO ME.

THE POWER TO MANIFEST

If we think in philosophical and esoteric terms, realize that money is not required to survive. What is actually required to survive is to manifest what is desired. Remember that as you co-create in partnership with Source, anything is possible.

Say what you really want is a house. Focus on the house, not the money needed to buy it. The universe can find all sorts of ways, unimagined by you and me, to get you a house.

For example, you could:

- inherit a house
- assume someone's mortgage on their house
- find a partner to co-create a house
- go live with someone who has a house
- house-sit for someone who is away for several years
- care for someone in a house
- marry someone who owns a house
- get a job promotion and transfer which includes housing
- win a house in a contest
- live in a house while working on it
- qualify for a house under a special grant
- have your existing apartment turned into a house
- receive an unexpected gift to help pay for a house

and all sorts of other ways that might surprise you. There are *no limits* as to how this house can come into your life.

It is far better to focus on the *end result*. After all, that's what you really want anyway! Don't necessarily try to manifest the means (for example, money), ask directly for what you want. Let the universe figure out how it will get delivered to you. This will give you a great advantage when manifesting.

THE ENERGY OF YOUR THOUGHTS

The process of intention as it affects manifestation can be illustrated by a helium balloon. When you first fill up a helium balloon, it is ready to fly. In this example, the balloon is your intention. Once the balloon is let go, it begins to rise. You are happily on your way in the manifestation process.

But wait. As time passes, you have a second thought. Perhaps you aren't sure. Doubt comes in. And in allowing doubt to enter your thoughts, you tug downward on that string of the helium balloon. "Yes, that feels a bit better. Slow it down. Come back a bit, that seems safer," you say to yourself.

But in doing so you are slowing your manifestation, and now you come to realize that. So you clear yourself of doubt, and your balloon starts to rise again.

But wait, you are a bit afraid now. You've never really done this before, have you? And with the fear and self-doubt comes another tug on the balloon string, and it comes back down a bit.

"Okay, enough of this nonsense," you admit. And you let the balloon rise again, and begin to soar toward your intention.

So, with this up-and-down process, releasing and returning, allowing then pulling back, you are sending out a type of sine wave, energetically.

an oscillating sine wave
Verbal expression: "I don't know, I'm not sure about it, I could go either way"

This kind of up-and-down wave will slow and delay manifestation. This happens when you are unclear, unsure, or uncommitted to your intention. A wavering, unclear thought projection will bring about haphazard results due to lack of clarity. Far more ideal is a steady, straight line of intention, with a clear focus. To achieve this superior way of thought projection, do not waver with your intention and conviction.

---

straight line image thought projection
Verbal expression: "I know exactly what I want"

AFFIRMATIONS

I NOW OPEN TO A WHOLE NEW WAY TO VIEW THE WORLD. I NOW BRING IN NEW INFORMATION AND AWARENESS TO MY BEING, AND I NOW RELATE TO THE WORLD IN AN EXCITING NEW WAY.

HIGHER LEVELS OF WISDOM, KNOWLEDGE AND UNDERSTANDING NOW COME TO ME. I NOW INTEGRATE THIS NEW INFORMATION INTO MY BEING FOR MY HIGHEST GOOD.

QUESTIONS AND ANSWERS

Q. I'm not quite sure I believe all this. Is it really true that I can manifest what I really want?

A. Yes. Very much so! Probably the best way to see that these methods work is to try out a few of the ideas in the Manifesting Worksheets at the end of each chapter. See what happens, and decide for yourself!

Q. How come everyone doesn't know about this?
A. Our third dimensional world draws us into the illusion of limits and a finite world. The truth is that our universe is unlimited, and that there is much more to life than what can be seen. This book explains these universal concepts.

Q. This all seems too good to be true, Pollyanna-ish, and airy-fairy. How is it possible to do all these things you claim?
A. Read on, and find out!

CHAPTER SUMMARY

1) By understanding and using the flow of energy, you can manifest in your world.
2) Manifesting can include both physical and non-physical things.
3) You can manifest using the energy available from the world beyond the physical.
4) Understanding how the universe works helps make the manifestation process easier.
5) You can consciously create with your intentions.
6) Your thoughts literally shift the universe to create your physical, emotional and spiritual life experiences.
7) What you dwell upon becomes your reality.
8) Decisions made in every moment of every day greatly affect your life.
9) You attract to you the same kind of energy that you project out.
10) Challenges in your life right now are expressions that are out of balance, and seek to be put back into balance.
11) You are only limited by what you believe.
12) Focus on the end result, not necessarily on how to get it.
13) A clear, steady, straight unwavering intention helps facilitate manifestation.

MANIFESTING WORKSHEET

If you had a magic wand and could create anything you want in life, list three things that you would manifest right now (these can be both physical and non-physical):

1) _____
2) _____
3) _____

Extra Credit—Here are some ideas and sample intentions to practice your skills at manifesting. Try one of the following:

1) You are going into town and would like a convenient parking space at or near your destination. As you leave your house broadcast out to the universe that you would like a nice spot to park right out front of your destination. (However, of course, if an elderly, handicapped, or person with a small child also needs a parking spot, you gladly offer it to them.)

2) You have been trying to get in touch with someone but continue to miss them. Next time it is convenient for you, put out into the universe that it is a good time for that person to contact you. Imagine them picking up their telephone to call you.

3) You are trying to get something done, and need help. Visualize someone coming to you and offering assistance with your project, just at the right time.

CHAPTER 2

Developing Your Personal Power

"One school is finished, and the time has come for another to begin."
—Richard Bach

DEVELOP YOUR PERSONAL POWER

In developing your ability to manifest magnificence in your life, you will simultaneously attain personal power. One of those powers is the power to create. We are creators and co-creators, and with that we have the power to change our world. When we work alone we have personal power. When we gather together in groups we have a collective force with capabilities for group manifestation.

WAKING UP TO YOUR PERSONAL POWER

Some people use the terms *asleep* and *awake* to describe the current state of consciousness of a person at any particular moment. Most of us go back and forth from time to time from being asleep or awake. Here are some definitions.

Those moments when you are *asleep* are those times you are focusing on primarily third dimensional issues, and you are involved with the day-to-day processes of making a living, competing for resources, and performing other daily tasks. We all do this. In this state, you focus on doing things and taking action to bring about results. Being asleep at any given moment suggests that you are not necessarily asking for help from the spiritual and metaphysical worlds, in a conscious way.

In times in which you are *awake,* you have "woken up" to the world of life beyond the third dimension. It means that you have acknowledged your divinity and connectedness to Source. Being awake means you are open to spiritual guidance, that you begin to feel Spirit. It means that you are now viewing the world in a holistic way, reserving judgment of people, *knowing that all is part of the plan, in its perfection.*

Being awake allows you to view the world in a more conscious, compassionate and understanding way.

For example, say you are at a stoplight in your car, and the traffic light then turns green. The driver in the car in front of you seems distracted, not paying attention, looking out the side window in a daze. You are in a hurry, and lean on your car horn and yell out a few choice words. You are unaware that this man is driving home from the cemetery where his wife was buried the day before.

When you are awake, you can often see deeper into the reality of a situation, and can see things more for what they truly are, or may be. It allows for additional levels of compassion. In times when you are awake you often realize that there is a *reason* beneath the surface of what appears to be what is real. You exhibit a bit more patience and compassion for your fellow human beings.

Waking up can be a very dramatic and enlightening time in a person's life. It can cause people to suddenly and dramatically change jobs, careers, relationships, living arrangements, priorities and personal goals. Generally speaking, waking up helps you develop, remember and reclaim your personal power. It also allows for keen insight. Where perhaps once you did not fully understand a situation, you are able to see clearly through other people's smokescreens and half-truths. One of the strongest personal powers that you develop upon waking up is increased *awareness*. Find below some factors which may trigger "waking up."

WAYS AND REASONS PEOPLE WAKE UP

1) Encountering nature, finding spirit in nature, seeing the energy of living things in nature, being overcome by nature
2) Meeting a guru or spiritual leader, Buddha, priest, rabbi, gifted healer, etc.
3) Becoming sick of a job or relationship, time to get out, crisis event
4) Losing a loved one
5) Going through a crisis in the family unit and re-prioritizing what is important in life
6) Surviving a near-death experience, auto accident, choking, near drowning, loss of consciousness, etc.
7) Acquiring a sudden unexplainable interest in spiritual or religious matters
8) Aging, getting older
9) Giving up control, putting one's faith in Spirit completely
10) Having an out of body experience, astral travel
11) Reading a book or seeing a movie that is transformative
12) Reaching your time to "graduate" to the next step in your personal growth

13) Having a striking premonition, prophesy, or psychic feeling which comes true
14) Experiencing a devastating natural disaster
15) Witnessing a sighting of a spirit entity (ghost), UFO, or other phenomena
16) Being told that you have only a certain amount of time left to live
17) Reaching a time in your life that you had previously agreed would be the time for your awakening
18) Making a conscious intention to manifest awakening

Realize, however, that you do not have to create a traumatic life-changing event to wake up. You do not need to bring about an automobile accident to "get the message." It can be a gradual process, with little fanfare, and lots of ease and grace.

If you feel ready for change or if you are feeling "stuck" or going nowhere, you can ask to accelerate your awakening and personal growth. Affirm the following if you like:

> I NOW CHOOSE AN ACCELERATED GROWTH PATH, AND GROW QUICKLY
> AND CORRECTLY IN ACCORDANCE WITH MY LIFE PLAN. I AM NOW READY
> FOR MY NEXT LEVEL OF AWAKENING, LEARNING AND GROWTH.

Some people wake up gradually, or go back and forth between being awake and asleep. This is because the world simply draws us back into the illusion, when daily activities and stresses bring us back to third dimension issues. Regular meditation is probably the best tool for staying awake.

HOW I WOKE UP

For me, I woke up suddenly and abruptly. Here's how it happened. While walking out in nature, while still in sight of my home, I experienced a dimensional shift of sorts. I astrally traveled to a place not of our third dimension. I journeyed through a kind of dimensional portal in which time and space as we know it did not exist. My journey was brief. It lasted just a few moments. And yet it lasted a lifetime. It was infinite. No time. Timeless.

During that experience, my reality shifted. And all sorts of things were shown to me. This awakening brought me to a place of knowing. I truly understood that we are all one, and that we are all connected. I came to know the eternal nature of our soul. I came to know that love is the energetic fabric that ties us all together. I came to know the Universal Spirit. And I came to know that we all have many from the other side helping, guiding and assisting us as we go through life.

And when my journey was complete, and I returned to the physical plane of our third dimension and back to my physical environment, I was forever changed.

AN UNLIMITED UNIVERSE

One of the universal laws we live under (see Chapter #6 on Universal Laws and Truths) speaks about unlimited resources. Everything in our world is made up of energy. And our universe is continually expanding. Our universe, as one big expanding void of darkness and stillness, is ready and waiting for you to create, manifest, and use its energy as you see fit.

If you accept the false belief that resources are limited, then you accept that someone or something can have a certain level of control over you. When you come to understand that our world has unlimited energy, then you realize that you have complete control over your life and your situation.

> I NOW LOOK TO THE UNLIMITED SOURCES OF THE UNIVERSE TO PROVIDE FOR ME IN GREAT SUPPLY. I DO NOT DEPEND ON PERSONS OR CONDITIONS FOR MY ABUNDANCE. THE UNIVERSE IS UNLIMITED, AND IS MY SOURCE OF ABUNDANCE AND CREATION.

BALANCING MASCULINE AND FEMININE ENERGY

Energetically, manifestation can be thought of in terms of a mix of both masculine and feminine energy. However, this has little to do with gender.

The feminine energy is said to be the creator of the dream. The masculine energy is the energy that manifests it. They are both critical to manifestation. By accessing both the yin / yang feminine and masculine energies at the same time, you rise up to a greater and even more powerful sum of the two separate elements. By accessing this combined energetic feeling, you are accessing your personal power and are able to manifest more easily.

Try to think about yourself, and your own strengths. Are you good with ideas, concepts, dreams, visions, and future plans? If so, you have strong female (creator) energy. Are you an action-oriented, get it done, driven type of person? If so, then you possess strong masculine action energy. By being aware of and applying a mixture of both the feminine and masculine aspects that we all have, you can better manifest and create positive change in your life.

MAKING A COMMITMENT TO YOURSELF

It is important that you make a commitment to yourself. This is not being selfish; it is honoring your truth. If you do not honor yourself and make a commitment to yourself, you will be at the wish and whim of others around you. You will be directionless. Your life will be like a beach ball on a windy day, being tossed about here and there, from one place to another. If you do not consciously try to go your own direction, you will be like a rudderless ship on the ocean, pushed about by wind, waves and tides, not having any true sense of direction or purpose. In fact, without any clear sense of direction, the winds and tides of life will steer you onto the rocks, serving as a harsh wake-up call for you to take some action and get back onto your correct path.

Evidence of this may be if one day you wake up and find yourself:

- in a job that you do not like
- in a relationship which is no longer fulfilling
- in a city that you wonder how you arrived there
- with friends who do not support you

If this is how you view yourself, it's time to change. It's time to put your priorities first. Your personal journey is yours alone. If you haven't done so already, it may be time to cast off the lines securing you to the shore, and sail out into a world of hope and adventure. It's time to *trust* that the journey will go well. It's time to *believe* in yourself. It's time to *activate* your personal power.

AFFIRMATIONS

I AM NOW COMMITTED TO MY HIGHEST PURPOSE. IT IS MY FIRST PRIORITY. I MAKE A PLEDGE TO HONOR MYSELF AND MY WORK, NOW AND ALWAYS.

I NOW GROW IN BODY, MIND AND SPIRIT. I NOW OPEN UP TO AN EXPANDED WAY OF KNOWING, LOVING AND BEING.

MY TEACHERS, GUIDES, AND SPIRITUAL MASTERS ARE NOW WITH ME. WITH THEIR GUIDANCE, I NOW PROCEED WITH MY NEXT LEVEL OF LEARNING.

QUESTIONS AND ANSWERS

Q. I think I am more asleep than awake. Yet I feel perfectly fine, I think. Will I wake up? Do I really need to wake up?
A. Trust that everything in your life is unfolding naturally and completely, with divine timing. But if you want to speed things up and grow to your next level, you can do so. Just ask! Affirm changes and growth for yourself. Study the universal laws in this book, as well as the steps to manifestation. These things will help you create change in your life. Create an intention to awaken and grow, in order to manifest it.

Q. How can I make a commitment to myself, when I have so much going on in my life? I am a parent, spouse, child, student, employee, and more. Are you saying I should put myself first?

A. Yes! Absolutely. Because you have so many roles and influence so many people, it is vitally important that you commit to yourself and become balanced, centered, and in alignment with your highest potential. By growing and helping yourself first, you are helping all those around you who rely on you so much.

Q. Isn't this whole manifesting thing a bit selfish?

A. Yes, of course! And why shouldn't you receive everything you want in life, and more? The fact is that you are supremely deserving, and the gifts of the universe are ready and waiting to come into your life once you allow them to. Remember, only if you buy into the false belief that the universe has limits would you want anything less than what you desire in life.

CHAPTER SUMMARY

1) By consciously manifesting, you make use of your personal power.
2) When you are awake and aware, you can see deeper into the reality of a situation.
3) Waking up can help you view your personal situation, your life, and your place in the world for what it truly is.
4) Waking up can be dramatic, enlightening, and life changing.
5) The universe is unlimited, and is continually expanding.
6) Manifesting often includes a combination of both feminine and masculine types of energy.
7) You can accelerate your personal growth by simply asking and intending to grow.
8) It is important to make a commitment to yourself, and honor your truth.
9) By putting yourself first and committing to yourself, you are helping those around you who rely on you.

MANIFESTING WORKSHEET

List three ways in which you are giving up your personal power to others in unhealthy ways in unhealthy situations (examples: over-commitment, unbalanced relationships, not speaking your truth, saying yes when you mean no).

1) _____
2) _____
3) _____

Now list three ways in which you can reclaim your power which is rightfully yours (examples: speak your truth and stand behind it, call someone on their "stuff," be true to yourself, do what you want to do).

1) _____

2) _____

3) _____

Extra Credit:

If you feel that, no matter where you are in your own personal growth right now, that you would like to grow and expand to a higher state, use this powerful affirmation to affect that change:

> I NOW CHOOSE AN ACCELERATED GROWTH PATH, AND GROW QUICKLY
> AND CORRECTLY IN ACCORDANCE WITH MY LIFE PLAN. I AM NOW READY
> FOR MY NEXT LEVEL OF AWAKENING, LEARNING AND GROWTH.

REFERENCES

1. Quote from Richard Bach, *Jonathan Livingston Seagull: A Story*, (The Macmillian Company, 1970), p. 47.

CHAPTER 3

Personal Responsibility

"Make It So"—Captain Jean Luc Picard, "Star Trek: The Next Generation"

BEING RESPONSIBLE

As a result of living in the third dimension and physically "watching" the way things appear to happen, people have a somewhat confused view of the world. This is because sometimes things are not always what they appear to be.

Many people think, more often than not, that things "just happen" in the world. As a result, they think that they are simply a victim of circumstances. Simply put, people are all too willing to blame *someone else* for their troubles, challenges or difficulties, thus shifting the blame or responsibility outside of themselves.

Well, the truth of the matter is that things do not just happen. We make them happen. We cause them to occur. And even when it appears that it is not something we could possibly have chosen, we have.

Many people simply don't believe that they are the source of their own problems. It is so much easier to pass it on to someone else, blame it on random events, or write it off as bad luck rather than take responsibility. However, if you choose to be a victim, you are in fact choosing to give away your power. In giving away your personal power, you are choosing to give away your power of manifestation.

If you can view your situation in a different way, that of being responsible for your life, you come from a place of power. It is far better to take full responsibility for creating the world around you, and all the ramifications of your creations (both positive and negative). It is refreshing to assume responsibility for everything around you. It is empowering. In fact, *everything* in your life is something that you brought into your life, and attracted to you.

Placing the blame or judgment on someone else leaves you powerless to change your experience; taking responsibility for your beliefs and judgments gives you the power to change them.—Byron Katie

TAKING PERSONAL RESPONSIBILITY FOR YOUR CREATIONS

One of the things to be aware of when you manifest something is that you are creating. And when you create you are responsible for the creation. Be mindful of what it means to be personally responsible for those creations. Depending on what you create, this can be a great personal responsibility.

- If you and a partner decide to become pregnant and bring a child into the world, you are both responsible for this creation of life.
- If you hire a new employee at your job, you are responsible to do your best to help that person succeed in their job.
- If you agree to meet someone at a certain time or place, and they are relying on you to be there, you should be there.
- If you are giving important advice to someone, you are responsible to do the best you can with your advice and guidance.

You are personally responsible for things you choose to do, and things that you choose not to do. This is a free will planet and you have the ability to decide to do or not to do everything. In fact, there is no control over you. Everything you are experiencing is something that you have chosen. Everything you intend and create has an impact on you and those around you. It is only when you give away your power to others that you allow them to exercise their free will over your free will.

I NOW RECLAIM MY LIFE, MY DIRECTION, MY PATH, AND MY GOALS.
SPIRIT NOW GUIDES ME AS I LEARN AND GROW.

TAKING PERSONAL RESPONSIBILITY FOR LONELINESS AND SEPARATION

Knowing that we are fully responsible for the situations we find ourselves in, and subsequently how we feel about it, we can more accurately understand various feelings we have as humans. Loneliness is a common feeling people experience.

There are two main reasons that people feel lonely. One is a lack of self love. The other is feeling separated from Source.

Self Love: If you can love yourself unconditionally, you will never feel a lack of love. When you love yourself unconditionally, your light and love vibrates out a warm and genuine love energy that attracts others to you. If you can take personal responsibility for your loneliness, you can also take the steps to overcome it, and fill your world up with loving, caring people.

Connection to Source: People feel lonely when they feel they are separated from Source. Know that you are never truly separated from Source. This is because we are all one. If one feels connected to Source then one is *never* alone. If you feel lonely or separate from Source, turn your yearning inward. Go back to your self. Open to your own divine love that resides within, and let it fill you. This is true love.

If you rely on *anything* or *anyone* outside yourself to give you love, it will never be enough. This can create a neediness in relationships. Any time in which you feel you need love, then do the loving yourself. When you express love through service, volunteer work, or reaching out to a friend, your love expressed will bring love back to you.

TAKING PERSONAL RESPONSIBILITY FOR INACTION

Just as creating something from nothing takes a decision, the decision to *not* do something or *not* to take action is also a decision. The world is full of people paralyzed and afraid to take action on anything. If they understand that they have no one to blame but themselves for situations or difficulties that they find themselves in, then they can accept responsibility and be empowered by it.

If you witness an accident or see someone who needs help, and you choose not to render assistance, you have made a choice. How does that make you feel?

Many people in the world do not have a clear direction, path or goals. The result is that they are affected and influenced by people around them who *do* have a clear intention. Thus, the people with no plan end up contributing to other people's manifestations and co-creative efforts. There is no judgment of this. However, if you are unhappy with the "way things are," you need to accept responsibility for your situation and inaction.

RECLAIMING YOUR LIFE

Today, there are many technological communications methods to steal you away from the moment (your moment!). Your cell phone rings, emails come in, you get instant messages, alarms and pagers go off, you hear a news story on the radio, and the television plays everywhere you go. In fact, it is becoming harder and harder to disconnect from the information-rich world. Sometimes you will even hear the same news story several times in one day through several different sources. As a result, we now know every "important" event in the world in a matter of minutes, even if it is occurring thousands of miles away, on the other side of the planet, with no direct connection to our own lives.

We all suffer greatly from information overload when it takes us out of living in the moment. And that makes it harder to find your power center. How can you relax, unwind, and go deep within yourself when you are in constant contact with everyone around you?

Make an effort to make time for yourself. Time in which you cannot be disturbed. Time in which you can reconnect with your essential nature. Time in which you can commune with the outdoors and nature. Time in which you can be fully present and in the moment. Time in which you can communicate with your higher self. (Your higher self can be described as a spirit-like part of you that is highly evolved. It is also sometimes called the oversoul, inner-being, inner-self, expanded self, or soul essence. It is the sum of all your lifetimes, past, present, future.)

You have a higher self who is very wise and is with you at all times.

LIVING IN THE MOMENT

A Warrior Mantra

> I have no future
> I have no past
> My goal is to make the present last
> I am in the now

Have you heard that it's best to live in the moment? Why is that? What's wrong with thinking about the past, or planning for the future?

Living in the moment allows you to access all of the power, immediacy and passion of the present. Living in the moment connects you with All That Is. Living in the moment is living truthfully, and not in some state of reflection on the past, or a fantasy of the future.

Living in the moment is about loving yourself, and doing what is right for you in each moment of every day. When confronted with a question or decision, ask yourself a few questions: Is this right for me or not? Is this loving for me or not? Is this the most loving thing for myself?

Many people, rather than living in the moment, live by emotion. Normally these emotional energies are from the lower chakras such as greed, fear, jealousy, and other more primary survival emotions. (A chakra is an energy node in the human body. There are believed to be seven chakras of spiritual energy in the human body which go up the spinal column from the base of the spine to the top of the head.)

The other thing people do rather than live in the moment is to live by societal expectations. Are you making certain choices because they are what society would look well upon, or because they are the right decision for you?

If you can live truthfully in the moment, then you have given yourself a great gift. Focus on the present moment and your surroundings as you directly experience them. Release distractions. Enjoy the bliss of being fully present. Engaging your senses and becoming hyper-aware of your surroundings and how your senses observe and experience your surroundings can help you live in the moment. Here are some ideas on how to reconnect with yourself:

- take a short walk or hike out into nature
- draw a picture, write a poem or verse

- listen to relaxing or inspirational music
- meditate
- sing, hum, whistle, or play an instrument
- light a candle or build a fire in the fireplace
- receive bodywork, massage, or energy healing
- turn off the TV, radio, computer, portable devices, video games, etc.

Also, remember that when you are in the company of other people, the best gift you can give to them is your full attention. Be *fully in the moment* when in the presence of others. When others are speaking, listen carefully to what they are saying to you. Listen with your heart to the meaning behind the words. Try not to be racing ahead with your mind with what you are going to be saying back to them. Be fully in the moment with them by connecting with them not just with your mind, but also with your eyes and especially your heart. This gift of presence is healing, especially if it contains unconditional love.

GUIDING YOUR DOMINANT THOUGHTS

When you focus on something long enough, it becomes a dominant thought. This is good, assuming that it is something desirable that you wish to bring into your life.

Have you ever considered buying a certain kind of car, or perhaps purchased a certain make of car, and then all of a sudden you begin to see them *everywhere?* This is because your dominant thought has become that kind of automobile, and they now come into your awareness much more. Another example is numbers or a series of numbers. For those inclined to see things that way, you may suddenly begin to see a certain series of numbers seemingly everywhere.

Make sure that your dominant thoughts are positive ones. For example, if you worry constantly that you will be robbed, you put that unconscious thought out into the universe and thus attract that possibility to you.

An example of this is if you are a bit afraid of dogs. If you walk by a house and the dog out front senses your fear, he will bark at you and chase you. But if the dog senses that you are strong and confident, he will be much less likely to bark at you. Your dominant thought while walking by the dog will help determine the dog's response to you.

One way to guide your dominant thoughts is to carefully pay attention to how you receive information. You may find that after a time, you cannot easily watch some violent television shows, read certain newspapers, or listen to radio news or talk shows. It causes too much discomfort for you. There is just too much reporting of violence, murder, and suffering. The sounds of gunshots and screeching tires, images of blood and gore, and stories of deceit and malevolence are just too unsettling for you.

The reason for the discomfort within you is that the energy of these things is just too low. You are now in a higher place. Your vibration is higher now. You've changed! But sometimes it can make it hard when the lower energies around you seem to be everywhere.

You do not need to buy into the mass mind, group consciousness, or someone else's concept of reality. It may be theirs, but it certainly does not have to be yours. Refuse to allow negative thoughts and people to affect your life. Make clear boundaries.

Strive to surround yourself with positive dominant thoughts including peace, serenity, empowerment, compassion, and love. Strive to surround yourself with people who support you and your highest path. Surround yourself with inspirational music, artwork, paintings, books and more. Focus on ideas, topics and conversations that inspire you, uplift you, and challenge you to explore the highest expression of your being. Engage in activities that help you grow as a person, and expand your relationship with your higher self.

Most importantly, connect with your higher self through quiet time or meditation each day. When you are filled with positive thoughts from your higher consciousness, lower thoughts cannot enter. Two thoughts cannot occupy the same space. Thus, keep filling yourself with positive things and over time, you will actually repattern your mind, making optimism and peace your new "norm."

DO IT OR DO NOT

"Do or do not, there is no try"—Yoda, "Star Wars"

Much of the effort in accomplishing something is getting it started. There can be so many reasons, both good and bad, why something takes time to get started. But sooner or later a decision must be made. Do it or do not!

And when you take responsibility and choose to do it, you are not alone. It may feel that way at first, but know that you have many angels, spirit guides, teachers and others in the world of the unseen who would help you get started, work with you, help arrange coincidences, and help see you through to your intended result. And in knowing that, feel confident about getting it started.

The first way to put inertia, the tendency of a body in motion to stay in motion, to work for you is to get a project started. For some people this can be a big challenge. But start you must.

I NOW STEP FORWARD BOLDLY. I NOW REASSUME MY ROLE AS CREATOR.

The other way inertia can come into play is the effort you make to keep a project going. Sometimes you are thrown curve balls, given hurdles, and presented with delays. Again however, remember that you literally have many in both the physical world and the spirit world who are assisting you every step of the way. *As long as your intention is strong,* people will come into your life to support you.

No matter how greatly you wish to manifest, your first steps may be small. Be sure to take that first step, even if it is small and modest. You are not settling for less. In fact, it is just the opposite. You are starting out on something grand, great, and wonderful.

As you create, realize that you will benefit from the unforeseeable, unknowable, and incalculable. You have *no idea* how grand and great your manifestation may grow to be. You have *no idea* of the lives you will touch, the people you will assist, and the positive effect you will have on those around you, and the other people around them. When you begin, you set waves in motion that will be felt by others you may never meet in places you may never go.

Of course the history books are full of people famous for great inventions, cures for life-threatening disease, and heroic acts of leadership and inspiration. But there are millions more examples of ordinary people who made an extra effort to make their world better with simply a kind word, reassuring gesture, or simple act. What will you do?

APPROPRIATE USE OF WILL

It's important to use powers of intentional manifestation appropriately. These methods work, and work powerfully.

When creating and formulating your intentions, ask yourself a series of questions about who your intention will affect. Will it affect your spouse, partner, children, parents, friends, relatives, coworkers? And if so, *how* will it affect them? Will they be pleased with your intention, and the results of it? Be ready for the changes that are sure to come.

Apply these methods of manifestation for the greater good. This includes the greater good of yourself, and those people whose lives you touch, and those new people who may come into your life.

As you develop these powers of manifestation, you will become better at it. Your skills will improve. The manifestations will come more quickly. And as a result, time will seem to speed up. The delay in time between intention and manifestation will shorten. And with that increase in speed comes increased responsibility.

Can you imagine for a moment if manifestation were instantaneous? This is a huge responsibility. For example, how terrible it would be if you wished harm for another person, and moments later they experienced that harm? This is not anything any of us wish to see occur. For what if you change your mind, and decide later that you really did not wish to harm this person? Too late, the damage has been done.

Or what if this person had agreed to come into your life to challenge you, in order to help you on your growth path? This is something that you in fact asked them to do on a soul level, for your benefit. And now you intend to harm them?

You see, there are untold energetic pathways, threads of lives intertwined, and so many lifetimes of karmic exchanges and back-and-forth interaction. As much as we think we know, we often have *no idea as to the complexity of the interdependence of people's lives*. (Karma can be defined as unresolved issues, or also the effects of a person's actions throughout a lifetime.)

What you *can* do, and *should* do, when confronted with a challenge that seems so great that you wish to harm someone, is to rise above it. Use your powers of awareness, understanding, and insight to *forgive* them for what you feel has wronged you, *allow* them to continue on their way, *accept* that things transpired the way they did, be *honest* with yourself about your feelings about the situation, and then *release* it all to the perfect outpouring of the universe.

> I NOW RISE ABOVE LOWER CHALLENGES. I NOW FORGIVE THAT WHICH
> NEEDS FORGIVENESS. I NOW ALLOW WHAT MAY TRANSPIRE TO OCCUR
> FOR THE HIGHEST GOOD OF ALL. I NOW RELEASE THIS SITUATION TO
> THE DIVINE WILL OF THE UNIVERSAL SPIRIT.

In doing so, you rise above the karma. You can overcome lifetimes of pain, strife, worry and battle by simply forgiving the person, rising above the situation, and releasing it back to the universe. You have learned the lesson. You have completed the karma. You have chosen to rise above the fight. You have taken the high road. (Karma can also be thought of as cause and effect, or the total effect of a person's actions and conduct during the successive phases of the person's existence)

> I NOW RELEASE AND AM RELEASED FROM EVERYTHING AND EVERYBODY
> THAT ARE NO LONGER PART OF THE DIVINE PLAN FOR MY LIFE.
> EVERYTHING AND EVERYBODY THAT ARE NO LONGER PART OF THE
> DIVINE PLAN FOR MY LIFE NOW RELEASE ME. [1]

Energetically, what you have accomplished is that you have raised your vibration. You have climbed up from the lower expressions of battle, fight and survival, and popped your head up above the fog in the valley to see clearly for miles around. You have stepped out of the mud, and washed the dirt off your feet.

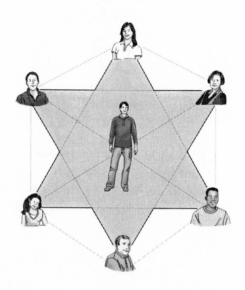

You constantly affect people all around you, and they affect you too!
This network is much larger than you would think.

A HIGHER STATE OF BEING

Energetically, when you rise above a particular situation, you enter a new and higher vibrational state. When you rise up from a challenge like this, you bring these new energies, feelings and vibrations into your being. And these are all good things to attract to yourself. These things bring you closer to your higher self, closer to service, and closer to the Infinite Intelligence. And these things will help you easily hurdle challenges in life that are simply no longer needed. No longer will you be "sleepwalking" through life, challenged by those who just want to pick a fight, push your buttons, and ruffle your feathers. You will be more "awake," aware, knowing and understanding.

Try to identify a time in your life, either now or in the past, when you were challenged by someone in a significant way. What were your feelings about the situation then, and now? Is it still something you struggle with? If you have not already done so, see if you can work through this issue. See if you can rise above the interchange, and put it behind you.

- understand the situation for what it really is
- forgive the person for the perceived wrong
- release the person and issues to the universe
- trust that all will transpire in perfection

If you like, choose a small topic or issue first to release. Then later, work up to the big ones. You will find that after it has all transpired, you will be much lighter, happier, and at peace.

AFFIRMATIONS

I NOW TAKE FULL RESPONSIBILITY FOR MY CURRENT POSITION IN LIFE AND WHERE I AM IN THE WORLD TODAY.

THE FORGIVING LOVE OF SPIRIT NOW SETS ME FREE FROM MY PAST, AND MISTAKES I HAVE MADE IN THE PAST. I FACE THE FUTURE WISE, FREE, UNBOUND AND UNAFRAID.

I NOW TAKE FULL RESPONSIBILITY FOR WHO I AM AND MY RELATIONSHIPS WITH OTHERS IN MY LIFE. I NOW UNDERSTAND AND ACKNOWLEDGE THE DIVINE WORKING WITHIN ME AND THROUGH ME.

I NOW FULLY ACKNOWLEDGE THE DIVINITY IN ME, AS I AM GUIDED IN THE CORRECT WAY.

QUESTIONS AND ANSWERS

Q. So you mean to tell me, that if something bad happens to me, that it's something that I caused myself?
A. Yes. You attract to you what it is in life that you project out, or that you need to learn from. So yes, there is a reason why you attracted something undesirable to you. Your job is to figure out *why* you attracted that to you, learn from it, and correct it.

Q. What if another car smashes into my car while I'm driving, or if another kind of accident happens to me that's obviously not my fault?
A. You attract to you energy and experience that *you need to learn from.* In these cases, you have decided to be in a certain place at a certain time, and be involved in that experience. Thus you have chosen it. It's true.

It can be very difficult to come to the awareness that seemingly random or somehow unintentional things are really the result of something that you have chosen for yourself.

And although you may struggle to fully believe this concept of taking responsibility for these kinds of things in your life, it is equally rewarding and personally empowering to accept that in fact these things are the result of your doing. The *real question* is not did you attract this experience to you, but *why* did you attract this experience to you?

Q. I have trouble making up my mind, so I delay, or I don't make a decision. Is that bad?
A. By deciding not to decide, you are still deciding. Know that if you are simply delaying making various decisions because they are hard to make or hard to share with others, you are only delaying the inevitable. Check in with your heart, and make the decision!

Q. If I don't actually believe that something will manifest, will it?
A. Probably not.

Q. What about superstitions? Are these real?
A. To the extent that you believe something, it is true for you. So, if you believe in various superstitions, you will create those events and realities in your life which support your superstitious beliefs. If you refuse to believe in superstitions, they will not become part of your reality.

Q. Am I personally responsible for things on a larger scale, like war or disasters?
A. These are group manifestations. So, for example, as part of a country that chooses to go to war with another country, we are all responsible.

Q. What about big companies that pollute our environment? Or countries which choose to overfish our oceans? I'm not responsible in these situations, am I?
A. Yes. You are responsible. I am responsible. We are all responsible.

CHAPTER SUMMARY

1) The third dimension can give you a confused view of how the world really is.
2) Things do not just happen, we cause them to occur.
3) "Victim mentality" consciousness gives away your personal power.
4) When you take responsibility for your creations you come from a place of power.
5) This is a free will planet, and you have the ability to decide to do or not to do everything.
6) You should never feel lonely, knowing that you can love yourself, and that Source is always there for you.
7) If you rely on anything or anyone outside yourself to give you love, it will never be enough.

8)   Take care not to let modern technology steal you away from the present moment.

9)   Living in the moment helps you be passionate about life.

10) You may guide and shift your dominant thoughts for positive outcomes.

11) Inertia, combined with a strong intention, will bring people into your life to support you.

12) You are personally responsible for your creations.

13) We often have no idea as to the complexity and interdependence of people's lives with one another.

14) As you create, realize that you will benefit from the unforeseeable, unknowable, and incalculable.

15) Use your powers of manifestation for the greater good.

16) Rise above challenges, become more awake and aware, and attract more positive things and situations to yourself.

MANIFESTING WORKSHEET

List three things in your life right now that are not working, where you can take personal responsibility to make your life better. What aspects of your life are not working to serve your highest good (example: loneliness, stress, overload, career problems, friendship problems, relationship issues, health challenges).

1) _____

2) _____

3) _____

Now write down three ways you can start to overcome and address these challenges.

1) _____

2) _____

3) _____

REFERENCES

1.   Catherine Ponder, *Open Your Mind to Prosperity*, (DeVorss & Company; 1984), p. 40.

CHAPTER 4

Making Way for the New

"We cannot become what we need to be, remaining what we are."—Max Depree

PREPARING FOR MAGNIFICENCE, PROSPERITY AND ABUNDANCE

Before you go through the actual steps on intentional manifestation in Chapters 8, 9 and 10, make sure there is room in your world for all the wonderful new things, people and opportunities just waiting to come into your life.

Probably the *easiest* and single most important thing you can do to insure that your new manifestation will occur quickly and correctly is to make room for it. You do this by creating a vacuum, an empty space, or void.

The universe hates a vacuum. And the universe will do everything it can to bring new and exciting things to you, once you have cleared out the old. If your house, apartment, closets, garage, basement, attic, desk, file cabinets, computer, workspace, and book shelves are all chock full of clutter and stuff, there may literally be very little room in your life for the new to come in. It's time to make some space in your life. Here's how:

1) Clean out your basement, attic and garage. Have a yard sale, or give stuff away.
2) Get rid of books and magazines you are finished with. Pass them along.
3) Go through your closets. Weed out anything you haven't worn in a year, and consign unwanted items or give them to charity.
4) Go through the kitchen. Look for things you simply don't use, and find them a new home (not in yours).

5) If you have put away things in a storage facility, rid yourself of them. Lighten your load. If they are yours, not matter where they are, then they remain in your mind.

6) Clean out everything: storage areas, shelves, desks, clutter, everything!

Feel good about it. Realize that with every object you rid yourself of, you are making way for the new. New people, situations, relationships, connections, and other great new things are actually just waiting for you to make some serious room for them in your life. So do it! Take steps large and small, and prepare the way. And after you are done, do some more. It feels good to get rid of stuff. Release it out to the universe; the universe will find the best place for it. Also, in clearing out the old, you are affirming your own power and ability to create whenever needed.

As an example of how this works, how many times have you cleared out some closets and donated old clothes to charity, only to be called on the phone a week later by a friend with some fresh new thing that they no longer need? It's all about the flow of energy. It works everywhere, with everything. Put it to work for you.

> I NOW RELEASE BACK TO THE UNIVERSE ALL THINGS, OBJECTS, AND CONDITIONS THAT ARE NO LONGER PART OF THE DIVINE PLAN FOR MY LIFE. I NOW RELEASE FULLY AND COMPLETELY, AND EXPRESS GRATITUDE FOR THE SERVICE THESE THINGS HAVE RENDERED ME UP TO NOW.

Then take a look at your personal schedule. Is it cluttered, busy, and over-booked? Are you one of those super-achievers who signs up for everything so there is not a free moment in your life? Is your calendar bursting with meetings, commitments, and appointments? If this is the way you are, make some changes and create some breathing room in your life. It will feel great to get your life back, won't it?

Helen, a longtime friend, learned about the magic of affirmations and clearing out the old in order to make way for the new. So she set aside a whole week and got rid of all sorts of extra stuff that was no longer needed. She also affirmed to get things going. As a result, the following week she received five unsolicited job offers seemingly out of the blue! And she wasn't even looking for a job! Helen got offers to be a teacher, receptionist, salesperson, tutor, and an interpreter. She took the tutoring job, and enjoyed the unexpected extra income in her life.

This technique of clearing out the old works even better if you have any kind of pent-up demand or unclaimed good that is due you. If you have been through a time in your life where things have been stagnant with nothing happening, get to work and start clearing things out. The results may surprise you!

AFFIRMATIONS

I NOW FULLY RELEASE ALL THAT IS NO LONGER PART OF MY DIVINE PLAN BACK TO THE PERFECT OUTPOURING OF THE UNIVERSE.

I NOW LET GO OF THOSE THINGS, CONDITIONS AND RELATIONSHIPS WHICH NO LONGER SUPPORT MY HIGHEST GROWTH. YOU ARE NOW RELEASED. I NOW ESTABLISH DIVINE ORDER IN MY LIFE AND IN MY WORLD.

I LET GO AND TRUST.

QUESTIONS AND ANSWERS

Q. This concept of clearing out seems counter-intuitive. Are you telling me I should give away things to get more?
A. Yes. You have to make room for the new, and get the flow of energy going through you and your surroundings. It's all about the flow of energy.

Q. Does it matter if I give stuff away, or sell it?
A. No, not really. Just release it from your life. (See chapter #11 on the Flow of Energy)

CHAPTER SUMMARY

1) Get rid of the old in order to make room for the new in your life.
2) The universe hates a vacuum, and will do everything it can to fill it.
3) Donate to charity, give to friends, have a yard sale. Get the energy flowing.
4) Clear out your schedule if you are simply doing way too much. Allow for balance in your life, and time for yourself.
5) People with unclaimed good and pent-up demand often experience major change after clearing out.
6) Clearing out allows for a new flow of energy to you.

MANIFESTING WORKSHEET

1) Choose at least one room in your house that you will "thoroughly" clean. This means removing (for good) a substantial amount of "stuff" in order to help get the flow going in your life.

2) Select some clothing from a closet or storage to remove, and go do it, now! Free yourself. If something (anything) is in your physical space, it is part of you, and in your mind. It's time to clear it out. You don't want it in your consciousness anymore.

Now, list one or more major physical spaces or areas in your life in which you will make space for the new.

1) _____

2) _____

3) _____

CHAPTER 5

Forgiveness

"Sometimes the heart sees what is invisible to the eye."—H. Jackson Brown, Jr.

FORGIVENESS

Along with having too much old and unwanted stuff cluttering up your life, the other major barrier that can hold you back from manifesting what you want is seemingly a bit less physical. Besides cleaning out your closets, you must clean out feelings of hurt, anger, jealousy, abandonment, and being wronged. You must clean out your mind and heart. *You must forgive.*

If you are still holding onto people, situations, difficulties, anger, grudges, ties and other energetic elements that are not helping your personal growth, it's time to release them to the universe for the perfect outpouring and resolution. In doing so, you are doing yourself a big favor, and lightening your burden.

Know that when you forgive others you are not excusing the other person, nor does it mean that what the other person did is okay. You are not condoning their actions. You are simply releasing it out to the universe, rising above it all, and letting it all go. It is actually a selfish act, in a way. This is because when you forgive others, you free yourself.

Holding on to anger for someone or a particular situation can be very harmful. In fact, being angry at someone can be compared to taking poison yourself, and expecting your enemy to die. It is much more difficult to move forward when we harbor negative feelings of anger, hate, revenge, and criticism towards others. These things hold us back, and keep us out of balance.

- Were your parents a bit less than perfect while you were growing up?
- Were your brothers and sisters unkind, and unfair?

- Did someone else make poor life decisions, which ended up hurting you?
- Did your parents have "favorite" children?
- Has a former lover left you scorned?
- Did your parents set you up for failure, with limiting beliefs, poverty consciousness, restrictive lifestyles, and narrow-mindedness?
- Were you abused, neglected, abandoned, forgotten, or left to fend for yourself?
- Has a spouse been abusive, angry, unsupportive, or unfaithful?
- Did your parents have problems of their own, like alcoholism, abuse, addictive behaviors, and jealousies?
- Have you been passed by at the workplace, with someone else getting a promotion which should have gone to you?
- Have friends or business partners taken advantage of you?

All of these issues, and more, can make for a heavy burden. There is absolutely no reason to hold on to these leftover unhappy feelings representing lower energies. It's time to forgive these people, the situations, and forgive yourself for being the "victim."

MAY THE DIVINE LOVE IN ME MEET THE DIVINE LOVE IN YOU FOR A BETTER UNDERSTANDING.

When you express anger for another person, *your anger binds you to that person or condition by an emotional link that is stronger than steel.* The only way to dissolve that link is through forgiveness. You must forgive that person or condition, and you will be set free. [1] Release it all back to the universe. Rise above it all. Set yourself free.

ALL THAT HAS OFFENDED ME, I FORGIVE. WITHIN AND WITHOUT, I FORGIVE. THINGS PAST, THINGS PRESENT, THINGS FUTURE, I FORGIVE. I FORGIVE EVERYTHING AND EVERYBODY WHO CAN POSSIBLY NEED FORGIVENESS IN MY PAST AND PRESENT. I POSITIVELY FORGIVE EVERYONE. I AM FREE, AND ALL OTHERS ARE FREE, TOO. ALL THINGS ARE CLEARED UP BETWEEN US, NOW AND FOREVER. [2]

Forgiveness frees you from the damaging image of yourself as a victim. It dissolves resentment. When you choose a new understanding of your situation, you are free to be compassionate to yourself and to those who you feel have wronged you. In forgiving these people, you feel lighter, and you raise your vibration.

It is entirely liberating when you release resentments, perceived wrongs, and old grudges. Additionally, it makes room for new feelings in your life, much better and more loving ones. If you have trouble forgiving people, pretend that today is the last day you will see them alive. Does that change it for you?

THE DIVINE LOVE OF SPIRIT NOW FREES ME FROM ATTACHMENT, RESENTMENT, AND CONDITIONS WHICH HOLD ME BACK AND ARE NO LONGER PART OF THE DIVINE PLAN FOR MY LIFE.

One great way to forgive and release others is by visualizing a knotted rope that is connecting you to the person you feel anger toward. And the more you struggle with it and think about them and the difficult situation, the tighter the knots in that rope become.

Visualize that you have a sword, a mighty divine sword, and that you and your angels together cut the rope which ties you to this other person. See it happening. Feel how great it is to sweep down with your razor-sharp sword and cut the ties that have bound you to this person and this situation for far too long. Now you are free. If you do this visualization once a day for a month, you will have completely cleared these energetic ties.

You can cut the energetic cords that bind you to another.

Forgiveness is a very important lesson for us all. After you forgive your relatives, friends, coworkers and others, don't forget to forgive the most important person of all, *yourself*. In fact, this may be the hardest thing to do. You must forgive yourself for not being the perfect person, parent, wife, husband, lover, teenager, student, brother, sister, boss, or employee. Start forgiving, and free yourself!

AFFIRMATIONS

I NOW FORGIVE AND RELEASE EVERYTHING AND EVERYBODY OF THE
PAST AND PRESENT THAT IS NO LONGER PART OF THE DIVINE PLAN FOR
MY LIFE. I LOVE YOU, AND RELEASE YOU.

DIVINE LOVE AND FORGIVENESS NOW RADIATE OUT FROM MY BEING TO
THOSE I RESOLVE WITH NOW. I LOVE YOU AND I FORGIVE YOU.

I FORGIVE EVERYONE AND EVERYTHING THAT CAN POSSIBLY NEED
FORGIVENESS IN MY LIFE NOW.

I FORGIVE MYSELF FOR NOT BEING EVERYTHING I THINK I SHOULD BE.

QUESTIONS AND ANSWERS

Q. If it's money I want to manifest, why do I have to go around forgiving people? That doesn't make sense.
A. You don't have to. But you probably should anyway. It will help with the flow of energy to you and through you. Forgiving others will make you that much clearer, centered, unburdened, and unencumbered with things that just don't need to be part of your life anymore. Isn't there someone in your past or present whom you can forgive? Forgiving others will help get the flow of good coming into your life again.

Q. Why should I take the time to forgive myself? I'm over it, I think.
A. Are you, really? Forgiveness is something you cannot overdo. Was there any time in your past when you were less than perfect? Have you ever done anything that was a bit embarrassing, that you still remember to this day? Have you released it? Have you really forgiven yourself? Forgiveness is similar to the vibrations of gratitude and love. Forgiveness is one of the highest expressions of energy you can emanate.

CHAPTER SUMMARY

1) Besides cleaning out household clutter, you must clean out your mind and heart. The best way to do this is with forgiveness.
2) When you forgive others, you free yourself.
3) Holding onto anger and intolerance makes it difficult to move forward.
4) Anger for another person binds you to them with an emotional link that is stronger than steel.
5) Forgiveness frees us from the damaging image of ourselves as victim.

6) We cannot be forgiven until we first forgive others.
7) Forgive old grudges, resentments, and anger, and be liberated from them.
8) Cut harmful energetic ties with others with your own "divine sword."
9) Don't forget to forgive the most important person of all, yourself.
10) Forgiveness is a very high energetic expression.

MANIFESTING WORKSEET

1) After careful consideration, choose one person to forgive. This person may be a person that you are angry, upset, or challenged by. Those strong energetic clues are telling you that the energy of this situation needs to be resolved.

Now start using some affirmations to begin the process of forgiving this person. Here's a sample:

_____(NAME OF PERSON TO FORGIVE), I NOW FORGIVE YOU. I NOW RELEASE YOU FROM THIS DIFFICULT SITUATION BACK TO THE UNIVERSE. I NOW LET GO AND RELEASE THIS SITUATION TO A HIGHER POWER. THINGS ARE FREED UP BETWEEN US, NOW AND FOREVER.

REFERENCES

1. Catherine Ponder, *Open Your Mind to Prosperity*, (DeVorss & Company; 1984), p. 36.
2. Catherine Ponder, *Open Your Mind to Prosperity*, (DeVorss & Company; 1984), p. 35.

CHAPTER 6

Universal Laws & Truths

"Dare to be different. Say no to the illusion."—Anonymous

PUTTING THE UNIVERSE ON YOUR SIDE

Knowing the universal laws that we all live under will help you to understand the process of manifestation, as well as other important concepts of life and love. You can make the laws work for you, and benefit greatly from them. Conversely, you can try to fight against these laws, but you will find that the struggle will be difficult. After all, you are fighting the universe!

Universal laws are laws that we all live under and are subject to. Universal laws are fair laws, and we have all agreed to be subject to them when we chose to be born into this lifetime.

Universal laws are laws that always work, without fail. You can try to "break" one of these laws, but it is only a matter of time before the law truly affects you, one way or another. For the universe is a perfect place, and always seeks perfection.

There are a few important points about universal laws:

1) they are eternal
2) they do not change
3) they cannot be violated
4) they apply equally to everyone and everything in the universe
5) they apply to non-believers as much as they apply to those who believe
(The fact that you may be unaware of a law does not make you exempt from it.)

You are no doubt already aware of natural laws. Natural laws include our understanding and complete confidence as "real" such concepts as gravity, magnetism, entropy, physics, and aerodynamics. These laws have been studied and defined by scientists observing and measuring how our world operates. These laws define life on earth as we know it, and we adopt these natural laws in our everyday life without a second thought.

Universal laws are a bit different. They relate to the *movement of energy* as it affects all life. Universal laws are essentially part of the blueprint describing consciousness and form. Where the laws of man are in a constant state of flux, universal laws remain the same for all levels of consciousness.

UNIVERSAL LAWS AND UNIVERSAL TRUTHS

Here are the universal laws separated out into four sections

- The way the universe works
- The way the world works
- The way humanity is
- The way you operate in the world

UNIVERSAL LAWS AND UNIVERSAL TRUTHS

THE WAY THE *UNIVERSE* WORKS

1) Everything in the universe is comprised of energy.

2) There is an unlimited supply of energy in the universe; it will *never* run out.

3) The universe is eternally expanding. It does so through a system of chaos, reorganization and order. This is an endless cycle of change, growth and expansion.

4) Creation is the result of thought applied to energy or thought focused on energy. Every thought has some impact in the physical universe.

5) There are a number of dimensions in the universe. The dimension most familiar to us is the third dimension.

6) The universe can and will provide you with anything and everything you could ever want at the right time, in the right way, in the perfect expression. Your ability to trust and believe this universal law will directly affect the extent that this law will be true for you.

7) The universe will match the energy you project out with the energy of what you get back.

8) The universe is fair and neutral, and seeks balance. When something is out of balance, the universe attempts to bring it back into balance.

9) Time and space are third dimensional constructs, and do not exist outside of the third dimension. Beyond our third dimension, there is no time, and everything is occurring right now, in the moment.

10) There is no good or evil, only experience. All there is are experiences designed to help you grow as soul. [1]

11) The universe seeks perfection. The universe attempts to make everything transpire and occur perfectly. The universe seeks the ultimate best solution for all involved.

12) The universe provides keys to the way it works through a concept called synchronicity. Synchronicity is a chain of seemingly unrelated or coincidental events that in actuality are quite meaningfully related. The universe is constantly and continuously sending signals, messages and hints to you, sometimes from people and things which casually come into and go out of your life.

13) There is a divine order in the universe. A higher spirit is at work in the universe and in all of our lives, even during times when it may not appear to be.

UNIVERSAL LAWS AND UNIVERSAL TRUTHS

THE WAY THE *WORLD* WORKS

1) The physical world we live in provides an ideal environment for all kinds of manifestation.

2) Over time, your thoughts become your beliefs. You can dramatically change your world around you simply by changing your thoughts and beliefs.

3) You get in life what you truly believe you can get. Your expectations and beliefs form and influence your results in a powerful way. Your expectations are a major influence on your results.

4) Living in the moment helps you to be centered, balanced, powerful and able to access your own personal divinity.

5) You grow personally through a series of "lessons" or personal challenges. If you do not learn a lesson, you will likely be given an additional opportunity to learn the lesson in another way (perhaps through another person or situation).

6) If you heal something in this lifetime, it also heals for you in all other dimensions in all other lifetimes. This is an extremely powerful concept to know.

7) People you meet sometimes consciously and sometimes unconsciously bring messages or learning situations to you. Sometimes it is you that has a message for them.

8) Those people in your life who you feel most strongly about are likely the people who you have the most unfinished business with (karma). You grow by working through your karma.

9) Our world is one of duality, with polar opposites such as good-bad, problem-solutions, and scarcity-abundance. When we learn from these polarized limiting constructs and grow personally beyond them, we evolve into divine love, joy and awareness. [2]

UNIVERSAL LAWS AND UNIVERSAL TRUTHS

THE WAY THAT *HUMANITY* IS

1) We are all connected to one another energetically, spiritually, multidimensionally, and infinitely. We are all One. We are also connected to All That Is.

2) Everyone wants to receive love and express love. It is natural to be loving and loved, and we all want to return to this divine expression. Love is an ultimate expression of being.

3) Your intuition is one way you can access universal wisdom. Meditation is the most common way that people connect with their intuition.

4) Your beliefs are some of the strongest and most powerful parts of your consciousness. Be mindful of all your beliefs, both those that are empowering and those that are limiting.

5) Negative emotions such as fear and anger work against manifestation efforts. These lower energies block the natural order and flow of energy through you and your life.

6) Gratitude expressed is one of the quickest ways to accelerate your personal growth. Gratitude helps get the energetic flow moving. The vibration of gratitude is a very high vibration, similar to that of love.

7) Personal expressions of divinity (singing, painting, dancing, writing, etc.) help us connect with the universal life force energy. Express yourself in joyful, divine, and creative ways in order to access your inner power.

8) When you are balanced, centered, and in alignment with your higher self and the universe, you can create and manifest whatever you want. When you are unbalanced and out of alignment, things can be more difficult.

9) When you are out of alignment, you may sometimes feel pain, discomfort, and discordance. Your body and energy patterns are telling you that something is not right. You may be able to fool your mind for a while, but your body knows, feels and expresses the imbalance.

10) One collective goal for humanity is to reconnect with one another and positively transform the planet into the next dimension. (see Chapter 23 on the New Age)

11) All negativity is a cry for love.

12) In the end you will find that for any question, love is the answer. (see Chapter 20 on Personal Spiritual Growth)

UNIVERSAL LAWS AND UNIVERSAL TRUTHS

THE WAY *YOU* OPERATE IN THE WORLD

1) You are a magnetic, energetic being, and you constantly affect the world around you.

2) You create with your thoughts. You experience with your consciousness. Energy coming into material form does so by thought.

3) You are free to have any thoughts at any time about any subject. This is an application of free will.

4) You attract things, situations and people of similar vibration to that of yourself.

5) You are creating and manifesting every moment of every day of your life, whether you consciously acknowledge it or not.

6) What you focus your thoughts and energy on persists in your life, and all around you. What you dwell upon becomes your reality. This works both positively and negatively.

7) You are worth no more or no less than any other individual.

8) Unresolved issues of anger, frustration, hate, jealousy, despair and dislike, if not addressed and dealt with, may manifest in your life outwardly in the form of disease or illness.

9) You were born into this world with all the resources, skills, and abilities to fulfill your life contract. (Your life contract is your agreement with yourself as to why you chose to incarnate in this lifetime, what you would attempt to complete, and the life lessons you would learn in doing so.)

10) When you consciously ask for help, it opens the door wide for your angels, spirit guides and others to come into your life and render divine assistance. They love to be asked, and they love to help.

11) To get love, be love. If you go "looking for love," you are looking outside of yourself and expressing the energy of lack or want. The best way to find love is to *be* love and *radiate* love; then love will be magnetized and attracted to you and find you.

12) You were born into this world with one or more God-given gifts of talent. One of your tasks is to discover, explore and express your talent(s) during your lifetime. As you express your talents, you reconnect with your divine nature.

13) As you go through life you will be confronted with your main life lessons. Try to discover them and complete them in a timely way, in order to accelerate your growth path.

14) What you resist, persists. The harder you push something away from you, the more the universe sends it back to you, in any number of ways. The universe has unlimited ways in which it can push things back to you until you "get the picture" and resolve the issue. There is no shortcut. Learn the lesson.

15) There is no such thing as an accident. We cause everything that happens to us. When we take responsibility, we claim our power. Otherwise, we choose to become victims and choose to be completely powerless over our lives.

16) When you are "dialed in," in right way, and manifesting easily, you are "in the flow." An example of this is when athletes are in "the zone."

17) You can look outside of yourself for the answers (books, crystals, tarot cards, oracles, psychics, etc.) but most likely your best and most truthful answers will come from within yourself. Often this can be discovered through meditation, or by checking in with your heart (understanding how you feel about something).

18) You cannot solve other people's problems for them. But you can help them see the problem, suggest various ways to address the problem, and support their efforts to manage and overcome the problem in their own way at their own pace.

19) Unconditional love is one of the greatest gifts and lessons available to us at this time. Bring unconditional love into a difficult situation, and watch it transform positively.

20) Emotion is energy in motion. Emotions occur when we attach a thought to a feeling. Feelings are when we attach an attitude to an experience.

21) You create karma by your intentions, thoughts, emotions, deeds and actions. When you do something (in this lifetime or others) that affects or involves another person, karma is activated (cause and effect). When you resolve the karma and complete the karmic cycle, you become balanced and centered and bring harmony back into your life.

22) To love yourself is to love others.

23) You are loved.

A FOCUS ON FOUR OF THE UNIVERSAL LAWS

There are four major universal laws:

1) the Law of Attraction—we get what we focus our energy on
2) the Law of Unity—we are all One
3) the Law of Reciprocity—what goes around comes around
4) the Law of Love—for whatever the question, love is the answer

Because these laws are the foundation for many of the other laws and truths, I will review these in greater detail.

1) THE LAW OF ATTRACTION

"That which you are seeking is causing you to seek"—Ancient Buddhist Principle

The basic premise of the Law of Attraction is that everything around us, including ourselves, is composed of energy. It is a basic law of physics that "like energy attracts like energy." Therefore, what we think about the most, we get more of!

You are using the Law of Attraction right now to attract everything in your life, even the things you don't want. You create your reality through your thoughts, words, and feelings.

All is vibration, be it mental, physical, emotional, or spiritual. What you believe sets up vibrations that draw situations to you that are within your belief systems. You are like a huge vibrating electromagnet that is always projecting out a certain frequency, based on what you believe and your current mental, emotional and energetic state.

This law of attraction can be seen in tuning forks. When you strike a tuning fork it begins to vibrate and hum, sending out vibrations of a specific pitch. When another tuning fork is placed nearby and calibrated to the same note, the second fork will begin to hum and vibrate in harmony with the first one.

This phenomenon is expressed in common sayings like: "birds of a feather flock together," "it takes one to know one," and "tell me who your friends are and I'll tell you who you are."

Though we travel the world over
to find the beautiful,
we must carry it with us
or we find it not.
Ralph Waldo Emerson

Every day, you attract people, situations and opportunities which are consistent with your energetic state. So, if you are having a great day, you will naturally attract more wonderful people and things into your life. You are on a roll, and everything is going your way. Don't you just love days like that? Every traffic light on your way to work is green. Everyone seems extra nice to you. Your boss tells you that you are doing a great job. Everything just comes together perfectly.

An example of this positive energetic state is when someone gets a new boyfriend or girlfriend. The new relationship makes them happy, and they broadcast an energy of happiness and love. And in doing so, they suddenly attract all sorts of other people to them who are attracted to their loving ways. Although these other people were around them all along, it was only when their energy became loving did they attract others to them as well.

On the other hand, if you are having a terrible day, figure that until you change your energetic projection, you will continue to attract difficult situations and people to you. In fact, some people actually reinforce the less positive energies when they proclaim to themselves and everyone who would listen, "I'm having a terrible day. Nothing is going right. I can't do anything right today. I got up on the wrong side of the bed. I'll be glad when this day is over." This self-fulfilling prophecy is the Law of Attraction in action, and it is a very powerful law.

Most people don't realize they have control over these personal circumstances. They believe that good and bad days just happen by chance. They attract by default. They do not realize that they can change what they attract and what comes into their life, just by changing their thoughts and feelings. It's true.

Sometimes you may experience the law of attraction when you don't want to. When you are confronted with challenges in your life that you keep delaying and putting off, you may experience the law of attraction unintentionally. What happens is that the more you keep pushing something away from you, the more the universe will find a way to keep pushing it back to you, in any number of ways, until the issue is resolved and the lesson is learned.

An example of this is when a person keeps attracting a certain kind of person to them. My friend Emily does this all the time. She continually attracts the "wrong kind" of guy to her, the type of guy who does not treat her well. Until she changes her own view of herself and her self-worth, she will continue to attract this kind of man.

One reason for this is that when you continue to push something away from you, you are actually continuing to focus on it (sometimes unconsciously). Thus the universe, in its quest to bring to you what you think about most (even if you do not want it in your life), does its best to keep sending it to you. The universe will continue to do this, until it is resolved one way or another, and you stop thinking about it and attracting it to you.

There is a story told about a young man who, in frontier days was looking for a place to settle down. As he approached the outskirts of a small western town, he came across an elderly rancher and asked, "What kind of people live in this town?" "What kind of people did you find in the last place you lived?" asked the elderly rancher. "Oh, they were a selfish and unfriendly bunch," replied the young man. "You'll find the same here," said the elderly rancher.

A few days later, another young traveler passed near the ranch and, seeing the elderly rancher, he put the same question to him: "What kind of people live here?" Again, the elderly rancher replied with the question, "What kind of people were in the town from which you came?" "They were a good group of folks: honest, sincere, friendly. I was sorry to leave them," replied the young man. "You'll find the same here," said the elderly rancher.

A ranch hand, who had heard both conversations, questioned the elderly man: "How could you give two different answers to the same question to two different people?" "Son," said the elderly man, "Everyone carries within himself the environment in which he lives. The one who found nothing good about his previous town will find the same here. The young man who found friends in his former town will find friends here. People and circumstances are to us what we find in them. Seek, from within yourself, and ye shall surely find."

What kind of people live here?

2) THE LAW OF UNITY

The Law of Unity simply states that we are all One. We are all connected, in Spirit, by the Creator. We are all connected to each other, and we are all connected to Source, as a divine expression of it. Furthermore, because of our collective awareness, we all influence one another. It is all too easy to forget that we are all connected, because in our third dimension it appears that we are not. Loneliness is the opposite expression of the Law of Unity.

This law helps us to understand that we live in a world where everything is connected to everything else. Everything we do, say, think and believe affects others and the universe around us. What we say and do adds to our collective consciousness as a society. People who are aware of this law understand that when there is crime or suffering, that it impacts us all. People who understand this law see things with compassion and understanding, since they know that someone else's challenges are essentially also their own.

Even if people consciously do not acknowledge this universal law, everyone does unconsciously. This is easily witnessed during a global disaster or crises, when people around the world instinctively and collectively share in the pain, and respond in compassionate ways. This is an example of humanity expressing unity.

3) THE LAW OF RECIPROCITY

The Law of Reciprocity, also known as the law of cause and effect, is an easy law to know and understand. Throughout time, it has been known as:

- The Golden Rule (do unto others as you would have them do unto you)
- What goes around comes around
- I'll scratch your back if you scratch mine
- You reap what you sow
- You get what you give

The principle is that others will reciprocate in kind based upon the way you treat them. The world gives you what you give to the world. By understanding and using the power of reciprocity, you can improve your relationships and avoid mistakes. In life and work, you get what you give.

However, when we try to invoke reciprocity directly, it does not work correctly. It is in helping others *without expecting reciprocity in return* that we invoke the power of reciprocity. You can't make "deals" for reciprocity. It doesn't work that way. Don't do something for someone only because you hope to get something in return. That's not the way it works. Your action or deed needs to be *unconditional.*

The reason the law of reciprocity works so powerfully is that *the universe looks to create balance from an imbalance.* So, if the universe keeps seeing you give to others, it will find ways to get things sent to you. The universe seeks a return to balance.

4)   THE LAW OF LOVE

The Law of Love states that for whatever the question or situation, love is the answer.

All living things require love to survive, including ourselves. We must first attend to our own needs for love before we can love others. When we neglect ourselves emotionally, we are incomplete and are not whole enough to give love to others. When we change our inner dialogue from an inner critic to that of an inner companion, we bring ourselves back into balance, and are then able to keep the flow of loving energy moving through us.

Unconditional love is the highest expression of the love energy. Unconditional love heals both yourself and others who are affected by your loving energy. [3]

> *Knowing and understanding the laws of life, also called truth,*
> *is not enough. A person must live the truth that he or she knows.* [4]

AFFIRMATIONS

THE INFINITE INTELLIGENCE NOW WORKS THROUGH ME TO IMPROVE ALL ASPECTS OF MY LIFE.

SPIRIT NOW GUIDES ME AS I OPERATE IN MY WORLD.

I NOW APPLY THE WISDOM OF THE AGES INTO MY LIFE FOR MY BENEFIT AND GREATER UNDERSTANDING.

I AM NOW GUIDED TO THE ESSENTIAL TRUTH OF SITUATIONS, AND UNDERSTAND HOW THEY WORK IN MY WORLD. I SEE EVERYTHING CLEARLY NOW, FOR WHAT IT TRULY IS.

QUESTIONS AND ANSWERS

Q. How can the universe be unlimited? Isn't there a finite amount of things like oil, gold, diamonds, etc.?
A. The important distinction here to understand is that *energy* in our universe is unlimited. So, if we need a type of fuel to power an automobile, it does not necessarily

have to be a fossil fuel. It could be hydrogen, solar, or another energy source not yet created by us. Because we create our own reality, individually and collectively, we can manifest any kind of energetic fuel source that we like, with the unlimited energy in the universe.

Q. The law of attraction seems awfully simple. Is that all there is? Can it really be that easy?
A. Yes, the law is easy to understand. But it can be a bit more complicated to put it into action. See subsequent chapters for instructions.

CHAPTER SUMMARY

1) Universal laws provide us with the framework under which we live.
2) Universal laws relate to the movement of energy as it affects life.
3) Universal laws remain the same for all levels of consciousness.
4) We are all subject to all of the various universal laws and universal truths.
5) There are four key universal laws.
6) By understanding the various universal laws, we can operate more effectively in the world.
7) The law of attraction states that you attract people, situations and opportunities to you that are consistent with your energetic state.
8) The law of attraction often works even when you don't want it to. If you keep pushing something away and it keeps coming back, it is because you continue to focus energy on it.
9) The law of unity states that we are all One, and that everything and everyone is connected to everything else.
10) The law of unity states that everything we say, do and believe affects everyone else and our collective consciousness.
11) The law of reciprocity states that you get what you give.
12) We invoke the law of reciprocity when we help others without expecting anything in return.
13) The law of love states that for whatever the question or situation, love is the answer.

MANIFESTING WORKSHEET—HAVING FUN WITH THE TOLLBOOTH TRICK

Here's a great way to initiate the law of reciprocity, and put it to work for you. If you live in an area where there are tollbooths on the highways, bridges, or tunnels, you can have some fun with this exercise. As you approach the tollbooth, project the thought out into the universe that you will pay for at least one additional car behind you. You may want to affirm that the person behind you will benefit most (in some way) from having their toll paid (by you).

As you go through the toll, pay double the amount so that the person behind you does not have to pay. (note: if you are feeling extra adventurous and prosperous, pay for two or more people behind you!).

Have fun knowing that by paying for an additional car behind you, that it can set many positive things into motion. You can change a person's bad day into a good one, you can start a chain of kindness, and you can influence many other drivers and passengers that day. Your act of kindness will be thought of long after the simple deed. This is all good karma.

Know that this simple act of kindness does many things:

- Helps your fellow man
- Reinforces your own personal abundance and ability to manifest payment whenever needed
- Gets the flow of energy moving through you
- Sets a chain reaction in motion which may affect an untold number of people
- Is fun!

Your loving energy from this simple act of kindness will be returned to you many times over in ways in which you may not even be able to imagine.

RESOURCES

1   Ellen Mogensen, Heal Past Lives, (www.healpastlives.com)
2   Ellen Mogensen, Heal Past Lives, (www.healpastlives.com)
3   Unity Principle number five, from the five principles of the Unity Christian Church
4   Unity Principle number five, from the five principles of the Unity Christian Church

CHAPTER 7

Science & Quantum Physics

The greatest discovery of our generation
is that human beings can alter their lives
by altering their attitudes of mind.
As you think, so shall you be.—William James

SCIENCE, QUANTUM PHYSICS, METAPHYSICS

Scientists in the field of quantum physics are making breakthrough discoveries that draw exciting connections between science, metaphysics, and spirituality. Quantum physicists are confirming what those who have studied metaphysics have theorized and believed for many years: the universe is composed entirely of energy, and as humans with a consciousness, we can consciously change our world with our thoughts.

As a human being, you are more than just a physical being of flesh and bones. Yes, you are much, much more. In fact, your life force energy is so powerful, encompassing and magnificent that it can be said that you transcend the third dimension. In other words, you exist not only in the third dimension, but in other dimensions as well, *all at the same time.* The term for this aspect of humankind is described as being *multidimensional.*

If you need some kind of proof or evidence of the multidimensionality of humans then think about your own experiences. Have you ever had a premonition, a hunch, or feeling about someone or something that later proved to be true? Have you ever thought of somebody, and then a moment later they called you on the telephone? Have you ever had a feeling about a situation that proved to be true? This is simply an example of your ability to access other dimensions and receive information. We do it every day. It is completely natural. Yet we don't always acknowledge that it happens.

By examining various theories arrived at as a result of studies in quantum physics, we can employ these theories and better manifest in our world.

QUANTUM PHYSICS

We are beginning to learn many new things about the world we live in from the study of quantum physics and quantum theory. And much of this is a result of two important inventions from the research laboratories of IBM Corporation.

In 1981, Gerd Binnig and Heinrich Rohrer of the IBM Zürich Research Laboratory invented the Scanning Tunneling Microscope. This device, easily one of the most elegant and unanticipated inventions of the 20th century, allowed imaging of individual atoms, and won Binnig and Rohrer the Nobel Prize in Physics for 1986.

In 1985, Binnig and Christoph Gerber of IBM Zurich, along with Calvin Quate of Stanford University, invented the atomic force microscope. This allowed imaging nonconductive matter such as living cells to molecular (although not currently atomic) resolution.

The powerful microscopy technique forms an image of individual atoms on a metal or semiconductor surface by scanning the tip of a needle over the surface at a height of only a few atomic diameters. This allows researchers to visualize individual atoms and their surface properties, like magnetism.

Binnig's contributions allowed science and industry to navigate the nanoscopic world. "I could not stop looking at the images," Binnig said in his Nobel acceptance speech. "It was entering a new world." [1]

These inventions allowed quantum theory researchers to see with their own eyes for the first time what was happening on a subatomic level in our world. Up to then, much of it was just theory. Now it could be seen. Quantum mechanics came to be as a result of the fact that classical mechanics and theory failed to explain, even approximately, such basic things as the energy levels and sizes of atoms.

As a result of their pioneering research, many quantum theorists have concluded that *many of the assumptions we have about the world we live in are actually wrong.* Although classical Newtonian theories of physics have done a good job of explaining segments of a large part of our observable world including chemistry and biology, these classical theories fall short when used to view the nature of light, magnetism, and matter.

Quantum physics tells us that the universe consists not of things, but of *possibilities*, and that *relationships* and *processes* are more fundamental than substances. We are learning that everything is much more fluid and malleable than we ever thought. We are learning that reality is far more mysterious than we have come to understand through traditional scientific thought. And at the center of this mystery is the *human consciousness*, and how it relates to a world of creation.

CONSCIOUSNESS IS THE KEY

As a person goes through life and makes observations, they do so with their consciousness. A person's consciousness and conscious observation is not a passive kind of thing, it is actually an actionable element. Thus, the consciousness of a person creates their reality. Quantum physics tells us that without our consciousness, our world does not exist.

Spirit and mind put together this energy into the physical shape you are used to seeing with your physical set of senses. If you look at yourself under a powerful electron microscope, you will see that you are made up of a cluster of ever-changing energy in the form of electrons, neutrons, photons and so on. And so is your wallet, your car, your spouse, and everything else.

Quantum physics tells us that it is the act of observing an object that causes it to be there and how we observe it. In fact, *an object does not exist independently of its observer!* This is because the observer has the consciousness. Some would even say that the observer *is* consciousness.

Although current quantum theory supports many of these theories, they are not really new. In the 1970's, Jane Roberts wrote the following in the Seth material, a study of metaphysics covered in a remarkable series of books, lectures and notes:

> *"There is a constant interchange between the realities, such as your world of physical construction and the worlds of construction which you do not consciously perceive.*
>
> *If five people stand observing that glass [a glass of water on a table], or rather if five people seem to be observing that glass, you have five different glasses, not one. Each person constructs that glass in terms of his own personal perspective.*
>
> *Therefore, given the five people, there are five different perspectives and space continuums in which a glass exists. Each of the five people is aware of only one space continuum, his own, in which his physical construction exists. However each of the five people has constructed a glass. In fact you have five physical glasses.*
>
> *Each physical glass is constructed of quite real molecules and atoms, which have their own generalized consciousness and capsule comprehension, and which form together in the gestalt called a glass. There is a point where five perspectives overlap.*

If you could find this one focal point, you could glimpse, and barely glimpse, the other four, using deduction from the point of overlapping.

The space continuums are created by each individual, in which he forms his own physical constructions. Now understanding this, you should be able to see how other planes, other reality continuums, can exist simultaneously with your own, and be unperceived consciously. This point of over lapse, or overlap, this point of overlap is extremely important, for there are points of overlapping in all universes." [2]

Scientifically speaking, *energy exists as waves spread out over space and time.* Only when you exercise observation do these waves become particles localized as a space-time event, a particle at a particular "time" and "space." As soon as you withdraw observation, the energy changes back from a particle to a wave. We know that atoms pulse on and off. When they are "on," they are part of our consciousness. When they are "off," they return back to a wave.

When you observe the quantum field with a certain expectation (such as a belief or intention), that quantum field performs to your expectation. You affect the quantum field, and do I, as does everyone else too. In fact, events are not things that happen to you. They are materialized experiences formed by you, according to your expectations and beliefs.

So, as you can see, your observation, your attention to something, and especially your intention, literally creates something in your life as a space-time event. And this is where your conscious intention, your will, and your affirmations actually work to change your life around you. We now know that thoughts are things. And every thought you have, whether it is conscious or unconscious, intended or unintended, shapes your reality *in every moment.*

SCIENCE IS SHIFTING EVERYWHERE

DNA

DNA is the molecule that carries genetic information in all living systems. Formed in the shape of a double helix from a great number of smaller molecules, the workings of the DNA molecule provide the most fundamental explanation of the laws of genetics. It has been estimated that there are approximately 125 billion miles of DNA in a human body, and that your personal DNA is long enough to wrap around the earth 5 million times.

Humans currently have two basic coils (helixes) of DNA. It is believed by some that at one time in human history, humans had a full consciousness compliment of twelve helixes. Humankind is now believed to be returning to the more conscious state of being, with all twelve DNA helixes activated. When this occurs, it will allow for interaction with the interdimensional spirit body (soul) contained within. [3] In other words, we will be more complete as humans, as we will consciously know, feel and communicate with our own soul essence.

Researchers have identified only a fraction of the total genome sequences. There exists much extra, unclassified DNA. The common name given to this mysterious DNA is "junk DNA" (also more accurately known as non-coding DNA). Junk DNA represents sequences that do not yet appear to contain genes or to have a function. Up to now junk DNA has been believed to be of little value.

Junk DNA constitutes approximately 95 percent of the human genome. Some scientists speculate that junk DNA may be archaic material left over from an earlier stage of evolutionary development. It has also been postulated to be involved in the evolution of new genes and possibly in gene repair.

In actuality, junk DNA provides a reservoir of sequences from which new genes can emerge. In this way, it is the genetic basis for evolution. Over time, as genetic mutations accrue, most will affect the junk DNA and not the functional DNA. Furthermore these mutations will likely modify parts of the junk DNA until they become functional, thus providing humans with new features or attributes. This is evolution in action.

Junk DNA is also theorized to be the storehouse of our conscious memory, also called cellular memory. This junk DNA carries all your personal, mental, emotional and physical properties from past, present and future lifetimes.

It is this junk DNA, which probably should be more accurately described as "divine DNA," which is beginning to come into the human consciousness and recognized for its inherent value. As humans evolve, we will achieve a state of glory that has been meant for humanity since the dawn of our species. This new DNA will give us increased levels of consciousness and many new exciting abilities. We are now entering a new stage of human evolution in which exciting new changes in our human composition will occur.

CHAKRAS

In Hinduism and some other eastern cultures, a chakra is described as an energy node in the human body. The seven main chakras are described as being aligned in an ascending column from the base of the spine to the top of the head. Each chakra is associated with a certain color, function, element, an aspect of consciousness, and other distinguishing characteristics. For example, the heart chakra relates to love, the throat chakra to expression, the third eye (eyebrow) chakra relates to intuition, and the crown chakra relates to divine expression. There are a total of seven main chakras.

The chakras are thought to vitalize the physical body and to be associated with interactions of both a physical and mental nature. They are considered to be a function of life energy, or prana, which flows along human energy pathways.

Many have observed a correspondence between the position and role of the chakras and those of the glands in the endocrine system. The Danish author and musician Peter Kjaerulff in his book, *The Ringbearers Diary*, describes the chakras in great detail, including the reasons for their appearance and their exact functions. He asserts that the seven chakras are said to reflect how the unified consciousness (the immortal human being or the soul), is divided to manage different aspects of earthly life. The chakras are invisible vortexes that root at the spinal column and extend into the seven layers of the aura.

Just as our DNA is evolving, our chakras are changing too. It has been theorized that additional chakras are now beginning to activate in the human body. It has been suggested that we will soon develop a new chakra system with a total of 12 chakras. As these new chakras activate, they will allow for increased levels of conscious awareness, improved communications, interdimensional relationships with the self and others, and a direct divine connection to All That Is. New chakras in and above the human head (chakra numbers 8-12) will additionally combine to form a new scalar wave antenna capable of enhanced multidimensional, telepathic communication. [4]

Humankind is now entering a new phase of evolution and is activating long-dormant DNA, chakras, and multidimensional capabilities.

CELLS AND SCALAR WAVES

Humans are changing on a base cellular level too. Human cells can now recognize light as an energy source. The new light energy coming into the body is measured by the amount of adenosine triphosphate (ATP) in the cells. Each cell has light focused directly onto it through the axial system. As light is received by the cells, the symmetrical head of the ATP molecule acts like a prism, reducing the light into color spectrums, which are then used by dormant junk DNA in a process of activation. [5] The axiotonal lines of light lie along the physical acupuncture meridians and connect up to your physical body through "spin points."

Contemporary cell research based on the principles of quantum physics shows the world as being created out of energy. Researchers have now demonstrated that our cells' membranes contain special proteins called Integral Membrane Proteins (IMPs) that respond to energy signals from the external and internal environment. These are important findings because they acknowledge that biological behavior can be controlled by "invisible" energy forces, which include thought. [6]

Practically speaking, when we shut off our internal mind-talk and concentrate our attention through things like intention, meditation, prayer, or contemplation, we tune ourselves into this subtle, spiritual, quantum-level energy matrix. When this energy is allowed to transfer to our DNA (without interruption from negative attitudes or limiting beliefs), it affects the molecular and cellular levels that drive all our physical metabolic processes. This is why we have the ability to heal ourselves through prayer, meditation or conscious intention. [7]

AFFIRMATIONS

I NOW AWAKEN TO AN ENTIRELY NEW DIMENSIONAL AWARENESS, FILLED WITH ASTOUNDING NEW REALITIES AND OPPORTUNITIES.

I NOW GROW INTO A WHOLE NEW STATE OF BEING, ACCESSING DIMENSIONS MULTIDIMENSIONALLY, AND RELATING TO MY WORLD IN A WHOLE NEW SUPERIOR WAY.

I NOW GROW AND CHANGE IN ALL WAYS ON ALL LEVELS FOR MY GREATER GOOD. I NOW DEVELOP AND EMBRACE THESE NEW CAPABILITIES AND GROW IN MY ABILITITIES OF WHAT IT MEANS TO BE HUMAN.

I NOW CALL UPON THE WISDOM OF THE AGES AND DIVINE GUIDANCE TO ASSIST ME AS I CREATE MY WORLD AROUND ME.

QUESTIONS AND ANSWERS

Q. Tell me more about quantum theory. It sounds fantastic. Can it really be true?
A. Yes! We are just beginning to understand the true nature of reality in our multidimensional world, and how we as humans can best operate in it. As the years pass, our awareness and understanding of these remarkable topics will increase greatly.

Q. How is it helpful to access higher dimensions when we need to live and manifest in the third dimension?
A. If you are entering a maze from the ground level, you may take several wrong turns before you find your way through the maze. However, if you can rise up to a higher level of understanding, and look down at the way things really are, you can more easily "see" your way through the maze.

Q. What does quantum physics have to do with manifestation?
A. When you consciously create change in your life with affirmations, visioning, and other similar techniques, you are influencing the subatomic world of the quantum field with your thoughts and intentions. You directly affect your own quantum field, whether you believe it or not.

Q. What do DNA and cells have to do with manifestation?
A. As we intend, we shift our dimensional awareness and we change ourselves in many ways on many levels. In doing so our DNA and cells change and grow to support our additional abilities.

Q. Why is everything activating now?
A. Humanity has evolved to this point in history where this is an option for us that we have created for ourselves. In a sense, we have graduated.

These "new" energies and experiences are actually very old ancient things that were created long ago. These energies have never gone away; only the memory of it was clouded and hidden from our conscious awareness. We have always had these abilities.

For example, there was a time when people didn't know they had a chakra system until someone brought it to their conscious awareness. Then people remembered and would feel and access the chakra systems easily themselves. Now people are starting to understand that we are just beginning a whole new journey of discovery that combines ancient knowledge, modern science, nature, reality and Spirit.

CHAPTER SUMMARY

1) With their consciousness, humans can change their world with their thoughts.
2) Humans are multidimensional beings, existing simultaneously in many dimensions.
3) Many of the traditional assumptions in classical physics we have about the world we live in are *wrong*.
4) Quantum theory supports metaphysical concepts of reality creation.
5) The universe consists not of things, but of possibilities.
6) Relationships and processes are more fundamental than substances.
7) The act of observing an object causes it to be there.
8) Our conscious observation and intention essentially changes energy from a wave into a localized space-time event.
9) Every thought you have, whether conscious or unconscious, intended or unintended, shapes your reality in every moment.
10) DNA is beginning to be seen as potentiality. Junk DNA provides a reservoir of sequences from which new genes can occur. Evolution is the result.
11) Chakras are increasing in number. New chakras will allow for increased levels of conscious awareness, improved communications, interdimensional relationships, and a direct divine connection to All That Is.
12) Human cells can now recognize light as an energy source.
13) Humans are changing on a cellular, dimensional, and consciousness level.

MANIFESTING WORKSHEET

One way to understand and apply the concepts of quantum physics is by considering your own physical body. Your body completely regenerates itself every seven to ten years. During this period, every cell in your body completely regenerates and is replaced with a brand new cell. This means that you can and do actually influence your body, your level of health, and the way you look, simply by your beliefs and expectations about your level of health, and what you think you should look like.

Furthermore, when you stand in front of a mirror and gaze at yourself, realize that the cells of your body are actually constantly blinking on and off. Only your consciousness focusing on your perception of the reality of your physicality causes it to be visible to you as you see it.

So, by understanding this, know that you can actually change things like your level of health and the way you look simply by changing your conscious awareness of the way that you think about your health and the way you should look. The dimension of time may make it seem that the process of change is slow, but it is a process just the same. As you gaze in the mirror, realize that the person you are seeing looks the way they do because that is your conscious understanding of the way that you think you should look. Not only that, but it can be changed in a moment, with a completely new thought!

Look at your complete body in a full-length mirror. List three physical things that you would like to change about yourself (even if it takes seven years to occur). Example: youthful appearance, different facial appearance, different posture). Know that these physical characteristics *can* be changed if you really want to.

1) _____

2) _____

3) _____

REFERENCES

1. *Small Times Online*, August 5, 2003
2. The Seth Material, the Early Sessions, Session 66
3. Sheldon Nidle, *You Are Becoming A Galactic Human*, (Spiritual Education Endeavors, 1994), p. 58.
4. Sheldon Nidle, *You Are Becoming A Galactic Human*, (Spiritual Education Endeavors, 1994), p. 68
5. Tashira Tachi Ren, *What Is Lightbody?* (New Leaf Distributing Company, 1999) p. 39.
6. Lipton, B., *Insight Into Cellular Consciousness*, Bridges, 2001, Vol. 12(1):5
7. The Heart of Health; the Principles of Physical Health and Vitality by Stephen Linsteadt, NHD

CHAPTER 8

Intention

"To think what you have not yet thought, is your real work."—Mike Dooley

STEPS TO INTENTIONAL MANIFESTATION

The following are the actual steps to intentional manifestation. We'll discuss each of these steps in this chapter and in the following chapters; this chapter focuses on intention and clarity of purpose.

Step 1—Create your Intention
Step 2—Clarify your Purpose
Step 3—Create your Affirmations
Step 4—Create your Visualizations

To create and manifest smoothly and effectively in the world, it helps to go through a process. This process of conscious, deliberate and intentional manifestation is defined and explained below. This process helps clarify and accelerate your manifestation. If you do not consciously create what is around you, then you create by default, and thus attract less desirable things and situations into your life.

By consciously and deliberately intending, you create what you want in life. It isn't hard to do. It simply takes some conscious awareness of what you are doing. As we learned in the previous chapter, this consciousness and intention is the actionable element which creates the third dimensional realities from energetic wave forms. Put simply, the energy goes from mind into matter.

The first step to manifestation is *understanding what you want to manifest*. This becomes your intention. With that understanding you become very clear about the picture that you are creating of the reality that you wish to live in.

Manifestation is a process of asking yourself internal questions. This is done to help clarify that which you truly desire. So the first question will be, what is your intention? What is the purpose of whatever it is you wish to create? You may have more than one intention, and you can use these steps for each one.

One important thing to remember is that *what you say and what you intend is what you receive.* So be careful of negative emotionally charged words. The phrases "I can't," "I should have," "I wouldn't," "I couldn't," "I didn't," should all be avoided if possible. A second thing to be aware of is that you should be certain that you are *ready for what you are going to create.* It will come.

STEP 1—CREATE YOUR INTENTION

Your first step to manifesting magnificence in your life is to create your intention. *This is the most important part of the entire manifestation process.* It must be done accurately, appropriately, and consciously.

1) Start by **writing down your intention**. Start with just one intention. You can add more later. *State your intention as clearly and precisely as possible.*

Note: Your intention is a bit different than your affirmation (next chapter). Your intention is what you intend. Your affirmation is the process of setting the intention into motion.

Here are some sample intentions:

I intend to change to a new career that brings me joy in my work.
I intend to bring a new person into my life for a long-term romantic relationship.
I intend to look at life in a positive way and see the good in things and situations.
I intend to become wealthy so I no longer worry about money.
I intend to change my physical body in a way that makes me look and feel better.
I intend to find a wonderful new home for me and my family to live in.
I intend to make wonderful new friends to share my life with.
I intend to overcome my sickness and become healthy again.
I intend to become more loving in all my ways.
I intend to be kind, compassionate and forgiving.
I intend to repair and improve relationships with relatives.
I intend to discover and strengthen my relationship with God.

2) **Address questions that arise** as a result of your manifestation. This will allow the manifestation to occur appropriately. For example, does this make sense for me right now in my life? Does it affect others? If it comes quickly to me will

I be ready? Your answers should be such that you feel good about them, and thus they are in alignment with you.

3) ***Understand the details of the manifestation and the impact it will have*** on your life and others in your life as a result of your intention. Be clear about the details.

4) ***Clearly word your intention*** to reflect your true thoughts. Consider the thoughts, wording, and beliefs in the intention. Choose your words carefully.

5) Check to see if your intention is ***in alignment with your heart.*** Do you really feel good about it? Do you feel good about all of it, and not just a part of it?

6) Check within yourself to feel if you ***deserve this gift*** of the manifestation. Are you worthy? Are you deserving, really?

7) See if you truly ***believe*** that you will receive it. All of it? Not just part of it? If you do not truly believe it, the manifestation will be more difficult to bring about.

8) Decide if you are willing to ***take responsibility*** for your intention. Are you willing to be personally responsible? Do you fully understand what it is you are trying to create, and do you *accept responsibility* for it?

9) Confirm with yourself that you are ***open to receive*** this in an unconditional way. Is there anything still blocking this from you?

10) Check in with yourself that you are in fact ***ready*** for this. Are you ready, now?

11) Once the manifestation occurs, be sure to acknowledge receipt and ***express gratitude*** for the manifestation.

CHECKLIST FOR FORMULATING YOUR INTENTION

Ask yourself:

1) Is this in alignment with my highest good?
2) Is this in harmonious balance with my life plan?
3) Is this intention specific enough?
4) Is this something I truly desire?
5) Is this something that I really believe can come about?
6) Is this something that I am fully open and ready to receive?
7) Is this for the good of all and harm of none?

When doing intentional manifestation, be clear about what your desires are, and about what you are willing and not willing to accept. Are you ready and willing to claim what is rightly yours?

I NOW MANIFEST MAGNIFICENTLY. I DISSOLVE ALL LIMITING
CONDITIONS AND BELIEFS, AND CREATE WITH EASE.

When you use your intention, you realign energy into a positive thought form. And in doing that, you set universal energy into action. *The greatest decision you must make in the process of manifestation is deciding on your intention.*

TO THINK WHAT YOU HAVE NOT YET THOUGHT

Spend some time exploring, imagining, creating, daydreaming, wondering, and visioning. Give yourself some time. And in doing so, try to think of new things, and new ways to look at things. Explore the unknown, the incalculable, the unforeseeable, and the unknowable. Think about what direction you wish to take in your life. *You are only limited by what you can think, and believe.* And that's why you need to take time out to *think.*

It is in times of personal reflection that you are able to see into and create your future, where you want to go, and who you want to be. You are able to open doors to other possibilities, and you are able to receive divine guidance as to which path to take. In doing so, you are consciously creating your life (rather than creating by default), and you are on your correct path of personal growth.

WHEN A PERSON IS UNCLEAR WITH INTENTION

If you are not clear about what you desire, you will get whatever comes along. You may know someone who has no clear goals, vision, or plan for the future. What kinds of things does this person manifest?

They often manifest a mish-mash of things. Often they support others until they are ready to venture out on their own, if they choose to. And actually, this is often perfectly acceptable!

Sometimes people are in an important learning phase or challenging stage of their lives. It may be important for them to experience various realities and interpretations of another's manifestations. Others amass real-world experience on how to accomplish or create something. They may be co-creating with someone else. They may be learning by doing. And they may be discovering ways in which they do not want to choose to do things.

Many people learn valuable lessons from one another in the co-creative process. There is no judgment about who is learning from whom, or about who is the teacher and who is the student. The world is a perfect place, and just as teachers seek out students to teach, students seek out teachers they can learn from. Realize too that these teacher and student roles may well have been reversed in previous lifetimes! That said, if it is time to put your own thoughts into action, do so!

> IF I AM NOT CURRENTLY ON MY DIVINE SPIRIT PATH, PLEASE SHOW ME WHAT IT IS. HELP ME TO KNOW IT, TO RECOGNIZE IT, AND TO DO IT.

SENDING MIXED SIGNALS

In the process of creating intention, indecision can cause delays, or an imperfect result. If the mind is sending confused signals (an oscillating sine wave), it makes the process more difficult.

For example, have you ever ordered something from a waiter at a restaurant, but realized as you ordered it, that you meant to order something else? Sometimes the universe brings you what you originally ordered, sometimes the universe brings you what you meant to order, and sometimes the universe brings you something else entirely. These are normally problems of clarity, because you are not being clear and decisive enough about what you want. If you are at a point in your life where things seem a bit stuck, it may be because you are unsure and unclear about which path to take. You are wavering and sending mixed signals. A lack of clarity brings about imprecise results, if any at all.

STEP 2—CLARIFY YOUR PURPOSE

Clarity is imperative if you want to accurately receive what you want to manifest. Clarity is all about getting to the essence of your directed thought, or intention. Clarity can best be achieved by introspection, reflection, and the process of questioning and listening to your answers.

For example, you may want to manifest a new friendship. But if you are unclear about why you want a new friend, and what you will do with this new friend, your new friend could be any kind of friend. It may be that you make a new friend who is extremely needy, or a friend who borrows money from you constantly, or a friend who talks about themselves incessantly.

Clarity of intention and purpose is critical to the accuracy of the thought progression of your intentional manifestation. Clarity allows for the illumination of pure Source awareness. Becoming clear on something can often be a sort of revelation. Such a breakthrough event may be fast and powerful, or it may transpire slowly, deliberately, and methodically. Powerful or subtle, discovering your clarity cuts through all distractions, attachments, and aversions to the direct experience of Source.

Try to match yourself to the energy of your intention. This allows for a time of checks and balances, soul searching, and a time to make changes and adjustments as needed. Take a pause to reflect, feel, and work with the energy of your goal. After working with the energy, you will arrive at a clarity of purpose and your intention will be much stronger.

AFFIRMATIONS

> I NOW CLEARLY INTEND THE BEST FOR MYSELF AND OTHERS, AND MY LIFE IMPROVES DRAMATICALLY AS A RESULT.

> THE DIVINE LOVE OF SPIRIT NOW ILLUMINATES MY PATH, AND MY INTENTION IS DIVINELY GUIDED.

> I NOW INTEND THE HIGHEST EXPRESSION OF MY BEING, THE MOST MAGNIFICENT EXPRESSION OF MY SOUL FORCE, AND THE CLEAREST MOST DIVINE MANIFESTATION OF MY LIFE PATH.

> I NOW CO-CREATE WITH SPIRIT.

QUESTIONS AND ANSWERS

Q. There's something I want to manifest, but I almost don't believe I can do it. What should I do?
A. It's good that you are being honest with yourself. You are coming up against resistance, a belief that is holding you back. Ask yourself why you do not believe it, then create another intention or affirmation for that. Alternatively, to release your feeling of doubt, visualize that limiting belief floating up and out of your body, back to the universe. You don't need that limiting belief anymore.

Q. What are the most common challenges people face with their intentions and manifestations?
A. Feeling that they are *deserving* of the manifestation, *believing* it can happen, and being *open to receive* it. Work on these three areas and it will help.

Q. Sometimes it takes a while for my intention to "gel." I don't always know exactly what I want. Sometimes it takes me a while to decide. What should I do?
A. This is why it is important to work with the energy of this new idea. It allows you to get comfortable. It allows you to see into the possibilities. It allows you to bring a

conceptual idea from the ethers into the physical. Ponder and meditate on it, in order to help bring it into the physical in a way that feels right to you. Once you are clear with yourself, your strong intention will follow.

Q. How long should it take for something to manifest?
A. There are several factors here:

1) The strength of your intentions, beliefs and convictions
2) Being clear and unwavering with your intention
3) Trusting that all will occur in due time

It is okay to be patient with yourself and the universe. Sometimes trying too hard will push it away from you. Things often occur with "divine timing," meaning that they transpire easily, effortlessly, and at the best time for all concerned. This is why it can be important to release it back to the universe for the perfect resolution.

CHAPTER SUMMARY

1) If you do not consciously intend, affirm, and deliberately create what it is you want, you will create by default.
2) An effective way to create what you want in life is by consciously and deliberately intending what you want.
3) Deciding on your intention is the most important part of manifestation.
4) Carefully formulate your intention(s) so that they reflect what it is you want.
5) Know that what you intend is what you receive.
6) Take time out to think. Sometimes it takes work to think. Make the time. When you can think of what you have not yet thought, you open new opportunities for yourself. If you can think it, you can manifest it.
7) Sending mixed signals of indecisiveness projects an oscillating sine wave of ineffective energy.
8) Clarify your purpose and intention for the best results. Clarity is all about getting to the essence of your directed thought or intention. Clarity allows for the illumination of Source awareness. A clear intention is like a solid, straight line.
9) Make sure you feel deserving of a manifestation, believe it can happen, and be open to receive it.

MANIFESTING WORKSHEET

You can intend certain outcomes and experiences as a result of various commitments and meetings that you may have. For example, next time you go to a meeting, conference, gathering, or celebration, create an intention for that event. You could intend that the meeting occurs smoothly, and that all business and communication transpires without incident, delay, or misunderstanding.

If you go to a celebration, you could intend that everyone there fully supports the celebration and accomplishment of those that the celebration is being held for, and that everyone there feels the joy and shares in the positive event.

You can set intentions before going out of your house each day, before meeting with your boss, or even before a workout at your gym. By setting your intention, you clearly communicate how it is you wish things to transpire in your reality and in your world, and thus are much more likely to achieve that outcome. By setting your intention, you literally influence your own quantum field and create a much more likely probable (desired) outcome.

List three intentions you plan to make at the next opportunity.

1) _____
2) _____
3) _____

REFERENCES

1. Mike Dooley, *Totally Unique Thoughts* (www.tut.com)

Chapter 9

Affirmations

"That which you dwell upon becomes your reality"—Anon.

STEP 3—CREATE YOUR AFFIRMATIONS

Now that you have your intention(s) clearly identified and written down, and you have worked with the energy to see if all is as it should be, it's time to manifest it! Affirmations are generally the fastest way to manifestation. An affirmation is a present-tense written or spoken statement which represents your intention. There are other ways to manifest (covered in the next chapter), but affirmations seem to work best for most people.

The intention that you formulated in the previous chapter identified exactly *what it is* you wish to manifest. This chapter on affirmations shows you how to *bring that intention about* and into your life, how to manifest it.

Affirmations have long been recognized as a powerful tool in manifesting desires. That's because the subconscious mind cannot differentiate between actual reality and suggestions. Therefore, the mind processes affirmations as being real, and then goes about using its powerful creative ability to bring those affirmations into your reality.

One of the best-known users of the power of affirmations was Muhammad Ali, the long-reigning boxing Heavyweight Champion of the World. Throughout his life and especially before he became champion, he constantly affirmed loudly and boldly, "I am the greatest!" And of course, he manifested that reality for himself. He was even known to proclaim in precisely which round of competition he would overcome his opponent. And sometimes, he did just that!

Affirmations are not new. Emile Coué, the 19th century French psychologist and pharmacist, became a pioneer of affirmation techniques when he introduced a method of psychotherapy, healing, and self-improvement based on autosuggestion or self-hypnosis. His book *Self-Mastery Through Conscious Autosuggestion* caused a sensation when it was published in England and the United States in the 1920s. He cured hundreds of patients in Europe and North America by teaching his patients to repeat the following affirmation each morning and evening: "Every day, in every way, I'm getting better and better."

FORMULATING YOUR AFFIRMATIONS

Here's how to create and use affirmations in your life.

1) Make your affirmations in the *present tense*.

Example: I AM NOW IN RIGHT WAY WITH PEOPLE AND OPPORTUNITIES WHICH BELONG IN MY LIFE AT THIS TIME, FOR MY HIGHEST PURPOSE. ALL IS AS IT SHOULD BE.

Do not state affirmations in the future tense, such as "I am going to get a great new job someday," or the results will always be waiting to happen. When you create your affirmations, act *as if* the desired result is already a reality. Because, believe it or not, it actually already is! Only the element of time in our third dimension is causing the appearance of delay.

Additional examples:

Poor: SOMEDAY I'LL GET A GREAT NEW JOB.
Better: I NOW MANIFEST A NEW JOB OPPORTUNITY FOR MY HIGHEST GOOD, AND IT MAKES ME FEEL WORTHY, HAPPY, AND VALUED.

2) Express your affirmations in a *positive way*. Affirm what you do want, rather than what you don't want.

Poor: I AM NO LONGER SICK.
Better: I AM NOW PERFECTLY HEALTHY IN BODY, MIND AND SPIRIT.

3) Get to the point and *be specific* about your intention, but do not be specific about the way in which you expect it to occur. That said, remember to also include key parts of your affirmations.

Good: I AM NOW IN PERFECT HEALTH.
Better: I AM NOW IN PERFECT PHYSICAL, MENTAL AND SPIRITUAL HEALTH.

TIPS FOR THE BEST AFFIRMATIONS

1) Impress yourself with your affirmations. Personalize your affirmations. They must resonate with you, and match your vibration. The more strongly you connect with your affirmations, the deeper the impression it makes on your mind, and the sooner you will experience positive results.

2) Recite your affirmations aloud to yourself repeatedly, such as once a day or several times a day. One to three times a day is usually best. This frequency is fairly easy to achieve for most people, and helps keep your affirmations in your consciousness.

3) Write down your affirmations repeatedly. This is another way to ground the energy into the physical.

4) When creating your affirmations, be careful to be clear and use detail. But don't use so much detail that you are limiting your manifestation. Use a level of detail that feels right for you and for your affirmation.

A major key to success with affirmations is to repeat them over and over again. Repeating your affirmations reprograms your subconscious mind to accept these thoughts as reality, and ultimately this creates changes in your life that will manifest this new inner reality. As a guideline, if you say your affirmations at minimum once a day for one month, you will have successfully reprogrammed your subconscious mind.

CHECKLIST FOR YOUR AFFIRMATIONS

1) *Write down your affirmations.* Put them onto paper, or type them into your computer. Feel free to use the sample affirmations included throughout this book. But also feel free to change the wording so that your affirmations are in your own words. Make them your own. Keeping your affirmations "in your head" is not ideal. Affirmations need to be written down so that they are "grounded into the physical," bringing them one step closer to physical manifestation.

2) *Speak your affirmations out loud*, slowly and clearly, with a strong voice. Speak confidently. Affirmations need to be brought into the third dimension.

3) Try to say your affirmations *at least once a day*. Repeat your affirmations often so they become part of you, and your subconscious mind. You can say your affirmations several times a day, if you like, for potentially faster results.

4) Speak your affirmations at the **same time every day**, if possible. Good times include: upon waking, before leaving for work, after the kids are dropped off at school, lunchtime, before dinner, or bedtime. You can also do them before or after meditation.

5) Try to choose a time and a place that is **private and quiet** to say your affirmations, where you will not be interrupted or distracted.

6) As you speak your words of affirmation, say them slowly and **feel the words** going out into the universe and being heard widely in all dimensions by those who are co-creating your new reality with you.

7) Say your affirmations for **at least one month**, longer if possible. If you can, start saying your affirmations at the start of a new moon period. This is generally a good time to start new things and ventures.

8) Modify and **change your affirmations** if needed to make them feel "right" to you. The stronger and more personal your affirmations are, the stronger the bond with your conscious and subconscious mind.

9) Feel free to **substitute** words if needed. For example, if you are uncomfortable with the word God in your affirmations, substitute that wording with Spirit, Source, Universal Life Force Energy, Infinite Intelligence, or simply leave out the reference.

10) **Write new affirmations** when needed. Remove older affirmations when you have manifested the desired change. Continue to use and modify your affirmations as needed.

11) Feel what the affirmations feel like as if they are already true. Capture that feeling of being **as if** you are already where you want to be when your affirmation is fulfilled. Feel and believe as if your affirmation has already happened. Be happy and filled with joy as you affirm.

12) Be **passionate** about your affirmations. Relax, get comfortable, and feel the affirmations fully as you speak them. Think carefully about the full meaning of them. See them "working" in your mind.

13) Be **certain** that you will achieve your intention. Be absolutely sure. Know that in some way, this affirmation will bring about your intended result, one way or another.

14) **Get ready** for some big and fast changes in your life!

MY HEART SINGS WITH JOY, AS I NOW MOVE INTO A WHOLE NEW WAY
OF BEING. I NOW CONSCIOUSLY CREATE MY LIFE MOMENT BY MOMENT,
AND I AM GRATEFUL FOR THE DIVINE RESTORATION OF MY AFFAIRS. I
NOW CONSCIOUSLY MANIFEST IN MY LIFE.

When you formulate and write down your affirmations, you are taking
a non-physical conceptual thought form and bringing it into your physical reality.

WHY AFFIRMATIONS WORK

It is important to understand *why* affirmations work, since affirmations work in many
ways on many levels. Here's why affirmations work so well:

1) Both your conscious and unconscious mind are hearing and working with your
affirmation, and helping bring it to you in a multidimensional way. Change
is beginning here in the physical world, but also in other unseen dimensions
of time and space.

2) When you affirm, your personal energetic vibration is changing. You are
broadcasting a different (and higher) energy. If, for example, in your
affirmation you release fear and replace it with love, your energetic vibration
changes as a result. Thus, you "broadcast" an improved energy field.

3) You are communicating with your higher self and spirit guides clearly and appropriately. An affirmation brings your intention out into the open. Your intention is clear.

4) You are communicating with the higher selves of those people who may be affected by your intention. The higher selves of people who may come into your life, go out of your life, or resolve issues with you will respond in some way to your affirmations. This is one of the "magical" aspects of affirmations. For example, if someone is "waiting" to be called to come into your life, the affirmation helps achieve this.

5) You are clarifying any incorrect assumptions. Believe it or not, those in the spirit world will not necessarily read your mind to know exactly what it is you truly wish to accomplish in your life! They will not violate your privacy. Your affirmation, spoken clearly and concisely, out loud, broadcasts your clear intention out into the universe and to all who are listening. This is very important.

6) Your spoken word helps put things into action. Where before you may have just been pondering something or debating with yourself in your mind, your stated intention and affirmation makes it real and sets the universe into motion to bring about your intended result.

7) You are coming into a place of balance when you intend and affirm. The push and pull of your busy life is placed into the background, while you relax, intend, and affirm your direction. When you affirm, you are centered and in your power.

8) By repeating your affirmations, you are prioritizing your unconscious mind. You are managing your unconscious. You are telling your unconscious mind what is most important in your life. It needs to know! You are filling your mind with a positive thought. You are consciously replacing any negative or limiting beliefs with positive, empowering ones.

9) You are consciously changing in a way that you wish to. You are placing more focus on your own life. Your affirmations will help you put your own goals into action. No longer will you be torn in different directions by those around you who have a stronger vision or intention than you do.

10) You are creating. You are reassuming your role as a creator being, as you co-create with Spirit and you manifest great things. After all, this is your divine right!

11) You are setting many people into motion. You call into action people currently in your world, as well as new people waiting to come into your world. You are also calling in angels, spirit guides, teachers, masters, and other co-creators who are just waiting to hear from you, who love you dearly, and who will do all they can to help you fulfill your dreams.

12) You are *asking* for assistance. Although those in the spirit world are always there to help you, they hesitate to involve themselves in a substantial way until asked. When you ask, you open the floodgates for all new things and opportunities to come in.

13) You are helping yourself on many levels, in many dimensions, throughout time. Like a domino effect, things fixed and resolved in this world are resolved throughout other dimensions and lifetimes simultaneously.

14) Your affirmations are helping clear up long-standing karmic ties with other people. Karmic ties are essentially unresolved issues, and are an imbalance in your life. Because the universe seeks balance, these issues want to be put back in balance. When it's time to complete karma with somebody and move on, almost nothing works as well as affirmations.

15) You are turning possibilities into realities. You are turning waves of particles and possibilities into a physical time-space event. Your consciousness is making it real in this dimension. You are bringing things into the "now" moment.

16) When you write and speak affirmations, you are grounding things into the physical, into the third dimension. This is why affirmations are not nearly as effective if just kept "in your head." They need to at least be written, and are even better when spoken.

Probably the single biggest reason that affirmations work so well, out of all the reasons listed above, is that you are clarifying your intention and projecting it out into the universe for all to hear and know. Not only are you changing yourself with your new vibration, your angels, spirit guides, teachers and others in the world of the unseen will also *hear your words* and *make every effort* to respond to your affirmations and assist you. Do not underestimate this great power you have!

Also, the higher selves of those people whose lives may be affected by your affirmations will also hear your words and respond to your affirmations (such as if you are forgiving someone, or if you are attracting someone new into your life). Your affirmations make it easy for your higher self to communicate directly with the higher selves of others. This is extremely important to know and understand.

Know that the universe will do all it can to support your intention, affirmation and vision. As we learned in the earlier chapter on universal laws, the universe seeks perfection, and will work its magic to search high and low into all the possibilities and potentialities in order to help you manifest what you want.

AFFIRMATION CONDITIONS CHECKLIST

Because intentions and affirmations can make things happen quickly, it is important to be clear about them. You can add any one or more of these conditional "switches" to the end of your affirmations for increased clarity and condition. This can be important, as you want your manifestation to occur in a way that is best for all concerned, especially you. See if any of these switches are appropriate for you:

- For the good of all and harm of none
- With ease and grace
- In alignment with my highest good
- In its perfection
- On all levels
- In harmonious integration with my spiritual path
- Multi-dimensionally
- In harmonious relationship with my family
- In harmonious balance with my life plan
- This or something better
- In alignment with my personal ascension
- In a manner transparent to the physical
- According to my highest good

These conditional "switches" are like computer subroutines, or like filters. It is like an "if, then" statement in a computer program. For example, perhaps a new career path is your intention, but only if "in harmonious relationship with my family." So, for example, a new job opportunity that you manifest in the same geographic area would be good, but a job offer from far away may be less than ideal if family members do not want to relocate. Here's an example:

Good—I NOW MANIFEST A NEW CAREER OPPORTUNITY.

Better—I NOW MANIFEST A PERSONALLY FULFILLING NEW CAREER OPPORTUNITY, IN HARMONIOUS RELATIONSHIP WITH MY FAMILY.

Best—I NOW MANIFEST A WONDERFUL NEW PERSONALLY FULFILLING
CAREER OPPORTUNITY WHICH BRINGS ME MUCH JOY AND ABUNDANCE.
I MANIFEST THIS IN HARMONIOUS RELATIONSHIP WITH MY FAMILY, AND
IN HARMONIOUS BALANCE WITH MY LIFE PLAN. THIS OR SOMETHING
BETTER COMES TO ME NOW, AND I REMAIN ETERNALLY GRATEFUL.

PERSONAL GROWTH AND CHANGES

If you are on the spiritual path and others in your life are not, it can create unique
challenges for both you and those close to you. You may want to have your spouse,
partner or family understand you and the spiritual path you are taking, and why you
are called to do what you are doing. This can be key if you make important career
changes, life decisions, and other choices which may seem like a mystery to others. You
can ask for understanding, acknowledgement, and compassion in your intention and
affirmations. Ask that things occur appropriately and for the best of all concerned.

I NOW ASK FOR COMPLETE UNDERSTANDING AND SUPPORT OF MY
JOURNEY ON THE SPIRITUAL PATH BY THOSE WHO KNOW ME AND
LOVE ME.

Know that as you change and grow personally, things will change around you. Your
relationships will be affected. Family, friends, and coworkers will be affected. If you
affirm that the changes will occur "with ease and grace," then things should transpire
more smoothly.

Write down your affirmations, work with them, and develop their energy. The more
you work with them, the more you build the momentum of the affirmation. Once you
become clear about what you want, and feel in your heart that it is right, that is the
best time to let it go. If you are still unclear with it, work with it a little more.

This can be similar to prayer, in that you pray for something but then let it go. Release
it to the universe. If it is for your highest good, it will manifest. Remember:

- Be specific enough about what you desire;
- Believe that it will be given to you; and
- Have no preconceived expectations as to the outcome.

USING AFFIRMATIONS FOR FORGIVENESS

One of the best and most effective uses for affirmations is forgiveness. Affirmations
make it easy and lasting to forgive anyone for anything.

One great reason this works is because as you affirm your forgiveness for someone, your higher self is communicating with the higher self of the person you are forgiving. The forgiveness is actually happening on an etheric level. Your higher self is a spiritual translator, so to speak, who does all the difficult work for you.

As a result, you do not necessarily have to forgive someone in person. You can if you want to, but oftentimes deep emotions can make it difficult to do. Because forgiving someone in person can be difficult, many people simply choose not to forgive someone at all. They hope that energetically, things will fade away with time. This is not the best resolution for unresolved issues. Sure, things can and do fade away with time, but not completely. It is so much better to get completely clear of something in this lifetime. Affirmations can do this.

> I NOW FORGIVE EVERYONE WHO CAN POSSIBLY NEED FORGIVENESS IN
> MY LIFE NOW. EVERYONE NOW FORGIVE ME.

As you speak your affirmations of forgiveness, try thinking of the names of the people you are forgiving, one at a time. This will help focus your attention on them, as you communicate with their higher selves.

THE MAGIC OF AFFIRMATIONS AND FORGIVENESS

When you express forgiveness for someone in an affirmation, you will *feel* it working. Energetically, things *will* change. Best of all, next time you see the person you have forgiven with your affirmations, they will somehow feel and act a bit differently toward you. They will *know* and *sense* that something has changed between the two of you, because it has! You have forgiven them. They won't necessarily understand what has happened, but they will view you and treat you differently And that's good!

What has happened is that you have cleared your karmic ties with them, and released the unresolved issues. You have set them free, and in doing so you have freed yourself. You have broken the chains that have bound you together for far too long.

AFFIRMATIONS

> I NOW AFFIRM MY GOOD, AND IT COMES TO ME IN THE PERFECT WAY,
> AT THE PERFECT TIME, FOR MY HIGHEST GOOD.

> I AM NOW BALANCED AND IN HARMONY WITH THE UNIVERSE. THINGS
> COME TO ME EASILY NOW.

> I NOW CREATE IN HARMONIOUS BALANCE WITH MY HIGHER SELF AND
> MY LIFE PLAN.

I NOW CALL IN MY TEACHERS, GUIDES, MASTERS AND ANGELS. I NOW EMBARK ON MY HIGHEST SPIRIT WORK, AND NOW ACCEPT AND APPRECIATE DIVINE SUPPORT AND GUIDANCE.

THE LOVING SPIRIT OF GOD NOW WORKS THROUGH ME TO BRING LOVE AND LIGHT TO ALL.

QUESTIONS AND ANSWERS

Q. I'm not exactly sure how to word my intention. Any ideas?
A. Get a pen and paper and work through it. Here is one way:
First try: I AM GETTING BETTER GRADES
Second try: I AM IMPROVING MY PERFORMANCE AT SCHOOL
Third try: I AM GUIDED TO THE BEST COURSES, TEACHERS AND LEARNING OPPORTUNITIES
Fourth try: I AM GUIDED TO THE BEST COURSES, TEACHERS AND LEARNING OPPORTUNITIES FOR MY HIGHEST GROWTH, AND I NOW THRIVE AND EXCEL IN THIS ENVIRONMENT WHERE I AM LEARNING ON MANY LEVELS.

Q. How many affirmations should I have? What is the ideal number of affirmations for the maximum results?
A. Any number from 1 to 100 is appropriate. Probably 3-10 affirmations is typical. It also depends on the number of different topics you are affirming about. Many people find that ten affirmations are just right. However, as time passes, some affirmations go out and other new affirmations come in.

Q. I don't have months and months to wait. I need changes now! What can I do to get my affirmations to work fast?
A. The true power of affirmations is in the *repetition* of them, and the *feeling* of them. As you say them, feel them deeply. That will help. And say them often, too. But even though you are in a hurry, you must *release* your intention to the universe. Otherwise you will be chasing it, and in doing so you will be pushing it away from you. It's a delicate balance of intending, trusting, and allowing. But it is easy to learn with a little bit of practice.

Q. Aren't affirmations kind of like positive thinking? I do that already. Will affirmations really make a difference?
A. For many of the reasons discussed, affirmations are often far more powerful than positive thinking alone. The main reasons that affirmations are superior are:

1) you are grounding your intentions into the physical
2) you are affecting and influencing your quantum energy field
3) you are calling in help from all those around you (physical and non-physical)
4) you are putting your intentions into your conscious and subconscious mind

Affirmations are often a more "conscious" action than positive thinking. Affirmations can also be thought of as a type of ritualized prayer, if you prefer to look at it that way. Thus, if you are inclined to, you can emphasize and ask for divine assistance to help bring about your manifestation.

CHAPTER SUMMARY

1) An affirmation is a present-tense spoken or written statement which represents your intention.
2) Create your affirmations by writing them out and working with them.
3) State affirmations in the present tense for the best results.
4) Repeating your affirmations multiple times reprograms your subconscious mind with a new and better reality.
5) Understand that affirmations work for a number of reasons, on many levels (multidimensionally).
6) Affirmations work so well because they help to clarify your intention, broadcast it out to the universe, and share your vision with your higher self and others.
7) If desired, conditional switches can help your intention manifest more smoothly (example: "with ease and grace").
8) Use affirmations to forgive, release, and be at ease with people or difficult situations in your life.
9) Affirmations are magical in a way, as changes often occur mysteriously, unexpectedly, and divinely.
10) The true power in affirmations is the repetition of them and the feeling of them.

MANIFESTING WORKSHEET

If you have not already done so, choose something in your life that you would like to work on. Formulate an intention. Then, write out your corresponding affirmation below. Here are some examples to help you get started:

"I now _____"
"The divine love of Spirit now _____"
"I trust in the universe to _____"
"_____"

Your Affirmations:

1) _____

2) _____

3) _____

4) _____

5) _____

CHAPTER 10

Visioning

If you see what can be, it will become part of your future reality.—Andrew Lutts

STEP 4—CREATE YOUR VISUALIZATIONS

Another powerful way to manifest things into your life is to envision them. Where affirmations use the spoken word, visioning uses mental imagery, visions and picturing to bring about your intended result. You can use either affirmations or visioning, or a powerful combination of both affirmations and visioning to achieve your desired result.

A vision is the imagined manifestation of a deep desire of your life. Simply put, you can envision things the way you want them to be. And if you can be passionate about your vision, your results will be even better.

When we envision a thing or situation, we are "training" our mind and body to respond with feeling to it. Thus we are getting used to the feeling, and in doing so we are attracting the thing or situation to us.

Visioning is a simple, easy and effective way to bring the new into your life, by helping you get the feeling of what it is like to be there. And by the way, you can't fake these feelings. If you want to use visioning effectively, you must do so in truth. You cannot deceive yourself, or take shortcuts with this process.

The exact same concepts associated with spoken affirmations apply to visioning. That is, the extent to which you both *feel* and *believe* they will happen profoundly affects the outcome.

Here's how to use visioning to manifest in your life.

Step 1—Collect photos, magazine pictures, brochures, catalogs, postcards or other images of what it is you want to manifest. You can even draw a picture if you are good at that. Choose images that are big, colorful, vibrant, joyous, happy and inspiring. Do not choose small, dull, depressing images (unless that is what you want to manifest).

If you want to bless your images in a natural way, add elements from nature such as leaves, pinecones, flowers, ferns, or shells. This will help harmonize your vision with your environment.

Step 2—With your images, create a collage or collection of your images. You can add words (like love, joy, abundance, peace, etc.) to your collage. You can also add a picture of yourself into the collage. Place these images where you will see them at least once a day, but being able to see them all day is best. Surround yourself with these images. You can put your images in several different places. Here are a few ideas for where you can put your pictures and images:

1) bedroom mirror
2) bathroom mirror
3) refrigerator door
4) kitchen cabinet
5) the inside of the front door of your home
6) automobile dashboard or console
7) computer monitor
8) office workstation walls or panels
9) computer background "wallpaper"
10) purse, wallet, or briefcase
11) inside a pocket
12) the wall of the garage where you park your car

Step 3—Now visualize yourself with that manifestation as part of your life. See yourself in it, and it in your life. Picture yourself in that situation, with all that great energy, those happy people, and good things. *Feel that feeling* when you are part of that experience. Own it. Make it yours. Believe.

Connect with your higher self by pausing briefly, and thinking of your higher self. Share that vision of your future self with your higher self. Remind yourself that you are supremely worthy, and more than deserving, and that you are open and ready to receive. Be at one with your images, and be ready to live that moment over and over until you are fully one with it. Soak it all up, and make it part of your life. Bring it into every cell of your body.

*The process of visioning is the use of mental imagery
and picturing to bring about an intended result.*

If you see what can be, it will become part of your future reality. Anything that you can imagine is possible. Focusing your energy and attention on the vision makes it possible. Believing that it is possible further reinforces your intention.

There are additional things you can do with pictures and images besides creating a collage. You can create a bulletin board of images, you can find a box to put your images in, you can get a notebook and put all your images inside it. These various methods all do the same thing: help you focus your energy on what you are seeing in the pictures in order to draw that energetic reality to you.

I NOW SEE AND ENVISION AN ENTIRELY NEW REALITY FOR MYSELF, FILLED WITH DIVINE LOVE.

EXPLORING FEELINGS OF MANIFESTATION

Explore and capture the feeling of what it is like to have a certain thing or situation that you want. At the same time, avoid the feeling of lack, the feeling of not yet having what you choose to manifest. Once you can explore the feeling of "as if," it is already a reality, you are halfway there. The common expression "fake it until you make it" speaks in some way to this concept. Feeling "as if" it is already a reality in your life is the key.

- Feel what it's like to be in your new home, the perfect home, and having your first dinner there.
- Feel what it's like to be in a wonderful love relationship with a great partner, doing fun things, going to fun places, feeling completely loved and valued, feeling like time is standing still, being fully in the moment, and living as if nothing else in the world matters.
- Feel what it's like to be driving around in your shiny new car, feeling like a million dollars as you cruise down the boulevard.
- Feel what it's like to be wealthy and generous, giving money away to people, organizations and charities who deeply appreciate your generosity and kindness.
- Feel what it's like to be in deep, deep meditation, connecting up with Spirit, feeling love pour into your body, feeling all your problems and worries melting away into insignificance, feeling that you are the most loving and loved person in the world.
- Feel what it's like to be wearing new and stylish jewelry and clothing, and how it makes you feel so wonderful and alive.
- Feel what it's like to have all the time in the world that you need, time to spend with the young, with senior citizens, with disadvantaged people, and others who appreciate your kind ways, generosity, and companionship.
- Feel what it's like to be in a great work environment, where people are happy, smiling, working together well, and accomplishing great things together.
- Feel what it's like to spend some quality time with great new friends who share your interests, value your opinions, and enjoy your company.
- Feel what it's like to be going to your secluded vacation home, and how relaxed you feel as you arrive there for a long weekend of quiet serenity after a busy work week.
- Feel what it's like to create a grass-roots organization, where you mobilize people for a common cause and work to make our world a better place.
- Feel what it's like to open up your new store or business on the first day, with tons of new customers pouring in, and how it makes you happy that you've realized your dream.
- Feel what it's like to spend a weekend away with your family, with everyone getting along, happy, spending time together, and enjoying each other's company.

Once you are able to live and capture these feelings, you are well on your way to manifesting that reality into your life.

THE YARD SALE TEST

A good way to get started and test out your ability to manifest through visioning is through yard sales, garage sales, tag sales, church fairs, second-hand stores, and antique stores. Here's how.

If you have an idea of something you would like to manifest, create a vision of it in your mind, and put your thought out there into the universe. If it is something where it really doesn't matter if it is new or lightly used, so much the better. Perhaps you are looking to manifest a child's bicycle, a fishing rod, or table lamp. Give it some thought. Picture in your mind seeing that object. Ask the universe to find it for you.

Oftentimes, just weeks later, you will happen to drive by a yard sale and spot that perfect bike, fishing rod, or table lamp that you have been thinking about in your mind. There it is, the universe matching it up for you!

You can do this kind of thing in countless ways, with countless things. Have fun with it! Practice. The universe is more than ready, willing and able to accommodate you. Be sure to acknowledge and thank Spirit upon completion of the manifestation. By expressing gratitude you will only support more pleasant outcomes to experience in the future.

USING VISUAL CUES AS REMINDERS

Here's an example of a friend manifesting a new kitchen set. She wanted all new beautiful white matching kitchen appliances. She found a nice glossy brochure of exactly what she wanted, and put that brochure onto her refrigerator.

So, every time she walked by her refrigerator she would see the image of beautiful white matching appliances in her kitchen. By putting the brochure image onto the refrigerator in the kitchen, she was actually putting her new kitchen where it was going. She was visioning the new kitchen set, right where it would be. And then, the new kitchen manifested for her, easily and in right way.

Visioning helps pull the energy in. With the image of the matched kitchen set she was *putting out a slight loving reminder that she was ready, open and available to receive this.* In doing so, she was adding more love vibration to the manifestation. If you come from a *heart-centered* place, your manifestations will come to you much more easily.

CREATING A VISUAL VORTEX

Another way to use visioning is with an energetic vortex. First, visualize what it is you want. Then, create a small swirling vortex of energy inside your mind. Picture the vortex swirling and growing up from within your body up your spine and out the top of your head, like a swirling tornado, pulling in the things you want to you. Let the energy of the vortex run for a while, and feel the vortex reaching out into the universe, bringing in what you desire.

Your vortex is actually a powerfully energetic attraction tool. It reaches out into the universe, far and wide. Those things of matching energetic vibration feel the vortex, and thus come to you in physical form. This is a great way to use your natural powers of attraction to literally pull things, people and opportunities into your life.

You can activate your own Vortex of Attraction.

ADDITIONAL CREATIVE EXPRESSIONS

Besides visioning, other powerful ways to explore some of your thoughts, feelings and intuitive expressions are by drawing, painting, singing, composing music, building, constructing, and otherwise freely expressing yourself in unbounded ways. Use some of your God-given skills and abilities to explore your expression. After all, you are a creator, and co-creator.

If you are unsure as to what it is that you want to do, listen to your dreams. Dreams come to tell us something about our lives that we are missing. Dreams, thoughts, and daydreams all guide us. Keep current life questions in mind, and watch for directions in dreams or intuitive thoughts. Also, many of our answers mysteriously come to us from other people. Stay open to the possibilities. Be aware. Listen.

> *"Your vision will become clear only when you look into your heart . . .*
> *Who looks outside, dreams. Who looks inside, awakens."*—Carl Jung

For example, when you start a new day, ask to be shown a sign. Think about a dream, and ask for clarity and understanding about what that dream really means.

> THE LOVING SPIRIT NOW GUIDES ME WITH DREAMS AND VISIONS TO MY HIGHEST SPIRIT PATH, AND I REMAIN OPEN TO THESE MESSAGES. I NOW SEE INTO THE POSSIBILITIES AND DOORWAYS OF OPPORTUNITIES WHICH OPEN UP TO ME.

MAKING LISTS TO MANIFEST

There are other well-known ways to manifest. Goal setting, list making, positive thinking, and other techniques all work well.

One way to manifest appropriately is to make three lists:

1) What you want to eliminate from your life
2) What you want to manifest into your life
3) What you are grateful for

By writing down these three lists, and working through them, you will help accelerate the desired changes.

Another fun way to manifest is to make a list with two columns:

1) That which you are willing to do
2) That which you would like the universe to handle

This is a great way to shift some of the work to the universe; it is very happy to do it. One key with this exercise is actually *believing* that the universe will do its part.

Here's an example. Say you plan a long road trip in your automobile. On your side of the list, you write in "preparing your car, preparing your driving route, and packing your items." But you do not want to worry about finding a place to stay overnight along the way. Also, you do not want to worry about your home while you are away. So, on the column that the universe will do, you write down "finding me pleasing and comfortable accommodations along my path." You also write down on the side of the universe, "making sure that my home is cared for while I am away."

This way, when you embark on your journey, you have these two things that the universe will handle for you. And of course if you really don't believe that the universe will find you a place to stay and take care of your home, that will be your experience. But if you truly believe, know and trust that all will be taken care of, it will be. It is all about what you believe, and trusting in the process as it unfolds. So, if you truly believe it can unfold this way, don't be surprised when someone from the neighborhood just happens to call or visit, and offer to watch your house for you while you are away or just happen to mention that they have a close friend along the way that loves to have visitors.

Another way to manifest with lists is to write yourself a letter. In the letter pretend that you are writing the letter from sometime in the future, and that all that you wish to create in your life has occurred. In the letter, include descriptions of what things are like, and make a list of all the wonderful things that you have manifested for yourself. Then put the letter away, but read it to yourself from time to time. This will help bring it about into your reality. By writing yourself a letter from the future, you are bringing that future reality into your current reality.

It is perfectly acceptable to set goals, write down goals, use lists, and employ other more traditional techniques in addition to what has been included here. They all work by helping to bring something conceptual (an idea) into the physical (an intention, goal, or list).

AFFIRMATIONS

> I NOW ENVISION AND EXPERIENCE A NEW PEACEFUL LOVING REALITY
> FOR MYSELF, FILLED WITH POSITIVE PEOPLE, MEANINGFUL LEARNING,
> AND LOVING RELATIONSHIPS.

> I AM NOW A SWIRLING VORTEX OF ATTRACTION ENERGY, AND ATTRACT
> TO ME ONLY THAT WHICH IS FOR MY HIGHEST GOOD.

QUESTIONS AND ANSWERS

Q. When collecting images for my collage, should there be people in the images too?
A. This depends on what you want. Say you are looking to manifest a house. If you want a house and family with lots of kids, then find an image of a house with lots of happy smiling people doing things that families do. On the other hand, if you are surrounded by people all day long and you want to manifest a quiet, secluded, private home, then find that type of image.

Q. I love yard sales and second-hand stores. But why can't I just manifest something brand new?
A. You can! It's your choice. You can manifest whatever you like, new or used.

Yard sales are a fun way to warm up and practice your skills. It can be a great feeling when you follow your instincts and are guided to a particular yard sale, and find a special antique or unusual item that you have been searching for. Trust in the universe to provide, then follow your intuition.

Q. I like the idea of a swirling tornado vortex. It sounds powerful. But is it dangerous? Will I attract things I don't want?
A. The law of attraction is at work here, and the vortex magnetizes and multiplies the attraction. If you are projecting positive, loving peaceful energies, that is what you will attract to you.

CHAPTER SUMMARY

1) Visioning is an imagined manifestation of a deep desire of your life.
2) Visioning helps train the mind into accepting a new reality.
3) Surround yourself with images, and visualize yourself with the intended manifestation as part of your life.
4) Envision the situation as if the change has already occurred.
5) Connect and share your vision with your higher self.
6) Explore the feelings associated with your new vision.
7) Try visioning various things and then finding them at stores, yard sales, etc. in order to practice your skills.
8) Put up visual clues around you as loving reminders of what it is you want to attract to you.
9) Create a mental, energetic vortex of swirling attraction energy to draw people and things toward you.
10) Use lists to manifest in your world. Make a list of what you would like to do, and what you would like the universe to do.
11) Write yourself a letter from the future, with all that you wish to manifest having occurred.
12) If you want people in your life, make sure there are people in your images and visions.

MANIFESTING WORKSHEET

Answer the following five questions in writing in order to create a vision for yourself that you can manifest in your life:

1) What is your greatest talent or gift: _____
2) What is it that you like to do: _____
3) What is your deepest desire: _____
4) What is it that you absolutely trust and know to be true: _____
   _____
5) What is one thing to do now: _____

CHAPTER 11

The Flow of Energy

"I am a vessel in service. Spirit, flow through me."—Andrew Lutts

ENERGY IN MOTION

One important thing to do when manifesting and creating in your life is to keep the flow of energy moving. Do not hold onto things that are no longer wanted, as they block the way for new things coming into your life. (We discussed this a bit in Chapter 4, "Making Way for the New.") You must allow for a correct and easy flow of energies into and through your home, workplace, and life. Principles of the popular ancient Eastern practice called Feng Shui support this concept.

To make room for the new, let go of old things. Go through old belongings, and throw them out. Donate old clothes to charity. Create a vacuum (physically empty space) in your life so that grand and glorious new things can come into your life.

Today many people are such enthusiastic consumers and collectors that they literally fill up their houses with material goods. Our society has created shopping malls, mega malls, and specialty stores so that we can buy more and more things. And we need larger houses to put everything in, too! And when our houses are full, we put our possessions into storage facilities. In fact, consumerism is a kind of disease, born from the belief that we need external, material things in order to feel good about ourselves inside.

This concept of clearing works for things, but it also works for people too! Is there an old boyfriend or girlfriend that you are hanging onto, just because they are familiar? Do you have old friendships with people that just aren't going anywhere? Are there coworkers at your office who are unhappy, and should have moved on months or years ago? Do you belong to groups or associations that are stagnant? Make room for new people to come into your life by consciously releasing those other people back to the universe.

> I NOW RELEASE TO THE UNIVERSE THOSE THINGS AND PEOPLE IN MY LIFE WHICH NO LONGER SERVE MY HIGHEST GOOD. I NOW BRING NEW PEOPLE AND SITUATIONS INTO MY LIFE. I AM NOW WITH THE RIGHT PEOPLE IN THE RIGHT WAY, AND IT FEELS GREAT!

OWNERSHIP AND PHYSICALITY

Ownership of items can sometimes block energy flow. Be conscious about your feelings around ownership of physical things. Ownership of an item, such as a house, does not necessarily mean that you need to be attached to it. Own it, and enjoy it. But acknowledge it for what it is, a house. It is not you.

Realize that if you own a house, a more accurate way to look at it is that you are a caretaker of this house. It is yours, for as long as you choose to own it. But someday, for any number of reasons, you will likely no longer own it. Realize that now, and know the difference between owning something and being attached to it.

This is actually quite obvious with the concept of land ownership. Can we really "own" land? Can we take it with us if we want to move? Of course not. Embrace the responsibility of being a caretaker of things like a home, land, fine jewelry, collectibles, antiques, paintings, family heirlooms, family documents, etc., as long as you choose to own them. But know that someday these things will pass out of your hands and into someone else's.

For example, if you have inherited valuable family jewelry from your parents, know that although you "own" and can fully enjoy that jewelry now, some day you will pass it on to someone else. Knowing this, it subtly shifts some of the obligations and "ownership" of this jewelry back to the universe. It can help unburden you from ownership, if you develop an attitude of being a caretaker or custodian. Also, more importantly, it allows for the proper flow of energy.

However, also know that the real power in the process is knowing that you can manifest anything at any time anyway! So there is really no need to struggle with ownership issues when new things can be brought in easily.

Here's a story of a good friend named Katerina who inherited a beautiful and valuable set of European Hummel figurines from her mother. The figurines had passed through many generations of matriarchs in the family, and had significant sentimental and symbolic meaning to this woman.

But the time had come to divest herself of these figurines, and pass on the joy of ownership to another sibling in the family. Although it was extremely difficult for her to "give up" the figurines which meant so much to her, she did so with an enlightened view of the situation, realizing that her time as caretaker had passed to another.

Although Katerina had attached much meaning and personal feelings to this set of figurines, she eventually began to realize that these figurines were merely symbolic of her personal self-worth as a matriarch for her generation. She courageously passed them on, and learned a valuable lesson about the issue of ownership.

Two common expressions describe someone as "attached to his earthly possessions" or "a slave to her possessions." Do you sometimes feel that way? These phrases reflect an attitude, or belief. If you adopt the view that you are not attached to these possessions, but are instead merely the current owner or caretaker, it shifts much of the burden of ownership away from you and back to the universe.

TRUSTING THE UNIVERSE TO PROVIDE

When you keep the flow of energy open, you are trusting that the universe will provide for you perfectly. Not only that, but it will provide for you *in the perfect way, at the perfect time, with the perfect solution.* It is fully within the capacity of the universe and the Infinite Intelligence to do so. Believe it!

> I TRUST IN THE UNIVERSE TO PROVIDE APPROPRIATELY FOR ME NOW,
> IN A DIVINE WAY, FOR MY HIGHEST GOOD.

Here's a true story about when I was looking to manifest something in my life: a boat. After deliberating on what kind of boat I wanted, I found a colorful picture of exactly the kind of boat I was looking for. I taped the image to my computer monitor at work, so I would see it every day, all day.

During that time, I also began the physical search for the boat. I started looking in all the boat-for-sale advertisements. The boat I was looking for was fairly common, and should have been easy to find.

I called around on the phone, drove around in my car, and looked at many, many boats for sale over the next few months. I knew what I wanted. I had a clear vision of it. I had the money. And I wanted it badly. But none of the boats I looked at were just quite right. I drove around the whole state looking for this boat, driving hundreds of miles in the process. But I just could not seem to find the right boat.

So, with despair, I gave up looking. I consciously said to myself, "I need to let go of trying so hard to find this boat." And I let go of my search.

Well, just a few days later, while I happened to be driving through the next town, not five miles from my house, I spotted the perfect boat, and subsequently bought it. I cannot even remember why I happened to be driving there. All I know is that Spirit put me there so I would see the boat.

Sometimes we try too hard to "make" something happen, when something just isn't right. In this case, when the search for the boat was released to the universe, the universe found it for me quickly and easily, by placing me in the situation where I would see it.

We sometimes spend much time and effort chasing a fleeting goal which usually manages to stay just ahead of us, in sight but not in reach. We fail to realize that the reason it is fleeting is that we are chasing it. If we would only stop chasing it, release the search to the universe, and make a space for it in our lives, then it will find us. Just as in my hunt for the boat, once the search was given up, a void was created. Then the universe came in quickly to fill it. Trust in the universe to provide appropriately.

I NOW SURRENDER THE DETAILS OF THIS SITUATION TO SPIRIT. I NOW RELEASE AND TRUST IN THE UNIVERSE TO BRING THE PERFECT RESOLUTION, AT THE RIGHT TIME, IN THE RIGHT WAY.

A conundrum: It can be difficult to know the difference between trying too hard or just being persistent. How do you know the difference? There is no easy answer to this. But often times, you can check into your heart about how you feel about a situation. In my own case of looking for a boat, it had begun to feel like drudgery, and was no longer the fun experience that it should have been. That was a good clue for me to stop pursuing that path and strategy, and release it to the universe.

If you do not trust fully in the universe to provide for you in right way, you set up all sorts of blockages. For example, people who hoard or stockpile things are not fully trusting that when they need something, it will appear. People who are reluctant to give up things often use these things as a crutch to cling to safety and security. All this does is reinforce the fear of loss, as the focus is on scarcity and shortages rather than abundance. For example, people who grew up in the 1930's in America, during the

Great Depression, are often not fully trusting of an abundant universe. As a result, they are inclined to save, collect, and stockpile.

Remember that the ultimate in wealth, abundance, prosperity, and perfection is in *knowing that at any time you can manifest any thing for any reason.* The universe will provide for you whatever you want or need right now. If you have total and complete trust in this reality, it is true for you.

I TRUST IT WILL BE SO. AND SO IT SHALL BE. AND SO IT IS!

In fact, *if you trust completely,* all will be manifested for you. Parts of yourself that vibrate doubt, fear, mistrust, anxiety, lack, and other limiting beliefs are simply areas of your being that are in non-belief. Believe it or not, the universe can provide everything that you desire. It is a universal law.

I NOW ACCEPT MY UNCLAIMED GOOD. I NOW BRING TO ME AND MANIFEST THAT WHICH HAS BEEN HELD BACK. I NOW MANIFEST GLORIOUSLY IN MY LIFE NOW, AS I AM WORTHY AND DESERVING OF ALL THE ABUNDANCE THAT SPIRIT HAS FOR ME NOW.

Here's a true story from a woman named Judy Panko which illustrates the flow of energy, generosity, and trust in the universe:

I work in a parking garage near the University of Nebraska, so I see it all the time: A driver will pay the parking fee for the car behind him, then that driver will pay for the next car, and so on. It's a bit of a tradition, especially at sports events. A random act of kindness that makes people smile.

One night there was a ballet at the campus performing arts center. A man gave me double the fee and asked that I let the people in the next car know that he'd paid for them too. "You're all set," I told the teenagers in the next car. Then they paid for the next guy. The chain reached the tenth car. A new record!

Car number eleven pulled up: A mom driving an old station wagon. She'd won tickets and wanted her daughter to see her first ballet, but didn't have money for parking. I told them the car in front had already paid. "No kidding! I prayed God would help me with this," she exclaimed. In this case, I guess it wasn't such a random act after all. [1]

I NOW THANK THE UNIVERSAL SPIRIT FOR SHOWING ME THE DIVINE WAY OF ALL THAT IS.

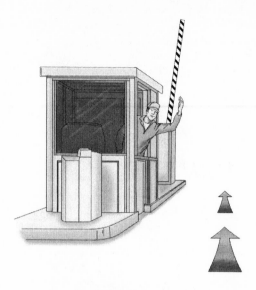

*"Go right ahead. You're all set.
The universe is waiting!"*

BEING AFRAID OF LOSS

People buy all sorts of insurance products to protect against losing something. But realize that the more you worry and fret about losing something, the more energy you put into that feeling of being afraid of loss. Thus you attract that possibility to you.

People who win millions of dollars in lotteries oftentimes discover that the money is gone just a few years later. Why? It is likely that they are unable to match the vibrational energy of being in abundance. They just can't see themselves as millionaires. It may also be a result of the fact that they may feel they are simply not *deserving* of millions of dollars since the money came to them so easily. And thus, the universe in its perfect way finds a way to separate them from their newfound money.

Another curious thing is that people who are very wealthy often have one major fear: that they will lose their money. Again, when people focus on something, it places energy onto that expression.

SPECIAL DELIVERY TO YOU

Today people feel that the more, bigger and better things they accumulate provide safety and security. Material wealth is one way we measure success in our society.

As an example of how we process the distribution of wealth and the flow of energy in the physical world, consider large companies selling products. Huge international retail companies pride themselves on their methods of distribution. Because of point-of-sale automated computerized inventory processes, even the largest companies know at any moment how much of an item is in stock, at which store, at what price, in which color, and how many days of expected inventory remain before more of that item is needed. These large companies have done a masterful job in creating systems which anticipate and track the flow of finished goods and materials to the hands of the consumer, in order to fulfill a desire of the consumer, and make a profit by doing so. The efficiencies of distribution are truly amazing.

Think of the universe like this, only even better, and far more perfect! The universe is not just limited to one store, one product, one color, or one low price. It can and does search the world over to provide you with just the right thing, at the right time, in a perfect way, in order to help you on your growth path. Not only that, but sometimes the universe will even deliver it right to you, and at no extra charge! The universe always seeks perfection, in its infinitely intelligent ways. Who could ask for anything more?

When you are in the flow, trusting, and connected to the universe, you:

- Allow for unrestricted flow of energy to you
- Open up to any number of possibilities
- Magnetize people, situations and opportunities to you
- Are co-creating with your higher self and with Spirit

True success and abundance is being one with yourself, one with Spirit, living in an unlimited universe, allowing for the flow of energy to you, and trusting that the universe will provide for you in great abundance whenever called to do so.

CHECKING IN WITH YOUR HEART

Energy wants to run smoothly and effortlessly through you and around you. When your energy is flowing naturally and you are in complete alignment and balanced, your pathway is smooth and easy.

However, if you forget to check in with your heart before you make a decision, and then make a decision which goes against your real truth, you are in effect putting up a kind of wall. The energy is unable to move, and must then seek out an alternative pathway.

Also know that sometimes things can take time to manifest. This is okay. Don't give up on your intention too early, especially if it is something that comes from the heart.

Additionally, sometimes the energy of a situation changes, and things can begin to become difficult. In this case, you will know that something needs to be changed, because manifestations do not occur, or do not occur in a desired way.

One example of this is someone who is in a job that they do not like. Perhaps things at work begin to become more difficult. Little things turn into big things. Work that was once fun and joyful becomes tedious and monotonous. The job may be exactly the same, but the perception of it and the work situation have changed. Energetically, the flow is being filtered and blocked. If you listen to your heart, you will know that some kind of change is needed. (Read more on this in Chapter 14 on Workplace Manifestation.)

"Your own heart and self is your best authority"—Chief Joseph [2]

GIFTS AND GIFT GIVING

Gift giving is another example of energy in motion. We have heard it said that the person giving the gift is actually the one benefiting from the giving. Now we know one reason why this is true. As one person gives a gift to another, the giver creates a vacuum, an imbalance. The giver is putting energy into motion. As long as the giver is giving from the heart, the giver will almost assuredly receive some kind of energetic return from the universe as a result of their generosity. This is the law of reciprocity in action. It could be in the form of anything really, but it will be positive. It could be something as simple as love.

If you are given a gift, refusing to accept it is not a good idea. By refusing to accept a gift, you are literally blocking the flow of energy to you from another. If someone has taken the time to try to give you a gift, you are helping them by accepting the gift.

LUXURY AUTOMOBILE SELF-TEST

One way to gauge the flow of energy to you is to consider your attitudes towards a luxury automobile. We can see the way energy flows to us and through us in physical ways, such as how we think about various automobiles and what they represent to us. When you see a beautiful luxury automobile like a Mercedes Benz, Jaguar, Lexus or BMW, what are your feelings toward its owner? Do you think to yourself "that rich jerk" or "arrogant snob?"

If you feel anger, jealousy or resentment towards that person, you are placing emotions onto that expression of abundance that comes with ownership of a luxury automobile. You probably realize that this is *not* the kind of emotional perspective that will draw that abundant experience into your life!

A better way to view the abundance and ownership of that kind of luxury automobile would be something like "that's for me" or "that's my kind of car" or "I love it, isn't it beautiful" or "I'll take mine in red." With these positive expressions, the feeling projected out is much more of an attraction energy.

Taking this concept even further, if you would like to manifest a luxury automobile for yourself, go for a test drive. Open the sunroof. Tune in your favorite radio station. Adjust the power seat. Adjust the mirrors. Make it fit *you*.

In doing so, you will develop, cultivate and practice the *feeling* of owning a fine automobile. And in doing so you will reinforce your attraction energy to it, and it to you. Sometimes it can take people a little time to "warm up" to the feelings of being deserving and worthy of something new to them. A "test drive" helps capture that feeling.

Of course this concept of "trying things out" is not limited to just automobiles, you can do this for anything:

- If you're looking to attract a new home to you (and you to it), try going to "open houses" in a neighborhood that you like.
- If you're looking for new employment opportunities, try going to a career day, or try going to a friend's place of business and spending some time there to get the feel of another work environment.
- If marriage is on your mind, visit a bridal shop or tuxedo store. Try on outfits and view yourself in the mirror.
- If higher education is on your mind, visit a college campus to feel what it is like to be a college student.

> I NOW RELEASE ALL LIMITING BELIEFS FROM MY BEING. I NOW RECEIVE ALL THE UNIVERSE HAS FOR ME, APPROPRIATELY. ALL MY ACCUMULATED GOOD NOW COMES FORTH TO ME AND SHOWERS ME AS RICH BLESSINGS, AND I AM GRATEFUL.

DOING WHAT YOU LOVE TO DO

One of the best ways to improve the flow of energy to you and access the abundance you deserve is to do what you like to do best. When you do what you love, you move into alignment with the universe. You live more "in the moment." Energetically, the signals you give out are positive and powerful, and attract abundance. Also, when you are doing what you love, you attract friends, family, clients, coworkers, and others who wish to be a part of it. If you are truly doing what you love to do, people are attracted to it, and respond to it!

Energy flows through you and around you.

BALANCE AND BEING CENTERED

When you are balanced, manifestation comes more easily. Another way to think of being balanced is being at the center in a quiet place, like in the eye of a storm or hurricane. While all around you is swirling and moving, you are in a very quiet place. You are in a position of power, at the center.

When you are balanced, you can manifest effortlessly. The energy in the universe flows smoothly around you and supports you. And the clearer you are, the more "perfect" the manifestation.

When you are balanced, you are like a solid, sturdy pillar of marble holding up a Greek temple. You are unshakable. In this way your transmission of energy is solid and your thoughts and intention go out to the universe in a perfect way.

When your energy is unbalanced, problems arise. You may adopt a victim mentality, or things may just seem to "happen" to you. When unbalanced, your solid, sturdy pillar of marble flexes back and forth. Bipolar feelings may arise, with extremes of emotions and feelings. As a result, the energy that you vibrate out is a less preferable oscillating sine wave.

When you are unbalanced, the manifestations may not come, or may not come in the best way. For example, if you are out of balance and try to manifest a new roommate, you may in fact attract a new roommate, but one who is very difficult to live with. Being clear and in balance is very important when manifesting.

MAGNANIMITY

If you are feeling "stuck" and that abundance is not flowing to you, think of someone you can give something to. This affirms your own abundance, and reaffirms your prosperity. It reinforces your strength, and your ability to manifest whatever is needed to take the place of what you are giving. It gets the flow of energy moving again.

It shouldn't matter at all what you desire in life; one way to obtain more of something is to give it away to somebody else who needs it more than you do. It can be money, it can be knowledge, it can be love, it can be anything at all you desire for yourself. The way to get it is to give it away, and create a new void.

As we have seen, by giving you create a vacuum in your life, a space that the universe is ready to fill. And that is where your abundance is created. When you create the vacuum for the commodity which is the media of exchange, you cause an imbalance which the universe will soon fill once more, *with interest.* The concept of tithing is founded on this universal law. In fact, many wealthy people create foundations and trusts in order to give money away and keep the flow coming to them. It can be a full-time job!

Some of the most prosperous people in the world are those who are the most generous. This is no accident. Although it may be difficult to know if these people became generous and giving before or after achieving abundance, it can be safe to conclude that keeping the flow of energy moving is a concept that they are fully aware of. No matter what level of prosperity you feel that you have, you can learn from these people by being generous. In doing so you affirm your own prosperity, and make way for much more abundance to flow into your life.

TITHING

Traditionally, tithing is the action of contributing or paying out a tenth of one's income. Customarily, this contribution is given to a church. The word tithing comes from the word ten.

While tithing is a noble concept, it can be charged with all sorts of emotions. There are usually two parts of tithing people feel uncomfortable with:

1) If you are trying to become abundant, how will it help to give away ten percent of everything you make?

2) You may or may not be particularly inclined to give your money to a church or other organized religion just because someone says it's a good idea.

Tithing is a completely personal choice. Here are some thoughts on the subject to help you decide if tithing is right for you.

First, if you choose to tithe, it is most powerful when you tithe to where you are getting your inspiration from. This may or may not be a church. Tithing is best done when you tithe to whomever, wherever, or whatever you are receiving inspiration, spiritual guidance, assistance, creativity, and divine help from.

Secondly, the *real power* behind the concept of tithing is this: God, the Universal Spirit, is the source of your prosperity, not persons or conditions. Thus, by tithing to where you get your spiritual inspiration, you are partnering up with the Universal Spirit. [3]

The people, channels, circumstances and conditions from which prosperity flows to you are always changing. They are not the ultimate sources of prosperity. The Universal Spirit is the ultimate Source. And this *never* changes.

Tithing is affirming your prosperity consciousness. When you give back to Source in a way that you personally align with, it reinforces your abundance in a powerful way. It completes the circle of energy flow. It keeps the flow of energy going through you strongly, as the universe supports your positive efforts. It is a very strong statement of trust and belief. Whether or not you make the decision to tithe in a conscious, deliberate way, know that *God is the source of your prosperity*, not persons or conditions.

BEING DESERVING

If you do not feel as though you are deserving, you will block the flow of energy to you. You must *feel that you deserve* what you wish to manifest. Many people say they want to win the lottery, but few people feel that they completely deserve it or are clear about what they would do once they receive it.

Jealousy is also related to being deserving. Jealousy often occurs when people feel that they themselves are not deserving. For example, people often become jealous of a neighbor who has something new. This is because they don't understand that they too can manifest for themselves.

TIPS TO OPEN AND INCREASE ENERGETIC FLOW

Be sure to do the following to help energy flow to you:

1) Take your time. Allow the universe to provide in its perfection, at the perfect time, in the perfect way. Trust in the universe!

2) Be open to virtually any idea or possibility of how your manifestation might come about. The universe may surprise you and provide you with what you want in a completely unexpected way! This can be a lot of fun when you acknowledge that the universe has brought you something in a way that is entirely and completely unexpected.

3) Keep your mind steady. Don't be wishy-washy. Being unsure broadcasts an uneven thought projection. If you begin to intend something and then later change your mind to something else, the universe must stop and start over to support your new choice.

4) Stay in your integrity. Don't take on other people's attitudes of disbelief, regret or doubt. They are not yours! There may be people you know who think that they are doing you a favor by suggesting that something is just "not possible." All they are telling you is that in their reality, it is surely not possible for them. Because that is their belief, their reality supports it. But you know better. It is not *your* reality. In your reality, it may be entirely possible!

5) Be true to yourself. Don't be tempted to "make a deal" with the universe. Don't make the manifestation contingent on something else happening or not happening.

6) Be confident and trusting. Don't worry and fret. Your manifestation involves a large amount of trust. Trust it and release it.

7) Guard your thoughts carefully. Don't focus on what you don't want. If you do, you will attract the unwanted to you. Be very careful with your thoughts, and what you focus your attention on.

8) Keep your faith. Don't give up. Even though you have "released it to the universe," you need to keep your intention in your conscious and unconscious

mind. Affirmations and visioning are important because they help you keep your intention in your consciousness.

9) Keep your intention clear, simple and direct. Don't make your intention complicated and convoluted.

10) Keep it positive and for the highest good of all concerned. Don't use these techniques to harm or hurt another. They will only come back to harm you.

11) Think big! It's okay to start out small to practice your skills. But ultimately, think big and go for it. There's no reason not to!

12) Express gratitude and acknowledgement once your manifestation has occurred. This will only bring in more good to you. Thank you, thank you, thank you.

ALL ABOUT RESISTANCE

Sometimes people are held back from manifesting because of one key concept: resistance. Resistance is a term used to describe the feelings, both conscious and unconscious, that are comprised of long-held beliefs about limitation, fear and lack. Resistance means you don't let the energy flow through you. Resistance is an aspect of fear. The opposite of resistance is harmony.

Often, resistance is the result of beliefs that you absorbed while growing up in an environment where you adopted the beliefs of others. Resistance can also come from limiting beliefs inherited from past lives. Left unchecked, resistance can sabotage your best efforts. Here is a list of resistance and limiting beliefs. You will likely recognize many of these, and you may even believe a few of these!

EXAMPLES OF RESISTANCE AND LIMITING BELIEFS

-   You have to work hard in life to succeed
-   Nothing good ever comes without working for it
-   Within every life a little rain must fall
-   The more you make the more they take
-   If it happens too easily, it can't be right
-   Life isn't fair
-   No matter how hard you try it won't make any difference
-   You can't fight city hall or the government
-   You can't have fun and earn money at the same time
-   Life is hard
-   You're not good with mechanical things

- That's the way of the world
- If you don't work hard at it, the results aren't valuable

Try to identify any limiting beliefs you have, and when you took on that certain limiting belief. It may have been an authority figure in your life (parent, teacher, relative, etc.) who passed this belief onto you. Naturally, you accepted it. It might have even sounded like good, reasonable advice at the time. But now you know better.

Belief patterns are normally deeply rooted in our emotional experience, and we must heal the wounds which cause unconscious and self-defeating behavior. Try to identify these limiting attitudes, remember where they came from, work through them, and release them back to the universe.

For example, you may affirm that:

ALL THINGS COME TO ME NOW, PERFECTLY AND EASILY,

and yet you actually believe deep inside that nothing really good can come "easily," and that anything really valuable comes only from hard work. Perhaps a parent gave you a work ethic of labor and toil. This is your resistance.

You may affirm that:

I NOW HEAL MYSELF ON ALL LEVELS IN ALL WAYS, AND AM NOW PERFECTLY HEALTHY,

and yet you are afraid of your illness, and fear the worst, and are reluctant to believe that you can actually make yourself better. Perhaps a doctor gave you a particular prognosis, and you find it hard to believe that another different outcome is possible.

You may affirm that:

I TRUST IN THE UNIVERSE TO PROVIDE APPROPRIATELY TO ME NOW, IN A DIVINE WAY, FOR MY HIGHEST GOOD,

and yet you don't really believe it, and are afraid to "let go and trust." Perhaps you have narrowed the ways in which abundance can come to you, because of various beliefs.

You may affirm that:

I NOW ATTRACT A NEW ROMANTIC PARTNER INTO MY LIFE, TO SHARE MY LIFE WITH, AND GROW TOGETHER IN LOVE, and yet you don't feel you are deserving of such a simple, easy wonderful loving outcome without a lot of searching, struggle and strife to make it that way.

Resistance can show up as internal roadblocks, outer roadblocks, or both. Inner roadblocks are often beliefs that you may have acquired, such as a poverty consciousness. Outer roadblocks can be physical manifestations such as sickness, handicaps, accidents, and other things which have manifested in your life and may prevent you from moving forward.

Be mindful of any and all limiting beliefs that you have which may be holding you back. They may not be new to you, and you may have struggled with them for years. Now it's time to work through them, and release them. They are no longer serving you. Release them. Let them go, now!

EXPECTING THE UNEXPECTED

It is important to have no preconceived ideas whatsoever as to how something may come to you. The possibilities are unlimited.

Looking for a new car? How about someone you know giving you their car because they temporarily lost their driver's license?

Looking for a romantic partner? How about suddenly realizing that your best friend means a lot more to you than just great friendship?

Looking for a new job? How about unexpectedly receiving a job offer from a previous employer, begging to have you back at any salary level?

Looking for a new apartment or house? How about your very reliable car unexpectedly breaking down in front of the perfect apartment or house, one that you have driven by a hundred times before without noticing it?

Looking for recognition for your efforts? How about unexpectedly being asked to speak as an expert in your field of knowledge?

WAYS TO OVERCOME RESISTANCE

To overcome resistance, first identify it. Then, think about it. Work with the energy. Feel your thoughts of resistance and disbelief come in, acknowledge them, and then rid yourself of them.

One way to rid yourself of resistance is to imagine yourself writing down on paper (you can actually write it down, too, if you like) your negative beliefs of resistance. Then throw the paper into a roaring fire. Watch your old limiting beliefs burn up into nothingness, and disappear from your life. Do this more than once if you need to. Know that your belief has been released back to the universe, you are done with it.

Here's another way to rid yourself of resistance and limiting beliefs. During meditation or a quiet time, imagine yourself at the bottom of a peaceful lake, deep under water, lying on your back, looking up to the surface of the water and the sun and clouds in the sky. One by one bring your limiting beliefs of resistance in from the side. Then, shape each belief into an air bubble and let it simply rise up slowly to the surface of the water. Watch it rise up, away from you. Visualize the bubble reaching the surface of the water, then just popping and disappearing into the atmosphere. It is now gone from your consciousness. You have released the limiting belief. Do this as much as you need to, or every time you feel that limiting belief arise.

With your affirmations, you are already bringing new and better realities into your unconscious and your consciousness. In doing so, you are reducing unconscious patterns of resistance. Because two thoughts cannot occupy the same space, your older limiting beliefs will be replaced by far superior new ones.

EMPOWERING BELIEFS WHICH OVERCOME RESISTANCE

Now that you have released any limiting beliefs, you can now bring new, superior empowering beliefs into your consciousness:

- You can be or do anything you want in life
- If you make your mind up to do something, you can't help but succeed
- You are always lucky
- You can have anything you want in life
- No one else has your mix of unique talents
- With God as my partner all things are possible
- You are completely unique in the world
- Things always come easily to you
- If you can think it, you can do it
- You're a natural
- Everything you touch turns to gold
- No one is as good as you at it
- You can do no wrong
- Go with God

AFFIRMATIONS

I NOW RELEASE THE OLD, AND BRING NEW INTO MY LIFE.

I NOW TRUST IN THE UNIVERSE TO GUIDE ME IN ALL WAYS THAT ARE
FOR MY HIGHEST GOOD.

I NOW MOVE TOWARD MY HIGHEST SPIRIT WORK, AND MY HEART SINGS
WITH JOY. THOSE THINGS AND SITUATIONS THAT ARE NO LONGER FOR
MY HIGHEST GOOD NOW SLIP AWAY AND OUT OF MY LIFE WITH EASE
AND GRACE.

I NOW LET GO AND TRUST.

QUESTIONS AND ANSWERS

Q. I'm an anxious person. I'm always afraid something bad will happen to me. I realize
that this doesn't help. What should I do?
A. By being afraid that something bad might happen to you (like a car accident), you
attract that energy and possibility to you. So you are attracting energy, but the wrong
kind! So you must take some time and explore that fear. Where did it come from?
Who gave it to you? What were the circumstances? When you are ready, release that
fear back to the universe. You are *done* with it! Acknowledge that you have learned
from that belief, and that you are moving on.

I NOW RELEASE ALL FEARS AND LIMITATIONS FROM MY BEING. I AM
CONFIDENT IN MIND, BODY AND AFFAIRS. ALL THINGS COME EASILY
TO ME NOW.

Q. Are you sure it's okay to be both very rich, and very spiritual? How can I achieve
enlightenment if I am making all sorts of money?
A. Yes, it is okay. Poverty consciousness blocks the flow of energy. It's time to release any
limiting beliefs. Remember, the universe is unlimited, so there is no reason you cannot
be both abundant and spiritual and anything else you want to be. Everyone can.

Q. I failed your self-test about those luxury automobiles. I always figured that everyone
driving a Mercedes Benz or Jaguar was a rich snob. But at the same time I wouldn't
mind having one myself. What's my problem?
A. Your personal beliefs are polarized. You must shift your attitudes about the feelings
you have about expressions of abundance. You need to get balanced and centered.
Don't be jealous or disdainful. Be loving. Be happy for these people. Imagine what
color your automobile will be. Imagine taking someone for a ride. Imagine cruising

down your street, and being seen in your beautiful luxury car. How does that feel to you?

Q. Hold on a moment. That all sounds nice. But I'm getting conflicting messages here, I think. Isn't wanting a Mercedes Benz or Jaguar a sign of gross materialism? Aren't there more important things in life than a shiny new car?
A. We live in a physical world, and physical things like our personal choices of the automobiles we drive are obvious examples of how we choose to project ourselves in the world. You can and should choose to express yourself in any way you like. There is no judgment of your personal choices.

Nonetheless, physical possessions like cars, clothes, jewelry, and houses often have a strong correlation to our ability to manifest situations and results in our lives. They are physical manifestations of the sum of our choices and beliefs.

What we can do is to practice on these physical things, and better develop all our manifesting skills. Once you feel comfortable with your abilities to manifest physical things, you can work on manifesting less tangible things like relationships, understanding and awareness, personal spiritual growth, awakening, and enlightenment.

Q. What's wrong with becoming wealthy by working hard, and saving carefully, and managing my money judiciously?
A. Nothing! That's a fine way to become wealthy. However, this question seems to imply a belief that it takes hard work, a certain amount of time, and a measure of sacrifice to achieve your goal. Many people believe this. Because it is their belief, it is also their experience. However, others may believe that they can become wealthy quickly and easily. And that is likely the experience that they will have. It's your choice.

Q. How do I know when something is not for my highest good?
A. Because it is not working, or it is not manifesting. If the greater love energy is supporting it, it will manifest. But if it is not for your highest good, it may not occur.

One other reason it may not occur is that you are not clear about what you want, or you are vacillating about what you want. Perhaps you keep changing your mind about whether or not you want this to occur. Perhaps mentally, you want to do something, yet in your heart you feel that it is not correct. The mixed messages will be ineffective.

Q. I understand that I need to "let it go." But I also want it to "happen." How can I do both? This seems a bit tricky. What's the real answer here?
A. The real answer is that it is a careful balance of intending, allowing, being open, and trusting in the universe to provide. Be sure you are true to yourself, that your heart is in it, and that emotionally it feels right.

Q. What are some of the things that manifesting works on?

A. It works on everything. It works on houses, health, romance, spouses, friendships, jobs, careers, everything! It will work on any situation or any thing, when appropriate. In every moment of your life, you create your own reality, and the life you choose to live.

However, if something is not for your highest good, or it is somehow in conflict with your life contract, it may not manifest the way you expected. Also remember that when another person is involved in or affected by your manifestation, it adds an additional dimensional component to the manifestation.

Q. What happens when what you are trying to manifest is in conflict with what someone else wants to manifest? What happens here? Who wins?

A. Great question! Firstly, if at all possible, the universe will try to arrange for an ultimate solution where everyone wins. However, sometimes this simply cannot occur. In instances in which a positive outcome is not possible for all, the universe will still attempt to serve the highest good of all. This means that your manifestation may or may not occur, or it may be delayed. Because others are involved, the situation becomes more complex. Relationships can fall into this category where there are many people involved and affected, with many possible outcomes.

CHAPTER SUMMARY

1) Keep the flow of energy moving throughout your life.
2) Release attachments to people and things. Clear out the old and make way for the new.
3) If appropriate, adopt the attitude of being a caretaker or custodian of something rather than the owner, in order to shift some of the burden or limitation of ownership.
4) Trust in the universe to provide for you in the perfect way, at the perfect time, with the perfect solution. It is fully within the capacity of the universe to do so.
5) The more you worry or fret about something undesirable (such as losing money, getting sick, etc.), the more energy you give to that possible reality.
6) Check into your heart before making a decision to insure that it does not go against your truth.
7) Gladly give and accept gifts in order to keep energy flowing.
8) Don't be jealous or disdainful of the prosperity of others. Instead, see yourself in that abundant situation and attract that possibility to you.
9) When you do what you love to do, you move into alignment with Source and the universe.
10) Focus your energy on success that you have had up to now, and it will bring in more.
11) Be magnanimous to reaffirm and reinforce your abundance.

12) When you are balanced and centered, energy flows smoothly around you, resulting in a more perfect manifestation.

13) Tithing helps you partner up with Source as you co-create for a combined good.

14) Get the energy around you moving again by overcoming resistance and limiting beliefs. Identify those limiting beliefs, remember where they came from, work through them, and release them.

15) Replace old, unwanted limiting beliefs with strong new empowering beliefs. If you can think it, you can do it!

16) You can be or do anything you want in life. manifesting worksheet

In order to increase the flow of energy to you and through you, do any one (or all three) of these activities below:

1) Do something nice for someone but do not tell them or anybody else. Keep it a secret. Know that the universe will somehow return the favor to you in some way.

2) Leave a dollar bill somewhere with a little yellow sticky note that says "God loves you and told me to leave this for you as a sign that all your needs will be met." Alternatively, your note could say something like "The Universal Spirit loves you dearly, and asked me to leave this note for you as a sign that you are loved."

3) Pick an address out of the phone book at random and write a letter to a stranger. In the letter, tell them you are involved in a spiritual project to spread love and that you picked their name at random. In your letter tell them that you want them to know God loves them and that you will keep them in your prayers for a day, asking that all their dreams come true. Know that your thoughtful kindness will be returned to you many times over in countless ways.

REFERENCES

1. *Guideposts,* July 2005, story by Jodi Panko, Lincoln, Nebraska
2. Quote from Chief Joseph of the Nez Perce Tribe, Great Western Publishing Company, www.greatwesternpublishing.com
3. Catherine Ponder, *Open Your Mind to Prosperity,* (DeVorss & Company; 1984), p. 102.

CHAPTER 12

Free Will

"It's choice—not chance—that determines your destiny"—Jean Nidetch

FREE WILL EXPLORED

Free will and choice allow you to choose what you want to manifest in your life. In every moment of every day, you have the choice to say yes or no to something. And even in choosing not to decide, you have chosen. There is always a choice involved.

In fact, every decision you have ever made in your life up to this very point in time has contributed to your situation and exactly where you are in the world right now. And that's one reason why you cannot honestly consider yourself to be a victim of anything. You chose it!

"I will choose free will"—Rush

Free will is the *biggest spiritual lesson* we have all come here to understand. That's because there are many, many people in the world who are afraid to make a change in their lives, afraid to venture out, afraid to claim their power, afraid to use their free will to create a life that will bring them joy. There is no reason to be afraid any longer. It is time to learn how to balance free will, power, and control.

What are people afraid to do?

- Afraid to end a relationship
- Afraid to change a career path
- Afraid to disagree with a parent
- Afraid to be home alone
- Afraid to go out with others

- Afraid to make a bold decision
- Afraid to allow a child to take their own path
- Afraid to make a major purchase
- Afraid to move to another location
- Afraid to tell someone the truth of a situation

Free will is a most powerful tool, and yet at the same time it presents all sorts of challenges for us. Should you seize the opportunity? Should you make a bold move? Should you move out of your comfort zone? You may be afraid to change a current situation until all the details have been arranged in your new situation. You may be reluctant to trust that another opportunity will present itself to you at the right time in the right way. Fears often come from a lack of faith and trust.

Free will is your tool to change things that are no longer working for you. When there is something in your life that is not moving and flowing in an appropriate manner, you are at odds with yourself. What's happened is that you are no longer able to accept what you have created as tolerable. You now find the need to change. Change is working through the steps of choice and manifestation. Because when something doesn't work in your life any longer, it's time for change.

SELF-JUDGMENT

Because we have free will and because we know that our every thought shapes our reality, be careful of the disempowering action of self-judgment. Self-judgment is an inner road block. For example, if you manifest a new job or opportunity for yourself, you may judge yourself harshly and say, "Oh, I can't do that job because . . ."

If you express this doubt, you are putting limitations on yourself. You see, this new job opportunity may be part of a huge leap of consciousness and positive change in you and your life. So be open. Do not allow your thoughts to race ahead of you with fear, doubt and imagined problems running wild in your mind. If you are able to let go of fear and overcome self-doubt, the flow of new opportunities will begin to come to you.

It is not a requirement that you stay the same. You can change. In each moment, things can shift instantaneously, and become very different. Those who have suddenly *woken up* can attest to this. One moment, they may have felt that they were unaware. The next moment, they felt something of great importance had occurred. In many cases, changing yourself is simply just a matter of changing your perception of yourself, and how you view yourself.

Things are given to you in the form of opportunity. Opportunities for your personal growth are everywhere, but your personal choice and free will determine whether or not you will accept them at this time. Look for synchronicities.

You are here to develop your higher self and your soul into a greater understanding, into a cosmic consciousness. It is not just a consciousness of the one individual person, or just the planet, but the entire cosmic consciousness with all life. With that understanding, you begin to fully understand the meaning of the words, "we are all One." Free will decisions which bring you to that knowingness bring you closer to your personal truth.

DESTINY VERSUS FREE WILL

Many people acknowledge feelings of destiny. They feel they are destined to meet someone, destined to succeed or fail, destined for a life of mediocrity, destined to live in poverty, destined to live with certain disadvantages, destined because of social status or race, etc. So which is true, destiny or free will?

By accepting the idea of destiny into your life, you are in effect giving away your personal power and choosing to be a victim. If you believe that you are destined to a life of poverty, you have surrendered yourself to that experience and belief. If you believe you are destined to be stuck in a dead-end go-nowhere job, you have in effect surrendered yourself to that dire situation.

People sometimes think that meeting someone is destiny, or that being in the right place at the right time is destiny. Oftentimes, in these situations, your divine guidance is assisting you with synchronistic clues and guidance. This is different from destiny.

Destiny is the blueprint, the roadmap. Destiny is the map of possibilities available to you. Free will is the path you choose to take, the door you choose to open and walk through, the choices you make every day, large and small. You can view life as a big long hallway with many, many doors lining the hallway on each side. These doors are various destinies available to you. But you and you alone ultimately have the free will choice to open and walk through any one of these doors. At any time in any situation, you are free to exercise your free will. It is your divine right!

*You have free will, which allows you
to make a number of choices every day.*

AFFIRMATIONS

I NOW CHOOSE AND RISE UP TO THE HIGHEST AND MOST MAGNIFICENT
EXPRESSION OF MY BEING. I SHED AND RID MYSELF OF LOWER LIMITING
BELIEFS. I SEE THE WAY CLEARLY NOW, AND FOLLOW MY BLISS AND
TRUE PATH.

I NOW PROCLAIM AND EXERCISE MY FREE WILL, AND INTEND AND
AFFIRM ONLY THE HIGHEST PATH FOR ME.

IF A HIGHER PATH IS AVAILABLE TO ME NOW, I NOW SEE IT CLEARLY.

QUESTIONS AND ANSWERS

Q. Can other people impose their free will on me?
A. Yes, of course. And people do this *all the time*. However, they cannot do this unless
you let them. So if your will is strong and unwavering, it is unlikely that others will
impose their will on you.

Q. What about my job? I have to work for a living. I have to eat and pay rent. But I hate my boss, and I hate my job. I didn't choose to work like this.
A. Yes, you did. There are any number of possible ways to earn a living. You chose the one you have now. You could have chosen others. But you chose to be where you are now. If you want to choose another reality for yourself, go right ahead.

Q. Can you give me some more examples of free will?
A. Probably the biggest example of free will is the fact that you chose to be born into a human body, and that you chose your life contract before you incarnated. You chose your major life lessons, and you decided that these were important lessons to learn from during this lifetime.

Q. Aren't some things just destined to be? For instance, I think that meeting and marrying my spouse was destiny.
A. In this instance, it may well be that before you chose to incarnate, that you and your future spouse agreed to cross paths in this lifetime. You may have done this to allow you to make this choice. So, in fact, there was a choice to do that. Also, when the two of you came to know each other, you both chose to marry. So there were two choices made. Oftentimes, things happen "behind the scenes" which may seem like fate, but they are more often the results of synchronicity or choices you have made previously.

Q. What are some good ways to ask for guidance from my higher self and my guides?
A. In meditation, ask to be shown. Formulate a question, and try to perceive the answer. Ask to be shown a sign. Ask which path is the best one to take at this time. Ask which path is your highest. Your inner knowing wants to come through, and wants to participate in your life, and wants to help you with the evolution of your consciousness.

I CHOOSE TO CONNECT NOW WITH MY HIGHEST SPIRIT GUIDES, TEACHERS AND MASTERS. I NOW MANIFEST GREATLY IN ACCORDANCE WITH MY DIVINE WILL AND THE PERFECT EXPRESSION OF MY BEING.

Q. It seems amazing to me that I am constantly creating in every minute of the day.
A. That is correct. Even if you are sitting idly by and doing nothing, things in other dimensions are always occurring. With every thought that you give off when you are sitting, except in the absolute silence of meditation, you are creating. You are creating with every thought you have, whether you utter it out loud or not.

Q. Sometimes I feel at odds with society. Sometimes I want to go one way, and everyone else wants to go another way. What's happening here? Am I losing my free will?
A. More and more, society is taking on responsibilities that were normally assumed by the individual. Responsibilities like food, clothing, education, healthcare, and

retirement are becoming more societal. This is a disempowering trend for the individual. How does society know what you truly desire? Do you really want to give up your power? Know that whatever happens in society and the world around you, you will *always* have free will choice.

Q. Is this free will consciousness directly at odds with group consciousness, and collective thought?
A. This is not to be confused with the worthy goal of an evolved society of group consciousness and group mind. In a situation of an evolved group consciousness, all participants have agreed to be as one.

Q. How do I know the difference between making a free will decision, and forcing my will into a situation that I am trying to make happen?
A. Check in with your heart. You will know by how it feels. The fact that you chose the word "force" is a good clue as to the appropriateness of that choice.

Q. I am not good at making decisions. It makes me nervous. I worry. Sometimes I just don't know. What do you suggest?
A. Check into your heart. How do you *really* feel about it? Meditate on it. Ask for a sign from Spirit.

CHAPTER SUMMARY

1) Free will is one of our biggest spiritual lessons.
2) Deciding to do something or deciding not to do something are both choices.
3) People are held back by fears, and are reluctant to make a change. This is often due to a lack of faith and trust.
4) Free will is your tool to change things that are no longer working for you.
5) Things are given to us in the form of opportunity. Opportunities to change, learn, and grow are everywhere. You must simply choose to see them and act on them.
6) Limiting yourself through self-judgment can hold you back from choosing a certain path.
7) Things that seem to be destiny are often a result of divine guidance or synchronicity.
8) Others cannot impose their will onto you unless you allow them to.
9) Check in with your heart; go with what feels right!

MANIFESTING WORKSHEET

You can visualize your future self. Take a moment and imagine what your life will be like at some point in the future. Make things as fantastic and great as you would like them to be. Be guided by your higher self about what this future reality will be like. Probe and explore until you get the revelation and epiphany of YES and feel it, feel the emotion. Your free will has imagined this future reality, now you can manifest it!

Now, let go of both your own and other's disbeliefs or doubts that this future reality is not possible. Believe that it can and will happen. Know that since you have now conceived this reality, that time is the only factor delaying this reality from occurring right now. Realize that with each passing moment that it is becoming more real for you.

List three characteristics and circumstances that describe your magnificent future self as you have envisioned it:

1) _____

2) _____

3) _____

Now, write down the three most important things that you can do right now which will help this become a reality in your life.

1) _____

2) _____

3) _____

CHAPTER 13

Group Manifestation

"No man is an island"—John Donne

THE POWER OF GROUPS

To this point in the book, we've looked at how you as an individual can manifest. But most of us spend a good part of our lives interacting with and working with other people to achieve group goals. Let's look at how manifestation works at a group level.

When two or more people gather together with a common goal, they create a group consciousness. This new creation of consciousness is normally comprised of the combined intention of the group's participants. The group consciousness can be very powerful, especially if the intention is clear, strong, and focused. Groups allow for increased levels of achievement and accomplishment. Groups also provide companionship and learning experiences for people while they co-create with one another.

A group consciousness is made up of various group dynamics. If there is not already a designated leader, a group leader emerges. This is usually the person with either the clearest or strongest intention. Sometimes the group leader is the person with the best and strongest communication style to express the goal of the group.

A group with a strong intention and purpose will find that new people come in to the group to support its efforts, and the group expands. Those in alignment in energy, vibration and purpose will join in and become part of the co-creative effort, adding their own special talents to the synergistic mix.

Manifesting in a group situation is different from manifesting for yourself, because all the experiences and feelings of other people in the group affect the outcome. Obviously, people have different motivations for being part of a group. Thus it is important for the group itself to have a strong vision, intention, and focus that everyone can align themselves with.

CREATING A GROUP

If you want to form a group, create a strong intention. State that you desire to connect with others with whom you have a co-creative agreement and who are resonating at the same levels as you are. Intention is everything. Put out the intention that you desire to connect with others now. Your group members will find one another (sometimes magically and with synchronicity), and form your collective effort.

> I NOW CONNECT WITH THOSE WHO CHOOSE TO CO-CREATE WITH ME AND WORK WITH ME TO ACHIEVE OUR COLLECTIVE GOALS AND GROUP VISION.

In simple terms, ask the universe to bring to you those people who are here to help you. Ask your guides to assist you in the process of bringing those people to you, to create those coincidences that bring two or more people together.

GROUP ASPECT AND DYNAMIC—THE COMMUNITY

Knowing that we are all one, and all connected to Spirit, we can see that we live in a kind of global community. There are also smaller groups and communities all around us. The community is an expanded expression of the self. Communities can often support both individual growth and growth of the community itself.

When the goals and focus of the community are strong, there is a kind of synergistic community "group mind." This is an evolved state of being. In this case, individualism and separatism are suppressed and the group mind and focus take priority.

Although the western world currently emphasizes individualism and personal achievement, the human race is now moving to a more evolved state of group consciousness. One example of this is when a natural disaster occurs (earthquake, tsunami, volcanic eruption, hurricane), and the worldwide community responds to render assistance. Other examples of group consciousness are international efforts to address climate changes, as well as efforts to improve human rights.

SYNERGY AS IT RELATES TO GROUP MANIFESTATION

Synergy is energy that expands through cooperation. With the power of synergy, we have an invaluable tool for helping each other work together in ways that support our common good. Synergy combines to far exceed the capabilities of any individual acting alone.

Through synergy, the universe assists relationships in their quest to provide purposeful service to the greater whole. Synergy is a key to the geometric expansion of consciousness, where the whole is greater than the sum of its parts. Synergy is natural magic which exists in our infinitely abundant and compassionate universe. Synergy helps us become conscious co-creators.

> I AM NOW IN RELATIONSHIP WITH THE UNIVERSE, CREATING AND MANIFESTING WITH THE UNIVERSE AND UNIVERSAL ENERGY.

> PLEASE DRAW TO ME THE PEOPLE WHO BELONG IN MY LIFE NOW, WHO WILL CO-CREATE WITH ME NOW IN A SYNERGISTIC CO-CREATIVE EFFORT. I NOW TAKE THE NEXT STEP. UNITE ME WITH THESE PEOPLE NOW.

STARTING A BUSINESS—A TYPE OF GROUP

Oftentimes when you start out to manifest something, you start out by yourself. Starting your own business is a great example of this.

If you are strong enough with your intention, will, and drive, you will find yourself on a path of being in business and providing a product or service to your customers. If you are passionate about what you are doing, so much the better. Being passionate about what you do will make it far easier to succeed with your efforts, because your emotion and energy will attract customers.

Because of your energetic projection, you will attract customers who match and compliment your vibration, people who are attracted to you, and want to buy from you. They may not even consciously realize why they are attracted to you, but they are! You will attract people into your world who match your vibration and energy, and who are similarly interested in working alongside you and co-creating with you in your company. They end up working with you.

If the co-creative effort is a well-matched one, things will go wonderfully. Your clients are happy. The sum of your efforts will be great. You will succeed. And not only will you succeed, but your coworkers will succeed. You will be enthusiastic, and it will be contagious. The sum of all individual efforts will be a collective greater good.

OTHER GROUPS IN ACTION

Another example of people working in groups together is a fundraising drive or walk-a-thon. When this happens, hundreds or thousands of people share a common goal, and seemingly create large amounts of money out of nothing. This is an example of powerful synergy created when many people are working for a worthy cause. Other groups include things like conservation groups, hobby groups, political groups, and networking groups. Even things like reading groups, birdwatchers, car clubs, and sewing circles are all groups in action. Some groups have an intention to learn skills from others in the group and to provide camaraderie; other groups have an intention to change the world around them.

Group consciousness and group manifestation have one great advantage over individual manifestation, and that is the power of the group. As mentioned previously, the group, when working together with unity of thought and purpose, has an exponential power many times greater than that of any one individual.

AFFIRMATIONS

> GUIDE OUR GROUP AS WE WORK TOGETHER AS ONE AND CREATE WITH EASE AND GRACE.

> BRING TO OUR GROUP THE GUIDES, MENTORS, LEADERS, FACILITATORS AND OTHERS WHO WOULD PARTICIPATE IN OUR MISSION, CREATING TOGETHER WITH US FOR THE GREATER GOOD.

> I NOW ALIGN WITH MY GROUP, AND WE ACCOMPLISH GREAT THINGS TOGETHER.

> I NOW FULLY EXPRESS MY PASSION AND ENTHUSIASM FOR MY MISSION.

QUESTIONS AND ANSWERS

Q. What if half of the people in my group want to go in one direction, and the other half want to go another way. What should we do?
A. With that kind of division, your group is projecting an oscillating sine wave. Your group will be far less effective until you get together and decide on a common goal. For example, in the workplace, retreats and brainstorming meetings allow for common goals and consensus building opportunities. Again, a solid straight clear line of intention is far more preferable to an oscillating sine wave that is constantly changing.

Q. Our group was strong and powerful once, but is now fading in popularity and influence. Why?
A. It may well be that your group has completed much of its essential mission and reason for being. It could also be a lack of leadership. Perhaps refocus or restate the mission of the group, or let the group dissolve.

Q. Someone tried to dominate, subvert and take over our group once. Why?
A. There may have been a weakness or lack or leadership at the time. The mission may have been unclear. Perhaps someone attracted this person to the group as a learning experience or wake-up call for the entire group. The cure for this is strong intention, leadership and vision.

CHAPTER SUMMARY

1) Group consciousness can be remarkably powerful when aligned.
2) Groups allow for increased levels of achievement and accomplishment.
3) To create a strong group, start with a strong intention. Ask the universe to connect you with others who align with you.
4) Groups can sometimes be community oriented, with a compassionate orientation.
5) Synergy is energy that expands through cooperation.
6) A business is an example of group consciousness creating.
7) A group is a type of community, and the community is an expanded expression of the self.
8) Generally speaking, the group consciousness when in complete alignment can be seen to be as a more evolved state than individuality.
9) Synergy assists relationships in providing purposeful service to the greater whole.
10) Groups can provide an environment for learning from others. Groups can also be focused with a unity of purpose, and a strong mission to create change.

MANIFESTING WORKSHEET

Think of a group that you might want to create. It could be a discussion group, a hobbyist group, a manifesting group, a political action group, an environmental group, a new business, or any kind of group at all. If you could create any kind of group, what would it be?

1) _____

Now think about the steps it would take to form, start and lead this group. What are the first steps?

1) _____
2) _____
3) _____

CHAPTER 14

Workplace Manifestation

"Work is love made visible"—Kahlil Gibran

MANIFESTATION IN THE WORKPLACE

In the workplace we manifest all sorts of things. We manifest a product or service, we manifest compensation (money) for our work, and we manifest all sorts of relationships with the people we work with. The workplace can be a dynamic place where people have opportunities to express themselves and learn from each other.

MANIFESTING A PRODUCT OR SERVICE

In the workplace, the obvious common goal is to provide a product or service to your customers. Ideally, each person in the group contributes to the collective effort in their own unique ways. The better that each group member does his or her job, the better they combine to create a collective good of the company. This is the power of synergy.

When people in a company experience problems working with others, the common goal of the company suffers. Conversely, when employees are in agreement and aligned with the goal and mission of the company, the positive and dynamic results can be breathtaking. For example, consider the positive dynamics of a fast-growing company where everyone wants to work passionately, where relationships are harmonious, where people work late into the night because they want to, and where great things occur. This is an example of manifesting occurring in the workplace when all are in alignment with the goal and vision.

INTERPERSONAL RELATIONSHIPS IN THE OFFICE

The workplace provides us with many opportunities for growth and learning. Interpersonal relationships, both good and bad, can help us learn a great deal in a short period of time. Here are some lessons often learned in the workplace:

- Tolerance for others
- Self worth
- Acknowledging various lifestyle choices
- Co-creative manifestation
- Acceptance of others
- Seeing the good in people
- Working together for a common goal

In the workplace, we are often confronted with people who challenge us. It may be a co-worker, supervisor, boss, client or other person you interact with. In the workplace, where we see people on a daily basis, some personality traits of others become obvious to us, especially the ones we see as less desirable. Make every effort to treat others with empowering thoughts. Be sure to treat people with these "less desirable" traits with compassion. Be sure to visualize the best for these people. They will rise to the occasion, and meet your expectations. See others you work with as multidimensional beings, similar to you, also experiencing what it means to be human.

Know that people you work with may have problems that you don't know about. Realize they may be carrying a tremendous burden that they are keeping private. They may be working on life lessons that are incomprehensible to you. They may be on a level of consciousness that is so alien to you that you simply cannot understand why they are the way they are, and why they do the things they do.

Treat your coworkers with respect and admiration, and be pleasantly surprised. Imagine for a moment that your coworkers are actually royalty, that they are noble, and extremely high-minded. Try to think of them in those terms, and they may turn out to be just so.

In the workplace, it is all too easy to get sucked into the lower energies of gossip, power struggles, and one-upmanship. Oftentimes these come about as a result of the perception of limited resources. You can waste much time and energy in activities that are not contributing to your own progress as a person. It is also not contributing to the greater good.

Small minds talk about people
Mediocre minds talk about events, but
Great minds think about ideas

You can easily rise above the fray at your workplace:

- Be true to yourself and high-minded in everything you say and do
- Help co-workers succeed with their efforts
- Be compassionate with others who are struggling
- Keep your own energy and spirit on a high level
- Be always willing to lend a hand to others
- Refuse to participate in petty struggles and gamesmanship

You should consider the fact that "difficult" people in the workplace may be there just for you. You may have "agreed" to encounter this person in your lifetime, and challenge each other with learning lessons. So, by being a thorn in your side, this person is actually doing what you may have asked them to, that is to come into your life and shake things up. And the better they shake things up, the more you will ultimately thank them later. Such a person may be helping you learn life lessons like:

- No one has a right to push me around
- I am worthy
- My time and energy are valuable
- My own priorities are the most important
- There are other things in life more important than work, such as God, family, love, health, personal growth, etc.
- Good business ethics are imperative; lying, cheating, and stealing are immoral.

Here's a story which involves some interesting workplace dynamics. I recall a time when I was working at a fine company, doing meaningful work, in a well-paying job. However, as the years passed by, I felt something was amiss. The work no longer inspired me. I slowly came to this realization and knew that ultimately a change was needed. Little did I know how that change would come about.

When Joanne was hired at the office, little did I know that she would be just the thorn in my side that I needed to help put me on my way, and allow me to move on. During that time when I was experiencing disharmony and Joanne was "challenging" me in the workplace, it was very uncomfortable. But after I left the company and moved onto another chapter in my life, I realized that Joanne did me a great favor by helping "shake things up." She gave me the nudge I needed to help get me back onto my true path of growth and learning. In looking back, the irony of the story is that I was the one who found and brought her into the company. Now we know why.

ENERGY IN THE WORKPLACE

We have all seen or worked with people with depressed energy, a defeated attitude, and a nay-sayer response to situations. Such people can negatively affect those around them. They can take a positive meeting and depress the energy in a minute. They can kill good ideas. They can be a problem. In energetic terms, they bring everything around them down.

Conversely, positive people uplift all around them. They inspire others and put things into action. They motivate people. They get people excited about being there, and they look forward to the challenges of the day. These types of people are great to work with. What kind of person are you?

Believe it or not, one positive person in an office can raise the entire energy of the office. They can uplift everyone around them, even without trying. If you are that kind of person, go forth with the knowledge that you are helping those around you just by keeping the flame of truth burning, and taking a high-minded path. *You take your individual spirituality to work with you every morning.* And that's great!

Interactions between people are as unique as people are.

Although it is not your job to save the world and all those around you, you *can* make serious and valuable efforts to improve your outlook on the way things really are in the world and seeing the good in things.

The workplace also gives us an opportunity to communicate with and do business with other companies. We can learn about other corporate cultures and the way other companies operate. In doing so, we can see that some companies and people operate with integrity, honesty, and trust, and some do not.

Those people and companies who perceive the universe to be limited focus more on competition, and beating the "other guy." However, the reality is that even in business, the world is unbounded, unlimited, and full of opportunity for everyone. Companies operating from a more evolved place create win-win situations, where everyone involved succeeds. It's not hard to do. If your company is more concerned with competition and a "limited" marketplace, shift the focus to a more enlightened expression of an unlimited universe with grand opportunities for all.

ATTITUDES CAUSING LIMITATION

Poor attitudes in the workplace can block the flow of energy. Carefully guard against your own attitudes, and also the attitudes of others who would gladly push their attitudes onto you if you let them. Here are some limiting expressions you may have encountered with others:

- We tried that before; it'll never work.
- Yes, but.
- We've always done it this way.
- If it isn't broken, don't fix it.
- Don't rock the boat.
- If you understood the full picture.
- Who made you the expert on it?
- That's a dumb idea!
- It's not worth the effort.

If you are surrounded by a workplace environment like this, change it! As things occur around you, realize that even though you cannot control all events and situations around you, you *can* manage your responses to situations. Carefully observe and become aware of your responses to situations around you.

EMPOWERING ATTITUDES

Try on some of these empowering attitudes below. Adopt these to your work environment and create change in your world.

- This is a great place to work.
- Everyone here is very friendly.
- It's great to be here.
- Your ideas and suggestions are always welcome.
- Your opinion matters.
- This is a co-creative environment.
- We couldn't get by without you.
- We work great as a team.
- If you can think it, you can do it.
- I love the people I work with.
- If this doesn't work, we'll keep trying until we find something that does.
- You're great to work with.
- What's your opinion?
- Anything and everything can be improved upon.
- That's a great idea!
- Let's give it a try.

AFFIRMATIONS

I NOW ALIGN WITH OTHERS IN MY GROUP FOR THE BEST POSSIBLE SYNERGY AND THE GREATER GOOD. WE NOW ACCOMPLISH GREAT THINGS TOGETHER AS ONE.

I NOW EMPOWER THOSE I WORK WITH TO BE AT THEIR BEST, AND THEY EMPOWER ME IN RETURN. I ACKNOWLEDGE THE DIVINITY IN EVERYONE I WORK WITH.

I AM WORTHY. NO ONE HAS A RIGHT TO FORCE THEIR FREE WILL ON ME. I AM A VALUED, WORTHY, LOVING, COMPASSIONATE PERSON.

QUESTIONS AND ANSWERS

Q. At the office, someone was dishonest and got the promotion instead of me. What should I do about it?

A. Release it. Get over it. Maintain high ideals. Trust that divine wisdom will prevail. Know that the person who apparently gained an advantage at your expense is amassing karmic debt at a rapid rate. Know that this person will eventually need to learn some important lessons about life. It may be that they learn the lessons from you, or it may be someone else in another situation that they learn from. The universe will ultimately rebalance an unbalanced situation, one way or another. Looking at it from this perspective can help you deal with a difficult situation like this.

Q. My boss steals from the company and it makes me extremely uncomfortable. Should I turn my boss in?
A. Be in your truth. If that means turning them in, then do it. You must live with your conscience, so do what you need to do so you can sleep at night.

Q. The energy at my company is very low. Nothing ever happens. It is stagnant. What can be done?
A. Just like on a personal level, you must get the energy flowing again. Clear out the old. Make big changes, and small changes. Move furniture around. Try some new paintings on the wall. Get the air flowing again. Shake things up a bit. It will help to get the energy flowing in and around your workspace again, and improve things.

CHAPTER SUMMARY

1) The workplace is full of group dynamics and interpersonal energetics from which we can learn and grow.
2) When employees are in alignment with the mission of the organization, positive results occur.
3) The perception of a limited universe fuels competition between employees within a company and between companies for business.
4) The workplace provides us with opportunities to learn about acceptance, self-worth, trust, personal responsibilities, personal boundaries, and community.
5) Know that coworkers may be in an entirely different "place." They may be experiencing a burden which they are keeping private. Show compassion towards them.
6) Treat your fellow employees with empowering thoughts. This will help them rise to a higher level of being.
7) You can shift your view of the workplace environment and change it. Often a certain job or situation may not have changed, but your perception of it has.
8) Attempt to create situations and opportunities in the workplace where everyone wins.

9) Although you cannot control all events around you in the workplace, you can manage your responses to them.

10) You take yourself to work every day in the morning, and you influence others just by being who you are.

11) Turn limiting attitudes into empowering attitudes.

MANIFESTING WORKSHEET

Think of one or more limiting beliefs you may have heard or are aware of at your workplace.

Example: "We tried that before, it will never work."

1) _____

2) _____

3) _____

Now turn those beliefs into new, empowering beliefs that you can bring to your workplace.

Example: "It's always worth trying, it will be a valuable experience for us no matter what happens."

1) _____

2) _____

3) _____

CHAPTER 15

Prosperity & Abundance

"The strongest single factor in prosperity consciousness is self-esteem: believing you can do it, believing you deserve it, believing you will get it"—Jerry Gillies

PROSPERITY AND ABUNDANCE

For many, prosperity and abundance are the ultimate expression of manifestation. Everyone wants to be rich!

What does being prosperous and abundant mean to you? A feeling of accomplishment? Impressing others? Buying luxury items? Feeling superior to others? Being good to yourself? Supporting family and relatives? Not worrying if you can afford something? Being philanthropic?

Our universe has a divine design which allows for everybody to have all that they need. We are all meant to live abundantly, and have and enjoy all we need in an unlimited way. Thus, prosperity and abundance are *available* and *waiting* for you now.

ATTRACTING WEALTH

The methods explained in this book for intention, affirmations and visioning work on virtually everything, but especially prosperity and abundance. So, to be that way, use affirmations and visioning to attract abundance into your life.

> I AM WEALTHY IN MIND, BODY AND AFFAIRS. I EXPRESS DIVINE ABUNDANCE IN MY LIFE NOW. I RICHLY DESERVE AND ALLOW ALL THAT THE WORLD HAS FOR ME NOW.

Because money is simply an expression of energy, it is usually more effective to *focus on the end result* of your personal expression of abundance. For example, if you want to be abundant so that you can care for and support family and relatives, explore that expression of helping your family in that way. Focus on that, but not necessarily the monetary expression. So, as a result, your manifestation could result in unexpectedly being appointed the trustee or beneficiary of a family trust, which then allows you to complete your intention of serving family and relatives.

Use the law of attraction to bring wealth to you. To be rich, feel rich. Act "as if" you are rich already. Explore expressions of it, and capture the feeling of what it is to be in rich abundance. By doing so, you will invoke the law of attraction and attract abundance to you.

> I NOW EXPRESS COMPLETE LOVING GRATITUDE FOR ALL I AM, ALL
> I HAVE, ALL I KNOW, ALL I FEEL, ALL I UNDERSTAND, AND ALL I LOVE.

POVERTY CONSCIOUSNESS VERSUS ABUNDANCE

Many people today have a poverty consciousness. Exactly what does that mean? It means that they identify with the feeling of being poor, and in lack or want. Thus, they attract that reality to them. One reason people feel this way is that they may feel more comfortable with this state of being.

Many feel that they are simply not deserving of material wealth. Others learned poverty consciousness from parents as they were growing up. Others may have spoken a vow of poverty in a previous lifetime. One very common reason people identify with poverty consciousness is that they feel that being both highly spiritual and abundant are mutually exclusive. In fact, nothing could be further from the truth! It is your divine right to be abundant!

OUR NATURAL STATE

Our natural state is one of abundance. When in right way we can manifest virtually instantly, and enjoy all that life has to offer. There is no shame in being abundant. If you acknowledge that in fact the universe has unlimited resources, everyone can be abundant and feel good about it! And in fact, everyone should be abundant if they want to be. Only if you think that the universe has limits would you feel guilty about manifesting in a grand fashion. A key component of personal growth is the mastery and understanding of the issues of abundant living, however you choose to express it.

> I NOW AFFIRM ABUNDANCE. I NOW BRING IN MY UNCLAIMED GOOD. I
> GLADLY ACCEPT AND RECEIVE ALL THE ABUNDANCE WHICH FLOWS TO
> ME NOW. I AM RICH IN ABUNDANCE NOW.

The major reason people are not abundant is because of limiting beliefs around abundance. These limiting beliefs, learned in both current and past lifetimes, are often embedded deep in our consciousness. One of the best ways to change and shift limiting beliefs is to use affirmations. Affirmations help replace limiting beliefs with new empowering beliefs in both your consciousness and unconscious.

Furthermore, to be abundant, express abundance. Accelerate the flow of energy to you and through you by being generous, and keeping the flow of abundance moving through you. Be thankful. Express gratitude for all that you have. Expressing gratitude tells the universe that you appreciate what you are receiving, and creates room for more good to come in.

Be careful of your beliefs, and your expectations around abundance. If you truly believe that abundance can only come from hard work and toil, that is the way that abundance will come to you. Alternatively, if you truly believe that you are deserving and that abundance is sure to come your way with a minimum of effort, it will!

We create for ourselves those lessons and experiences we need to learn in our lives in order to grow. If you feel you need to work multiple jobs for long hours, that is the experience you will have until you change your beliefs. Perhaps someday you will decide that you only need to work one job to be abundant. Or perhaps you will decide that being abundant is not really a certain amount of money in the bank, but that it is in fact fully appreciating all that you have now.

Know that there are certain responsibilities to having money. One of those responsibilities is to help others. When we are all of one consciousness, no person is an island. If you use your money to help others, it will benefit you. *It is then in a giving and sharing of your love and success that more prosperity and abundance flows to you.*

GRATITUDE FOR WHAT YOU DO HAVE

Along with capturing the feeling of abundance, the quickest way to get more of *anything* is to express gratitude for what you have in your life right now. Prosperity and abundance are much more than the acquisition of things, they are also about *fully appreciating all we have, in gratitude and joy.*

Unfortunately, greed and competition in our society have created an unbalanced environment. Instead of focusing on all that they do have, people focus on what others have or what they themselves do not have. Ironically, today we live in more luxury, splendor and convenience than royalty did just a couple hundred years ago. There are many, many things in your life that you can be grateful for, *right now.*

AFFIRMATIONS

I NOW ATTRACT CONTINUED AND EXPANDING PROSPERITY AND
ABUNDANCE TO ME, KNOWING THAT THERE IS AN UNLIMITED SUPPLY
IN THE UNIVERSE AVAILABLE TO ME NOW.

I REMAIN ETERNALLY GRATEFUL FOR ALL THE LOVE AND ABUNDANCE
IN MY LIFE NOW, AS IT POURS FORTH TO ME IN GREAT SUPPLY.

IN EVERY DAY IN EVERY WAY I ATTRACT ABUNDANCE AND PROSPERITY
TO ME.

QUESTIONS AND ANSWERS

Q. Some people are millionaires, and others are not. Why does this occur?
A. In somewhat simple terms, those who are millionaires have developed the feeling,
vibration and expression of that reality. In other words, they think, feel, and live like
millionaires. Conversely, those who feel that they "could never be rich" often manifest
that reality. How do *you* feel, honestly? Which expression of abundance is closer to
what you project and attract?

Q. If I can manifest lots of money in my life, doesn't that solve lots of problems?
A. Sure it does. It solves those problems that can be solved with money. But manifesting
is much more than just about manifesting money. You can manifest all sorts of things.
For example, if you have a serious illness, you will likely want to manifest robust health.
If you are lonely, you may want to manifest meaningful relationships. If you are unsure
about a direction to take, you can manifest clarity and understanding. Money cannot
normally buy you robust health, true friendship, and clear thinking.

Q. How can I be free and easy with my finances when I have spent a lifetime learning
to be frugal, cautious, conservative and deliberate?
A. It's all about the flow of energy to you and through you. By being generous and giving,
you allow more to flow to you, and project a vibration of trust that your generosity will
be returned to you. The universe will make it right, and support your kind, generous
ways. Start small, practice, and develop your skills at attracting and moving the flow
of abundance through you.

CHAPTER SUMMARY

1)   By design, our universe allows for everyone to have all they need.
2)   To be wealthy and prosperous, act as if you are already in rich abundance in
      order to draw that reality to you.

3) The quickest way to get more of anything is to express gratitude for it; express gratitude for the abundance you have now in your life.

4) Focus on the end result, what you will do with your abundance (such as create a trust or foundation, or get a house) in order to help manifest that reality.

5) Our natural state is one of abundance. It is your divine right to be abundant.

6) Replace any limiting beliefs you may have around abundance with positive affirmations to draw abundance toward you. Give up poverty consciousness.

7) Remember to keep the flow of energy (such as money) moving in order to bring in more to you.

8) One responsibility of having money is to help others. By helping others, you attract even more prosperity and abundance to you as the energy flows to you and through you.

9) Greed and competition in our society have created an unbalanced environment, where people focus on what they do not have, rather than what they do have.

10) Be fully appreciative of all you do have, with gratitude and joy, and more will flow to you.

MANIFESTING WORKSHEET

Look at your personal attitudes towards prosperity. Do you have a poverty consciousness, or a prosperity consciousness? If you have a poverty consciousness, make a bold move in some way. (For example: leave a really big tip, splurge on something you normally would not do, or buy yourself an expensive outfit). List three ways below in which you can think and act with prosperity instead of limitation:

1) _____
2) _____
3) _____

EXTRA CREDIT

Starting from a Single Idea: If you are in a situation where you feel it may be difficult to manifest, realize that you can change your whole life by just changing one idea, thought or belief. It can be one simple little idea. For example, for one minute of one day, you think prosperity instead of lack. The next day, you think of prosperity twice. By the end of the week or month, you are thinking prosperity and abundance many times over, in many ways, for longer periods. You are bringing that new reality into your consciousness. You are bringing a thought form into the third dimension. It is happening on a holistic, conscious level, but also on a cellular level too.

CHAPTER 16

Health

"The first wealth is health"—Ralph Waldo Emerson

MANIFESTING VIBRANT HEALTH

As you live your life each day and create your reality with your thoughts, you create your level of health. You likely do this unconsciously. However, know that you can create your level of health consciously, with intention. Using your conscious powers of thought, you can manifest vibrant, robust health if you choose to.

Many people begin to seriously reflect upon their lives when they come to a critical point around health. Unfortunately, that event often involves a serious sickness or disease. After years and years of putting less of a priority on health, people sometimes realize that it is time to make good health a priority in their lives.

Lack of good health is also called disease, or lack of ease. Disease is normally an outward manifestation of something that is out of balance on the inside. Often we can be out of balance for shorter periods of time without problems. But when we are out of balance for months, years and decades, it can result in an outward manifestation of illness or disease.

Because we create our own reality, this means that we also create sickness or disease in our lives. It's true! Here's a simple example: Have you ever been so busy, overworked, and overstressed that you became sick because you were trying to do so much? In this example, you actually made yourself sick for just one reason, to *slow down*. The imbalance known as a "nervous breakdown" is an example of a larger outward expression of this imbalance.

Louise L. Hay, in her breakthrough books *Heal Your Body* and *You Can Heal Your Life* theorizes about the mental causes behind physical illnesses. She asserts that outward manifestations of illness or disease are a manifestation of something not quite right inside the person.

For *cancer*, she asserts that it is caused by "deep hurt, longstanding resentment, deep secret or grief eating away at the self, carrying hatreds." [1]

For *heart problems*, she identifies the following as contributing to this disease, "longstanding emotional problem, lack of joy, hardening of the heart, belief in strain and stress." [2]

For issues of being *overweight*, she says, "fear, need for protection, running away from feelings, insecurity, self-rejection, seeking fulfillment." [3]

For *myopia* (nearsightedness, shortsightedness), she attributes to "fear of the future, not trusting what is ahead." [4]

Upon reflection, many of these mental causes offered by Louise Hay are refreshingly empowering. It is not someone else or something outside of us making us sick. We are making ourselves sick! Not only that, but sometimes the major causes of health issues are surprisingly obvious. Of course, it is usually obvious to everyone else but us!

The good news in all this is that if you can take responsibility for the fact that you have made yourself sick, then you can take the responsibility to make yourself well.

So, the way to "cure" yourself of a disease or illness is to find the "mental" source of the problem, and fix it. If you are unable to see yourself objectively, ask a close friend or two to give you an honest, direct appraisal of your situation. Keep asking until you get the answer. You may have to press people a bit on this, because the real truth of the situation may not be something that is easy for someone to tell you, or easy for you to hear. Also, using Louise Hay's approach as a guide, first think of the most obvious, apparent, and simple answer you can possibly think of. Start there, you may find the answer to your problems. For example, according to Louise Hay, problems with feet are often caused by a reluctance to step forward, or move ahead.

ALL THE CELLS OF MY BODY ARE BATHED DAILY WITH THE HEALING WHITE LIGHT ENERGY OF SPIRIT. I GET BETTER AND STRONGER EVERY DAY.

I NOW HEAL MYSELF IN ALL WAYS AND ON ALL LEVELS.

I AM WHOLE AND HEALTHY IN MIND, BODY AND AFFAIRS. I WELCOME EACH NEW DAY WITH GRATITUDE AND THANKFULNESS.

On your path of healing, be sure to address and fully resolve the root problem of the disease. With the power of the mind and conscious intention being so powerful you can actually "will away" disease before you have learned the lesson that the illness has brought to you. If you have not addressed the root source of the problem you could manifest the illness again, or manifest a different expression of it. There are no shortcuts. You must discover the root of the problem. You must learn the lesson.

> I NOW MANIFEST VIBRANT HEALTH AND LIFE FORCE ENERGY THROUGHOUT MY BEING. I NOW FULLY RELEASE ALL PHYSICAL, MENTAL AND EMOTIONAL PATTERNS AND ENERGIES THAT ARE NO LONGER CONTRIBUTING TO MY GOOD.

In your quest for robust health, be sure to ask for *what you want*, not the *means* to get what you want. If you want perfect health, focus on seeing yourself healthy and full of life. Don't necessarily try to manifest the right doctor or healer. Let the universe find a way to help you on the road to wellness. If a healer or doctor is what is needed, allow the universe to guide you in that direction.

> VIBRANT HEALTH AND BOUNDLESS ENERGY NOW FLOW THROUGH ME AS I CONNECT WITH THE HEALING POWER OF UNIVERSAL LIFE FORCE ENERGY.

THE HEALING POWER OF WORDS

A woman who was aware of the power of words had the occasion to prove it when her son became ill and was hospitalized. He was placed in a room with two terminally ill patients. He grew weaker every day in this depressed atmosphere.

Every day his mother visited and spoke encouraging words of life and health to him, but it did not help. Finally, the mother realized that if those administering treatment to her son also spoke encouragingly, it would help. She confidentially asked the head nurse to be sure that everyone in contact with him spoke encouragingly to her son. The nurse replied, "I will be glad to see that this is done, though I cannot see how it can help your son. He is getting weaker every day."

Soon a nurse's aide, following instructions, said to this woman's son, "You are looking much better than you were yesterday. You are on the road to recovery!" Later, an intern said the same thing to him. Immediately, the woman's son began to respond. The atmosphere in the hospital room improved. And the mother also continued her daily visits and words of encouragement and healing.

Her son's health improved dramatically, and additionally, as the days passed, the other two people in the room began to recover too! After a complete recovery, one of the men in the room told the woman's son, "Your mother not only talked you back to life, but her words gave me new life too. Had it not been for your mother's daily encouraging words, I believe we would both be dead today." [5]

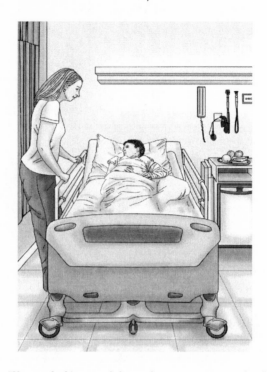

"You are looking much better than you were yesterday."

AFFIRMATIONS

EVERY DAY, IN EVERY WAY, I'M GETTING BETTER AND BETTER.

I NOW LOVE OPENLY AND COMPLETELY, AND RECEIVE LOVE OPENLY AND COMPLETELY.

I AM NOW HEALED ON ALL LEVELS IN ALL WAYS.

I AM NOW IN PERFECT HEALTH, ACHIEVING LEVELS OF HEALTH AND WELLNESS THAT AMAZE ME.

I AM WELL, I AM WHOLE, I AM STRONG, I AM HEALTHY.

I HAVE ALL THE ENERGY I NEED TO ACCOMPLISH MY GOALS AND TO
FULFILL MY DESIRES.

GOD'S LOVE HEALS ME AND MAKES ME WHOLE.

I AM FULL OF VITALITY AND ENERGY. I AM VIBRANT AND ALIVE, AND
LOOK FORWARD TO NEW OPPORTUNITIES IN MY LIFE.

QUESTIONS AND ANSWERS

Q. Say two people are diagnosed with cancer. One cures themselves of the disease, and the other dies from it. Why?
A. There can be many reasons and explanations. But if all else is equal, the person who cures himself or herself of the disease does so because they both *want to* and *believe* that they can.

Q. Don't genetics and heredity factors play a big part in the health of a person?
A. Yes, they do. But thoughts and beliefs are equally as important, if not more so.

Q. I'm not sure I believe that I can heal myself.
A. You can. Use affirmations, visioning, and see yourself in vibrant health. You can do this! People heal themselves every day, in every way, of all sorts of serious illness and disease. You can too!

Q. If I try hard enough, can I heal a loved one?
A. Sickness and health are personal choices. There may be far more to an illness than what appears on the surface. If you want to help, try to help the person discover and see the source of their problem that is causing the illness. However, true healing comes from within. The person who is sick and out of balance needs to want to heal himself or herself.

CHAPTER SUMMARY

1) Using your powers of thought, you manifest your level of health.
2) Oftentimes people wait until they manifest a serious sickness or disease before they put a priority on their health.
3) Disease is normally an outward manifestation of something that is out of balance on the inside.
4) If you can take responsibility for your sickness, you can also take responsibility to make yourself well.

5) Cure yourself by discovering the root "mental" cause of disease, and addressing it. Ask a close friend for an honest appraisal of yourself to help you uncover your "unhealthy" issue.

6) Use the healing power of words and affirmations to promote healing.

MANIFESTING WORKSHEET

Try to think of friends or relatives who have developed things like heart disease, cancer, or other major diseases. Looking at it objectively from the outside, can you see how it may be that this is something they may have created for themselves, in some way, for some reason? Often, looking at it with a detached point of view, it can be a bit easier to see the reasons and circumstances around someone else's health condition.

With this knowledge and understanding, you can now view your own life from a higher place. Write down five affirmative statements around even higher levels of health that you will now create for yourself:

1) _____

2) _____

3) _____

4) _____

5) _____

REFERENCES

1. Louise Hay, *You Can Heal Your Life,* (Hay House, 1984), p. 158.
2. Louise Hay, *You Can Heal Your Life,* (Hay House, 1984), p. 175.
3. Louise Hay, *You Can Heal Your Life,* (Hay House, 1984), p. 189.
4. Louise Hay, *You Can Heal Your Life,* (Hay House, 1984), p. 187.
5. Catherine Ponder, *The Prosperity Secrets of the Ages,* (DeVorss & Company, 1986), p 84.

CHAPTER 17

Gratitude

"Thank you, thank you, thank you."

EXPRESSING GRATITUDE

Expressing gratitude is one of the best and fastest ways to accelerate manifestation. When you express gratitude, you are projecting a vibration of thankfulness and love. This powerfully magnetizes more and similar positive experiences and opportunities to you.

The act of expressing gratitude identifies and projects good energy out into the world. In doing so, it reinforces the positive and attracts more good into your life. It is like starting up a big snowball of gathering good will.

By expressing gratitude, you are also creating a void or vacuum within yourself into which more goodness can flow. Additionally, when you express gratitude to others, you are raising both your and the recipient's vibration and consciousness. It is a synergistic, cumulative good.

> I NOW EXPRESS COMPLETE GRATITUDE FOR ALL THE WONDERFUL PEOPLE, MEANINGFUL RELATIONSHIPS, LEARNING SITUATIONS, WONDROUS OPPORTUNITIES, AND UNCONDITIONAL LOVE IN MY LIFE. THANK YOU, THANK YOU, THANK YOU.

When we are grateful and appreciate what life has to offer, it indicates to the universe that we accept whatever has been given to us. For example, if we want to attract more abundance into our lives, we need to start the process of being grateful for the abundance we have right now. All of this opens up the flow of supply into our world because whatever we give to life returns to us.

You can multiply the affects of your expressed gratitude by seeing everyone around you as expanding and growing. Express gratitude on behalf of yourself and others, and generate more good will all around you.

> THIS IS A TIME OF GREAT BLESSINGS. ABUNDANCE AND PROSPERITY
> FLOWS TO ME NOW IN A NEVERENDING WAVE. I REMAIN ETERNALLY
> GRATEFUL. THANK YOU, THANK YOU, THANK YOU.

One way to express your own gratitude is to write a list of those things you are grateful for, and put them into a *gratitude notebook*. Add to your list as you like. Focus on the good. Your gratitude notebook can include work, home, relationships and spiritual matters.

Expressing appreciation for others and appreciation for yourself is a very high energetic vibration. Gratitude, thankfulness, and love are all very high energetic patterns. If you are feeling "down" or "not right," try thinking of someone or something to be grateful for. Be especially sure to express gratitude to those who make a positive difference in your life. They will appreciate knowing that their contributions are valued.

ATTITUDES ABOUT MONTHLY BILLS AND INVOICES

Can you feel grateful for your monthly bills? When you receive an electric bill or car payment invoice in the mail, how do you feel about it? Most people dread having to pay bills. Most people begin to feel all sorts of worry, concern, lack, and emotional issues surrounding the payment of bills. It doesn't have to be that way.

For example, with your electric bill, focus on how much you enjoy having electricity, how convenient it makes life, and how it is always there when you want it. Think about how it powers your television, computer, radio, and refrigerator. For your car payment, focus on how happy you feel when you drive your automobile, and all the wonderful places it has taken you. By expressing gratitude for these things, you will shift the bill paying process into a positive experience, and benefit from it.

If you shift your view of the way the world works, paying bills can be more pleasant. First, you must thank your creditors. You should express thanks to the electric company that not only provides you with electricity, but also trusts you and has confidence in your ability to pay that it is willing to give you the service first and let you pay for it afterwards. In terms of your car payment, thank your bank or finance company for trusting in who you are, and your ability to manifest correct and proper payment when needed. Feel good about the fact that these people think you are worthy. Because you are!

AFFIRMATIONS

I AM TRULY GRATEFUL FOR ALL THAT HAS OCCURRED IN MY LIFE AND
THE LOVE, LEARNING, GROWTH AND INSIGHT IT HAS PROVIDED ME WITH.
I AM ETERNALLY GRATEFUL. THANK YOU, THANK YOU, THANK YOU.

I REMAIN GRATEFUL TO THE UNIVERSAL SPIRIT FOR THE ALIGNMENT
AND RESTORATION OF MY DIVINE SPIRIT PATH.

THANK YOU GOD.

I AM GRATEFUL FOR THE GIFTS I RECEIVE EACH MOMENT OF EVERY DAY.
I AM THANKFUL FOR ALL THAT I AM RECEIVING.

I REMAIN ETERNALLY GRATEFUL FOR EVERYONE AND EVERYTHING IN
MY LIFE NOW. THANK YOU, THANK YOU, THANK YOU.

QUESTIONS AND ANSWERS

Q. I'm sick, broke, and jobless. What is there to be thankful for?
A. That's for you to decide. Get a notebook, and every time you can think of something
to be grateful for, write it down in your notebook. Can you be grateful for a beautiful
sunrise? Can you be grateful for the smile or laugh of a small child? Can you be grateful
for a warm summer rain? Read back your gratitude passages to yourself from time to
time. Shift your focus to the things in life you are grateful for, and it will bring more.

Q. My sister has everything: a great husband, nice kids, and beautiful home, and yet
is thankless and miserable. What's the problem here?
A. Lack of gratitude. Sometimes people in these situations will manifest a dramatic
loss of some kind to help them understand feelings of gratitude for what they do have.
Hopefully your sister will not have to create some kind of loss before she can fully
appreciate what she does have now. The thing to remember is that it really doesn't
matter how much or how little you have. What is important is that you fully appreciate
all that you do have in your life, right now.

Q. Kids are spoiled rotten today. They have everything. And yet, they are grateful for
nothing. Why are they so ungrateful?
A. They have not seen strife and struggle. They have not seen world wars. They have
not seen shortages. So those things are not part of their reality and consciousness.
Generations who toiled before this one have in fact given them a great gift. Try not to
be in judgment of them. However, at the same time, try to help them truly appreciate
what they do have.

CHAPTER SUMMARY

1) Expressing gratitude reinforces the positive and attracts more good to you.
2) By expressing gratitude, you create a void or vacuum into which more goodness can flow.
3) Expressing gratitude raises your vibration.
4) When grateful, you indicate to the universe that you accept what has been given to you.
5) Consider keeping a gratitude notebook to emphasize the good.
6) Multiply the effects of gratitude by seeing others around you as growing and expanding.
7) Shift the process of paying bills from a place of resentment or fear to one of being thankful and grateful.
8) Help younger people appreciate and be grateful for all that they do have.

MANIFESTING WORKSHEET

Starting Your Gratitude Notebook: Write down 10 things you are grateful for, and then transfer them to your gratitude notebook. Find a notebook that is a bit special. Perhaps it has a colorful cover, or inspirational image on it, or is a handy size to carry. Use this notebook and add to it or read it whenever you are feeling a bit unsure of yourself, a bit down or depressed, or not sure which way to turn. Remember that you can be grateful for anything, even the simple things in life we take for granted, like a sunrise, a shimmering lake, a smile from a stranger, a meandering path through the woods, or a falling leaf.

CHAPTER 18

Love

"I now love openly and completely, in bliss"—Andrew Lutts

GROWING YOUR HEART-CENTERED ENERGY FIELD

Experience love and joy in your life, now!

By opening up to the expressions of creation and manifestation, you also open the doorway to love. The reason is that universal love energy comes from exactly the same place as creation energy: Source. And just as creation energy in the universe is unlimited, universal love energy is unlimited too! It is the same energy, simply expressed in different ways as it flows through you.

This means that if you can manifest things and situations in your life, you can also manifest love. You can have as much love as you want in your life, simply by opening up to it. Pure, true love, whenever you want it. Love that never runs out. Love that is without condition. Love with no strings attached. Powerful, sweeping, overwhelming love. The good stuff!

To receive this unlimited universal love energy, open up to it. Get quiet, get peaceful, and then visualize the love energy coming to you. Here are three ways to do this:

1) Imagine standing under a waterfall of love, where the water of love pours forth in a never-ending rush onto your head, shoulders and body, showering you with shimmering cleansing love energy for as long as you can stand under it and bathe in it.

2) Imagine lying on your back on a soft blanket in a wide open field. The sun is shining brightly. There is no one nearby. As you lie there, the rays of the sun beat down on you in wave after wave of love and compassion, flooding your body and filling you up with radiant, healing light and love energy. It makes

167

you feel so happy and light in your body that it feels like you could rise right out of your body.

3) Imagine sitting in a chair or sitting in the lotus position with your legs crossed, and you are in the middle of a deep fulfilling time of personal meditation. You breathe deeply, and go even deeper. You feel the crown of your head "open up," and you feel the golden white light of love pour down from the heavens, filling up every cell of your body with brilliant love and life force energy. It fills you up so much that you are overflowing. You are so radiant with love that you are glowing. Every cell in your body is radiant and shining. You feel a rush of energy up your spine, and the hair on your scalp tingles with excitement. There is so much love in you that you have become love.

LOVING OPENLY AND FREELY

As the love pours forth from the universe into your being, filling you up with light and love, project the love out into your surroundings to people in your life. It is important to share the love, and keep the energetic flow moving. The more you project it and share it, the more you get from the universe. It is a never-ending cycle that *never* runs out. It is available to us all, not just those who are "perfect" or "enlightened" or "in love." You can access it right now, as you read these words.

> I NOW OPEN MY HEART CHAKRA WIDE. I AM FULL OF UNLIMITED LOVE.
> I NOW LOVE UNCONDITIONALLY, OPENLY, AND COMPLETELY, IN BLISS.
> LOVE FLOWS THROUGH ME NOW, IN A NEVERENDING WAVE.

When you are loving freely and unconditionally, there is much beauty. This beauty shines from within, as you connect with your passion. You are connected to Source, and you are at peace with all things. You are in right way with the universe.

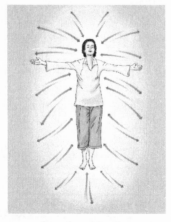

Loved and Loving.

Beauty in this context is not physical beauty, but a beauty that everyone recognizes easily. You feel it! It is a beauty that causes attraction. It is the kind of peaceful beauty that everyone wants to be around, feel, take in, and be part of. It is wonderful, and powerfully attractive! In a word, it is radiant. It is one of the highest energetic patterns you can vibrate at. As you develop this loving aspect of your being, don't be surprised when you start to become "popular," and that people want to be around you and in your loving presence.

> I LOVE MYSELF, HONESTLY, OPENLY, UNCONDITIONALLY, JUST THE WAY I AM.

When in the flow, feeling love and feeling connected, you:

- Feel a strong interconnectedness to all beings and things
- Feel unconditional love spreading throughout your whole body
- Feel at one with Spirit, and being loved by Spirit
- Feel a flow of universal life force energy from above, coming through the crown of your head (crown chakra)
- Feel a surge of energy rising up from the base of your spine and out through the top of your head (kundalini energy)
- Feel light and spirit-like (etheric) in your body, as if you are able to rise out of your physical body
- Sense your higher self, spirit guides and angels, and have a feeling and awareness that you are being assisted throughout the day
- Feel grace, blessings and a profound feeling of bliss

If you want to manifest meaningful, loving relationships in life, be love. Project love out from your being. Be loving in all your ways. You will attract people from all around who want to be in your company. They may not know exactly why, but they will be responding to your loving ways.

SELF LOVE

The energy of love can also work like forgiveness. We often readily and easily forgive others. We work through the issues, clear the karma, and are ready to move on. But we often forget to forgive the most important person of all, *ourselves!*

Love can be like that too. We love everyone else, deeply, honestly, passionately, kindly, and even unconditionally. But again, we forget. We must love ourselves too, and it must be done unconditionally.

Can you really love yourself unconditionally, knowing that you are less than perfect? Can you love yourself unconditionally when:

- Your job or career is less than perfect
- Your physical body or appearance is not ideal in your opinion
- You are going through changes in your primary partner relationship
- Your children are presenting you with daily challenges
- You have relatives or in-laws who will not speak with you
- You are not acknowledged at work or home for all the great things you do
- You are financially challenged, or in debt
- Your parents were never there for you, or never showed their love
- You feel like you have accomplished little in life
- You feel like you have no friends, or that no one loves you
- You feel like you are going nowhere, or going backwards

You must put these things behind you, and know that you are much more than the sum of your parts. You must love yourself, knowing that you are far from perfect. And you must love yourself so much that you can love yourself without condition or reservation. You must love yourself *just the way you are*, right now, in this moment. You must love yourself *unconditionally*.

I FORGIVE MYSELF FOR NOT BEING EVERYTHING I THINK I SHOULD BE.
I NOW FULLY ACCEPT AND LOVE MYSELF THE WAY I AM.

LOVE ENERGY AND UNIVERSAL CREATOR ENERGY

When we are in love with someone, we give them unlimited love energy. We give and give and give, and often don't even think about the energy of it. After all, it feels great! And the love can be so powerful it can be addictive. We are in love with the feeling of being in love. Time seems to stand still. We live fully in the moment, because we are completely immersed in it all. And nothing else in the world really matters anymore. Isn't it great?

Where at one time we may have looked to Source for love, we now get love in abundance from our partner. And, because of that, Source energy is not sought after as much. However, the intensity of the energetic transfer between two people may change. Sometimes in romantic love there can be an imbalance. A struggle for power and energy may arise. Personal dramas and issues may come into play.

Be aware of addiction to others and the addiction of love. It can be problematic when you depend on someone to provide loving energy to you in a significant way, and then the dynamic changes. At any time you can access all the love you want from Source.

Thus, you should never feel a lack of love, when it is always available to you. Love energy directly from Source will only add more love to your already loving life. Take that love from Source and recharge your batteries.

As you grow, change, and experience loving relationships with other people, issues surrounding love and the energy of love will become apparent to you. If you can feel, identify, understand, and appreciate the sometimes subtle differences between romantic love, friendship love, universal love, and unconditional love, it will help you become more aware of the situations that present themselves to you as you relate to other people in the world. That said, realize that all love is great!

> I BATHE IN THE UNCONDITIONAL LOVE OF SPIRIT, AND IT RADIATES FROM ME AT ALL TIMES.

ETERNAL LOVE

As the universe expands, so does love expand, eternally. As you reconnect with Source, that love comes to you, directly, powerfully, from the universal All That Is. You are *never* alone.

Love is an expression that transcends time and space. Love is an energetic vibration which lasts far longer than our physical bodies. Love carries the emotion and interaction of energy across timelines, generations, and dimensions. Love is eternal.

Eternal love for another can be defined as feeling a connection to someone throughout all time and space. The love may be for someone in your life in this incarnation, for someone from past incarnations, or for someone who is now in the spirit world.

If there is someone you love unconditionally and eternally who is for some reason denying your love, it a choice that they have made. It is not your "problem," it is theirs. The love is still there. The love will always be there, eternally. And although relationships and situations may be conditional, love is unconditional.

People who have loved you in your past, your present and your future all love you simultaneously, in the now, whether you know it or not. This is because time is merely our third dimensional construct which makes things appear to be linear (with a beginning and an ending). The love is there. Furthermore, your love is continually evolving, growing and expanding. It is a key part of your personal growth. Love is the ultimate expression of being.

I NOW LOVE ETERNALLY, ENDLESSLY, AND WITHOUT LIMITS. MY
BOUNDLESS LOVE TRANSCENDS LIFETIMES AND DIMENSIONS. MY LOVE
GROWS EVERMORE, WITH EACH PASSING MOMENT OF MY LIFE.

LOVE AS OUR TRUE NATURE

Saint Francis of Assisi best describes the Law of Love: "It is in giving love that we receive
love." When we fall in love with someone, it is not because we expect to receive love
back from them. It is simply because we love their being, their soul. We love them
because we *see the divine in them*, shining brightly. We recognize the God or Goddess
within them and consequently want to love and serve them. Some thoughts on love:

- Recognize and accept love as our true nature. It is natural to love and be loved.
- Be loving, gentle and respectful towards others in your thoughts, speech
  and actions.
- Surrender your ego to others. Rise above the limitations imposed by your ego.
- Value your relationships with others as sacred, because they are.
- Be centered and connected to your loving higher self.
- Love others unconditionally and support them in their personal and spiritual
  growth.
- Keep communications open and love consciously, actively and in the present
  moment.

It matters not
Who you love
Where you love
Why you love
When you love
Or how you love
It matters only that you love
John Lennon

UNCONDITIONAL LOVE

Unconditional love is defined by loving someone or a situation unconditionally, without
reservation, regardless of the circumstances or situation.

Can you love someone who does not seem to return love, or someone who has done
you wrong, or someone who keeps pushing your buttons, or someone who is fighting
with you? Can you love someone who you feel simply cannot love you back?

This can be one of our greatest challenges, and one reason why we are here today. It
may also be the reason we have brought certain people into our lives.

These are people that we likely feel strongly toward, both positively or negatively. These are people that will call us on our stuff, who will see through our personal shields and veils. We have attracted these people into our lives at this time in order to help us learn about unconditional love. And it is a valuable lesson, indeed.

Unconditional love is a step to enlightenment, ascension, all being, all knowing, with a direct connection to Source and All That Is. It is the feeling of interconnectedness with everyone and everything in the universe. Can it be that simple? Yes.

Unconditional love means not having preconceived expectations of what someone should say or not say, do or not do, be or not be, have or not have. *It is loving people for who they are.* Unconditional love means keeping your heart wide open, with love energy emanating freely and unconditionally from your being. "Unconditional Love is learning to be the source of love, rather than waiting for others to be the source." [1]

Unconditional love is a feeling, a state of being, and a magnetic vibration all rolled up together. It is the God Consciousness in action. Unconditional love, when put into action, has the power to heal, transform, and uplift both the person loving unconditionally and the person being loved unconditionally.

> I NOW OPEN MY HEART WIDE, AND LOVE OTHERS COMPLETELY AND UNCONDITIONALLY, KNOWING THAT LOVE HEALS ALL.

> I EXPRESS MY LOVE FREELY, KNOWING THAT AS I GIVE LOVE, I AM INSTANTLY SUPPLIED WITH MORE.

> I FEEL UNLIMITED UNCONDITIONAL UNIVERSAL LOVE POUR FORTH FROM MY HIGHER SELF, ANGELS, AND SPIRIT GUIDES TO ME, AND I SHARE THAT LOVE WITH ALL THOSE AROUND ME.

To achieve the state of unconditional love, use the step-by-step process below. Work through some of the primary levels of forgiveness, acceptance, release, awareness, and love, in order to raise yourself to higher and higher vibrations.

1) Forgive people and situations in your life that need forgiveness. Free yourself from the energetic connections which no longer serve your highest good.
2) Accept, understand and trust that certain things will transpire divinely. This is a key component of allowing the universe to rebalance and perfect situations.
3) Release out to the universe what is holding you back. Rid yourself of dysfunctional situations.
4) Address, overcome and release grudges and karma with others. Forgive others freely.

5) Rise above situations and view things from an enlightened position. View situations with detached objectivity. View things from a higher place.

6) Meditate, reconnect with Source. Come into your power, into the stillness and depths of yourself.

7) Open up your chakras, remove energetic blocks, get clear and balanced. Seek bodywork if necessary.

8) Connect directly with your heart, throat, third eye and crown chakra to be in full alignment with your higher self and highest potentiality.

You may find that someone comes into your life and helps you learn and explore this concept. They may be a friend, lover, or a guide of sorts. Remain open to the possibilities that you will receive help that guides you on your best path.

LOVE NOW ENCOMPASSES MY BEING FULLY AND COMPLETELY. LOVE WORKS THROUGH ME AND POSITIVELY AFFECTS ALL ASPECTS OF MY LIFE.

HOW DEEP CAN LOVE GO?

Love can go very, very deeply. You can experience love so deeply that you can take the expression to entirely new depths. You can love someone so much that you are connected with an incredible bond that transcends lives and lifetimes. You can love someone so deeply that you anticipate your lover's thoughts, that you finish each other's sentences, that you feel like two halves of a whole, that your life feels incomplete when you are not together. You can be so "in step" with someone that you complement their every strength and weakness with your matching complementary expression. In these cases there is almost always a soul recognition and complete familiarity and comfort with this person. This can be the result of having known someone for hundreds of lifetimes, and growing with them on your spiritual paths together. [2]

Everyone wants to connect with their soul mate, their twin flame, and their perfect life partner. But remember that *you do not need to* connect with this "perfect" mate in this lifetime in order to experience the perfection of deep unconditional love. There may be a myriad of reasons why your connection to the "ultimate" partner may not occur as you would hope in this lifetime. That said, you are limiting your personal growth if you let that be a reason to not fully experience the depths possible with true, full unconditional love that is available to us all. Don't place conditions on your love; don't wait for that perfect time, that perfect place, that perfect situation, that perfect partner. You can experience it *now*, fully and completely, without condition.

AFFIRMATIONS

I AM A VESSEL IN ALIGNMENT WITH SOURCE. I AM A HUMAN FULL OF LOVE. LOVE POURS FORTH FROM MY BEING, NOW AND EVERMORE.

I AM A RADIATING CENTER OF DIVINE LOVE. I NOW EXPRESS LOVE TO
ALL THOSE I MEET. I RADIATE LOVE TO ALL PERSONS, PLACES AND
THINGS.
DIVINE LOVE IS WORKING THROUGH ME NOW.

I LOVE MYSELF COMPLETELY, AND I GIVE AND RECEIVE LOVE EASILY
AND JOYFULLY.

I AM LOVE.

QUESTIONS AND ANSWERS

Q. How can I love myself when I am not perfect? I'm not exactly happy with the way
I look, I'm too tall / short, fat / skinny, light / dark, etc.
A. All is perfect. This is a lesson of self-love, and acceptance. Can you accept and love
others who are less than perfect? Of course. When you can truly love yourself for the
essence of who you are, then you will open the doorway for others to love you for
who you are. This is key. Loving yourself for who you are right now is one of the most
important things you can do.

Q. Why am I in such a complicated love situation right now?
A. You chose it. However, realize that things may be much deeper than what they appear
to be. For example, at another time you may have agreed to help someone at this time
now. So you may be participating with someone in a co-creative lesson, an agreement,
or an understanding. When you both receive this lesson you are then free to move on
to the next level of learning together. You may move on together, or separately.

Q. I'm a little confused with all this talk of love. Isn't it good enough to just love
someone truly and deeply?
A. Sure it is. There is no judgment. But all of us can love even more, love very deeply,
and we can love unconditionally. Can you love someone who has stolen something of
value from you? Can you love someone who has harmed someone close to you? Can
you love someone who has wronged you? Can you love someone who has lied to you?
Can you love someone from a country that is at war with your country? These are all
situations from which you can grow personally. Our true essence is deep, pure love, yet
as humans in the third dimension we sometimes hide it behind personal "shields."

Q. I have been searching my whole life for my life partner to love truly and deeply.
Why haven't I found this person?
A. It may be that in the searching and in your pursuit that you are chasing him or her
away from you. Try trusting and allowing. Try attracting. Try practicing your loving
ways with someone else. That loving experience may draw someone near to you. Or
you may find that the person you are "practicing with" is the real one for you. The

possibilities are endless. Try releasing it to the universe. Expect the unexpected. Allow the universe to work its magic!

CHAPTER SUMMARY

1) Loving unconditionally is very similar to manifesting and creating; they both involve Source energy.
2) Get quiet, and visualize universal love energy filling up your physical being.
3) The more you project love out, the more that love comes back to you from the universe.
4) When you love unconditionally, you are beautiful, and powerfully attractive.
5) When in the flow, you feel a strong interconnectedness with all beings and things.
6) Love yourself unconditionally first, then love others unconditionally.
7) Try not to be addicted to others for receiving love energy. At any time you can access all the love you want from Source.
8) Eternal love transcends time, space and dimension. Love is eternal. Love is the ultimate expression of being.
9) Recognize and accept love as your true nature. It is natural to love, and be loved. It matters only *that you love.*
10) If you are involved in an energetically imbalanced relationship, where one person is giving much more and one person is receiving much more, send love to it and change it in order to release and resolve the karmic imbalance.
11) Unconditional love is learning to be the source of love. It is a true and deep feeling of interconnectedness with everyone and everything in the universe.
12) You can experience love so deeply that it takes the expression to entirely new depths.
13) You do not need to connect with the "perfect" partner in order to experience the perfection of deep unconditional love.

MANIFESTING WORKSHEET—BEING LOVING IN ALL WAYS

As you go through your day, look for chances to reaffirm to yourself:

I am loving—I am loved.

Look for the small and large ways in which you can be loving. If someone cuts you off in traffic, or if they step before you in a line, send love to them. Know that your love may help them to become aware of their actions.

Look for the small seemingly insignificant things in life: a breaking wave at the seashore, a drop of rain from a leaf, a puffy cloud drifting by. See love in everything.

If you can identify this love all around you, *and it is all around you,* you will find this love amplified in your life in many, many ways. Because what you dwell upon becomes your reality, make an effort to see the love that is truly in you and all around you. You will find yourself truly blessed and loved as you go through life.

Also, focus on how you can love all people, *unconditionally.* Think of people in your life, perhaps people that challenge you, and practice sending love to them, and loving them unconditionally. List three people below that you will send unconditional love to:

1) _____
2) _____
3) _____

REFERENCES

1. Sanaya Roman, *Personal Power Through Awareness,* (HJ Kramer, 1992), p.100.
2. Ellen Mogensen, Heal Past Lives, (www.healpastlives.com)

CHAPTER 19

Enlightenment

"The river of grace longs to flow through you."—Eric Klein

THE DOOR TO ENLIGHTENMENT

When we learn the skills of manifestation and we are able to understand and work with concepts of an unlimited universe, it allows for the opportunity to become enlightened. The door to enlightenment is waiting for you to reach forward, pull it open, and step through. Do it!

What does enlightenment mean, anyway? On the surface, enlightened means being full of light. But it is much more than that. Enlightened people have awakened and developed a mastery of themselves: their spiritual selves, their humanity, their awareness, and their connection to Source. For many people on earth now, our goal is to achieve a state of enlightenment. By doing so, we positively affect not just those around us, but everyone on the planet.

Many times people who are enlightened take an obvious spiritual path, expressing themselves as a Buddha, minister, priest, rabbi, healer, or shaman. However, more often the enlightened people are those you see on the street, at your job, in line at the post office, and at the volunteer meeting. They are the ones with the twinkle in their eyes. They are the ones who are in their truth. They are the ones who are not afraid to be themselves and be in the moment. They have no problems seeing things the way they really are, and saying so.

The Door to Enlightenment.

Here are some of the qualities and characteristics of people who are enlightened:

1) ***Radiant***—Enlightened people affect people around them in many ways, almost always positively. Being in the presence of an enlightened person can be transformative. It can also be a bit uncomfortable, as your own issues sometimes come up when you are in the presence of someone radiating pure love.

2) ***Loving***—Enlightened people are full of and overflowing with love. They glow. You can recognize their divinity in the smile on their face, their compassion for others, their selflessness, and their service to humanity. You can feel their love just by being in their physical presence.

3) ***Aware***—Enlightened people normally have heightened abilities of intuition, foresight, and understanding. Enlightenment allows for a powerful understanding of the essence of other people and situations around them.

4) ***Complete***—Enlightened people feel complete and satisfied with what is. They are not in want or lack. They are who they want to be, and have what they want. They fully know and trust that whatever they need will be provided to them perfectly.

5) ***True***—Enlightened people are true to themselves. They are not saying one thing, and doing another. They are not doing something because they are supposed to, or because it is looked well upon.

6) **Present**—Enlightened people live fully in the now. They are completely in the present. They are not distracted by outside influences.

7) **Fearless**—Enlightened people are fearless. They know that they do not need to experience fear, and thus they are not interested in attracting fearful events and situations to them. They possess a total knowing, trust and acceptance in the universe and all that can be.

> I AM ETERNALLY GRATEFUL FOR BEING SHOWN THE WONDERS OF LIFE, LOVE AND SPIRIT. I NOW LIVE FULLY IN THE MOMENT. I AM FULL OF UNCONDITIONAL LOVE FOR MANKIND.

Enlightenment is often attained through the process of awakening. This can occur when you have cleared your karma, overcome limitation, and acknowledged that we are all one. Physically, things like meditation, a macrobiotic diet, Reiki, yoga and various forms of bodywork can also help contribute to this process. Mentally, things like solitude and a quiet mind can help a great deal.

Enlightenment also comes from emotional mastery. When you master your emotions, you quiet your mind to a state of deep stillness. Enlightenment can result when you are so purified that your energy rises from the base of your spine, up through your body, and up and out the crown of your head. The combination of these physical events, along with spiritual pursuits, can combine to bring enlightenment to the seeker.

An awakened and enlightened state can bring about certain realizations that there is no you, and that there is no I. It can bring you to an understanding that *you are awareness and consciousness itself,* and that "who you are" is peering out through your eyes. And although you do not lose your persona when enlightened, you certainly see things in a different way.

Enlightenment is an innate understanding of who you are, and that we are all God. It is one thing to understand this intellectually, yet those who are awake and enlightened *know this truth,* to the core of their being, from a deep state of understanding.

> *"The path to the doorway of ascension passes through the corridor of self-realization."*—Erik Klein

IN THE PRESENCE

One curious thing about enlightened people is this: try as you might, you normally cannot "bring down" or negatively affect their strong, high energy. Here's an example:

If you go to a guru and ask him or her why you are having problems with abundance issues, the reply will not be one of sadness or despair. They will not "take on" your problem. Their reply will typically be something like "Well, why have you chosen this experience for yourself?" or "What is it about yourself that is blocking the flow of abundance to you?" Although an enlightened person is certainly compassionate, they come from a place of knowing. They will not be drawn into your issues. And they will not give you a shortcut solution. But what they will do is try to help you see inside yourself, try to guide you, and help you to see into your own heart.

An enlightened person can seem as slippery as a brand-new non-stick frying pan. You can try all you want to lay some of your issues on them, but your issues will slip right off. An enlightened person will not be swayed or pulled down, but will help you discover, identify and address the truth behind your issues.

The reason it is important to understand the characteristics of an enlightened person is that we are all rapidly moving into an enlightened state. The veil of illusion between our physical world and the world of the unseen is now lifting. The truth of the ultimate nature of reality is beginning to become clearer to us. We can all learn from those enlightened people who have gone before, have done the work, and made the path a little smoother and easier for us all. Now it is your turn to take that step if that is the direction you choose to go.

The Path.

THE LIGHTWORKER'S JOURNEY

Upon awakening, many people feel called along the path of the lightworker's journey. In assuming this role, people find themselves in opportunities to help their fellow man. They follow their bliss. They feel an importance about what their role is, knowing that all are needed. The lightworkers are here on earth now to help shift the planet to the next dimension. The lightworker's journey sometimes manifests:

- as a bodyworker in Reiki, polarity, massage, healing
- as a counselor, social worker, life coach, business coach
- in service in any number of various religious capacities
- as a teacher of yoga, tai chi, meditation
- as a musician, poet, sculptor, author, painter, composer
- in service with children, the disabled, the disadvantaged, the elderly
- as a teacher, nurse, therapist, doctor, humanitarian
- and many more

Sometimes a complete turnaround of values and outlook on life will accompany those who make a career change to a new path of a lightworker. And oftentimes the pursuit of one of these career paths invokes much trust. Trust that the universe will provide appropriately during the transition into something that is joyful, meaningful, and fulfilling. The lightworker's journey is a noble one, and we are all grateful for those who work in the light on behalf of us all.

MASTERY AND EXPRESSION OF DIVINE SELF

When you are on the correct path of personal self-expression, things seem effortless. If you listen to a singer with a beautiful voice singing an inspirational song, the act is full of divine, soulful expression of personal talent. The same can be said for a masterful painter, capable poet, experienced ballet dancer, or champion figure skater. In these examples, it can be easy to see the energy of the divine working through them. However, many times the divine talents of people are overlooked because what they are doing appears commonplace.

- Have you ever watched a carpenter build something beautiful and functional from scratch in just a matter of minutes or hours?
- Have you ever seen a gardener grow vibrant plants and produce where virtually nobody could before?
- Have you ever watched a computer person work their magic on the computer keyboard and execute powerful computer programs quickly and easily?
- Have you ever watched a receptionist manage dozens of incoming telephone calls with masterful ease, calm, and professionalism?

- Have you ever watched a mechanic use their wrenches and tools with an amazing economy of motion in order to fix a mechanical problem almost effortlessly?
- Have you ever watched a parent manage dozens of daily tasks in the morning to get everyone in the home off to school and work?
- Have you ever watched a young child use crayons to color in a coloring book, being fully focused, immersed, and using extreme care to insure that it comes out just right?

All around us in a myriad of ways, we witness people expressing themselves and their divine connection to Source. Sometimes the act may seem a bit ordinary or commonplace, but it is actually far from it! This is Spirit working through these people. And Spirit works through you, too! Realize this as you go through your day, observing and acknowledging the divine work that people do every day.

A TIDAL WAVE OF LIGHT AND LOVE

You are fully and completely capable of creating a life which contains so much beauty, joy, splendor and love that you cannot wait for a new day to begin. Your life can be such that you feel like bursting out of your skin with unbridled bliss, joy, love and compassion for your life and all those around you. By taking in all the universal life force energy available to you, you can resonate and emanate this wonderful love energy out from your being and into the world. As you access golden white light coming in through the crown of your head, feel it come into your being and burst out in all directions from the core of your being in a tidal wave of light and love. Your day can be so meaningful that you send wave upon wave of powerful love energy out to those around you, transforming everyone and everything in your path. This is an enlightened state to strive for.

I NOW ACHIEVE A STATE OF MASTERY AND ENLIGHTENMENT, AND POSITIVELY SHIFT THE WORLD AROUND ME.

LIFE IS A PLAY

"Once the game is over, the king and the pawn go back in the same box."
—Italian Proverb

One enlightened way to think of life on this planet, with all its challenges, difficulties and opportunities, is to think of it as a play. In a way, *it really is.*

You are an actor, and the people on stage with you in the various scenes are there for only one reason: you asked them to be there!

That villain lurking in the corner is someone who agreed to come into your life at a particular time and offer you all sorts of karmic challenges. He agreed to play the "bad guy." Not only that, but the meaner and more terrible he can possibly be, the better. You don't just want him to be kind of mean, he needs to be *really* mean.

And there are others in your life who also agreed to play key parts in this play of life. The love interest, the trusted friend, the wise advisor, the children and young people, the eccentric uncle, the animals, and others. You chose the stage and the setting (to be born into). You chose the subject of the play (your life contract). Others in the play (your soul family) all agreed to be there for you, and to play their "role" (exchange karma) to the best of their ability, all for *your* benefit (your personal growth).

And after the play is over, the standing ovation has subsided, the actors are backstage at the cast party, and the set has been taken down, you will all congratulate each other on your fine performances in this "play" called life.

"You were a great villain," you will say to your longtime friend who chose to play the part of the bad guy this time around. "You really got my blood boiling!" you will admit. "Thanks for doing such a great job, and being so wicked! It helped me learn my lesson that much more quickly."

"And you were lovely," you will say to your love interest in the play. "When I looked deeply into your eyes I knew it was you," you will confide in them. "Thank you for being there for me, and being such a key part of my life," you will acknowledge, sweetly.

"And you came into my life at the perfect time," you will tell another old friend. "You helped show me the truth of a situation, and helped me move onto my next level of learning."

And those who played the parts of children, friends, parents and others will all be thanked, congratulated, laughed with, and scenes retold as people do when they reminisce and think back to happy, meaningful, and learning times.

For life on earth is a play, a *grand* play, that you helped formulate, write, cast, and one where you played the lead role. You chose the themes. You chose the conflicts. And you decided which scenes belonged where.

And when it is all over, and everyone has gone "home," you will look back with fondness for it all. Despite the blown lines in the play, the problems with props, and the improvisation here and there, you will be thankful. And the things that seemed so big at the time, those critical scenes, that big life lesson, will all seem a bit less critical now, knowing and understanding it all for what it really is.

"You will wake up from this life like it was a dream."—Sun Bear

AFFIRMATIONS

I NOW EXPRESS GRATITUDE FOR ALL DIVINE EXPRESSIONS OF MY LIFE. I AM COMPLETELY GRATEFUL FOR ALL THINGS THAT HAVE TRANSPIRED IN MY LIFE, AND ALL THE DIVINE LOVE, GUIDANCE AND SUPPORT I AM RECEIVING.

I NOW APPROACH LIFE IN AN ENLIGHTENED WAY, AND SEE WITH CLARITY.

I LIVE FULLY IN THE PRESENT, FULLY IN THE NOW, FULLY IN MY TRUE POWER.

QUESTIONS AND ANSWERS

Q. I think I may be a lightworker, but my job is not like one of those listed. In fact, I am doing just a regular type of job.
A. There is no judgment. You have free will choice. Follow your heart. Be where you need to be. Be true to yourself. It is perfectly okay, wherever you are in the world right now, whatever you are doing. We often learn in ways and situations that are unknown to us at the time.

It may be more important that you are with the people you are with at this time. Often we find ourselves in places in which we will have the most positive effect on others. Remember this as you go through your day. There is no judgment as to what current role you have, and whether or not it is "better" than someone else's role. Remember that you bring your divinity with you, wherever you go. And that's a good thing!

Q. Are you sure that I asked the villain in my "play" to be really mean to me? I don't really like all the meanness.
A. Yes. You asked them to play that role, and because they love you they agreed to do it. They are actually doing you a favor. Their job is likely to somehow get you unsettled so that you will learn whatever lesson it is you need to. It could be about self worth, love, or compassion. The lesson could be about moving on to your next step in life. Your lesson could be about anything, really. Try to find out what it is, and work through it.

CHAPTER SUMMARY

1) Enlightenment is a state of mastery of spiritual self, humanity, and connection to Source.
2) Enlightened people express characteristics of: radiant, loving, aware, complete, true to themselves, present and fearless.

3) Enlightenment is often attained through the process of awakening.

4) An awakened state can bring you to the realization that there is no "you," that you are awareness and consciousness itself, and that "who you are" is peering out through your eyes.

5) Enlightened people are not easily drawn into your own personal dramas.

6) Enlightenment is a worthy goal in your personal evolution.

7) The veil of illusion between our physical world and the world of the unseen is being lifted; this helps us all to attain enlightenment.

8) Lightworkers often express the qualities of enlightenment, and often seek opportunities to help their fellow man.

9) All around us every day we can see people expressing their divinity in seemingly commonplace ways.

10) You are fully and completely capable of creating a life which contains so much beauty, joy, splendor and love that you cannot wait for a new day to begin.

11) Life is a lot like a grand play, and you are the lead actor.

12) You will wake up from this life, like it was a dream.

MANIFESTING WORKSHEET

In order to move into the state of enlightenment, try these exercises:

1) Imagine for a moment that there is no you or me, and that what you truly are, your essential life force energy, is peering out through your eyes.

Imagine that "what you really are" is light and love, a kind of pure energy, loving and being, and fully conscious, aware, and enlightened.

Imagine that you are now in a state of human mastery, and that your heart is completely open, and that you possess endless love for humanity, and that your love for others is boundless and beaming out in all directions.

2) Meditate on the concept of "Who Am I," and answer "Who" is the one that is asking this very question. Perhaps your answers will follow this kind of development:

I Am a Man

I Am a Father

I Am a Husband

I Am a Human

I Am a Lightworker

I Am Pure Energy

I Am Connected to All That Is

I Am Unconditional Love
I Am Eternal
I Am Light and Love

REFERENCES

Quotes from Eric Klein, *Jewels on the Path* (Medicine Bear Publishing, 1999)

CHAPTER 20

Personal Growth

You are the Crown of Creation—Jefferson Airplane, 1968

GROWING PERSONALLY

As we become increasingly skillful with manifestation, other related things happen to us as a side effect. Good things.

Human form is the "Crown of Creation." In fact, all humans are ready and fully capable of full God-self activation. As evidence of this, when humans were created we were given the divine gifts of free will, creation and manifestation. We are now called to grow into that role, and fully express these abilities inherent in us all. *It is your time to step forward.*

Personal growth is all about expanding your consciousness. It's about accumulating experience, and learning from that experience. It's about making decisions, right or wrong, and moving forward with the knowledge and understanding that your accumulated life experience brings you closer to your truth. It's about taking responsibility for everything in your life. It's about living in the moment, and manifesting with ease and grace. It is skillfully mastering your existence, all of it. This chapter offers various ways to help you grow personally.

LOSING ATTACHMENT TO THE PHYSICAL

We often become attached while in the third dimension. It's easy to do. We can become attached to the homes we live in, houses of worship, favorite outdoor places, favorite articles of clothing, favorite foods, favorite music, and all sorts of other things in our material plane. To grow personally, it can help to lose attachment to some things physical.

One reason we get attached to things is that, energetically, they remind us of happy times. We feel comfortable with the energy of them. Perhaps we have attached positive feelings to the physical. For example, if we enjoy going to a certain park, it's often because we have had joyful times there. Thus, we attach our feelings of the good times to the park itself. Another example is a favorite vacation destination which reminds us of happy times spent there.

This is not necessarily good or bad. But it can be limiting. It can be problematic if you need to go to that particular park in order to feel joyful. After all, can't we feel good anyway, even if we aren't at that park? Understand that you can feel that feeling of being at a beautiful park on a sunny day at any time, anywhere, whenever you choose to. You don't have to go to the park.

Earth is a fast track planet. This means that we can learn and grow in an accelerated way. We can experience things, feelings, and situations that, although they may seem difficult at the time, help us learn and grow very rapidly. For example, if you visit your homeland, birthplace, or country of origin, you may receive senses, feelings, and an understanding of what it is to be a part of that country or geographic area. It allows you to "work through" the energetics of that experience.

Additionally, people often become attached to things like the earth, trees, or the ocean. We long for the physicality of it all. We long to plunge our hands into the warm earth. We long to listen to the wind through the trees. We long to stroll barefoot along the beach, and feel the sand and waves at our feet. It is perfectly fine to fully embrace and enjoy these physical things. But try not to become attached to or dependent on them for your happiness.

It is because of our attachment to things that we suffer. By letting go
we find that we have not lost anything except our attachment. —Sogyal Rinpoche

LOSING ATTACHMENT TO PEOPLE

Probably the biggest challenge people have with attachment is the attachment to people, or specifically a particular person. We also may find ourselves being attached to the feelings we have when we think of someone.

The attachment to a person creates an imbalance in the energy, and thus creates an emotional or ego-based response to situations. When we lose attachment we liberate ourselves from people and situations.

An obvious example is a romantic relationship. When a romantic relationship ends, often there is someone in the relationship who would prefer to keep the relationship going. It can be very emotionally painful to feel as though your love for another is unwanted, or not returned, because the flow of energy is incomplete.

Another example of attachment for someone is when someone dies. Often a mourning spouse, sibling or child will mourn for months or years over the loss of a loved one. They hold onto and grasp at fading memories, hoping that somehow their sadness and loss will fade with time.

In both of these examples, the person is simply unable to complete the flow of their expression of love for the other person. The love is not returned. And this can be very sad. However, try to look at it as a learning experience of sorts, a type of graduation.

When you are able to release that loved person back to the universe, through separation, breakup, or death, you liberate yourself. You become free and clear. You become unencumbered by the past, and unbound from your emotions, feelings, and especially attachment.

This does not mean that your love for this person is any less. You have simply shifted your perspective on the emotion that you have attached to that person who was in your life in a very meaningful way, but who has moved on. Additionally, as a result of losing your attachment to a person who is no longer in your life, you create a void, a vacuum. In doing so, you allow for a new person or people to come into your life.

> *"Those who have felt the depths of your true love*
> *will remember you forever*
> *and cherish you eternally. "*—Andrew Lutts

Please know that the process of mourning a death or feeling a sense of loss about a relationship that has ended is not unwanted or harmful. It allows us to acknowledge our feelings, come to terms with what has transpired, and "work through" the energy of it. However, where it can be harmful is when this process is stuck, or is preventing you from continuing on with your next level of growth, or your next relationship. This is where it can help to surrender to the situation, and trust that all will be well.

I NOW RELEASE ALL FEELINGS OF ATTACHMENT AND LOSS. I NOW RELEASE THIS SITUATION TO THE HEALING LOVE OF SPIRIT. I GIVE THANKS FOR THE DIVINE RESTORATION OF MY AFFAIRS AT THIS TIME.

I LET GO AND TRUST. ALL IS OCCURING IN DIVINE PERFECTION.

THE ROLE OF EGO

Ego is a function of the mind which creates your personality. Ego can sometimes confuse us into understanding what is important to us. In terms of personal growth, when we understand how the ego works on our behalf, it can be a great help to us.

One role of ego is keeping us separate from Source. The experience of being separate, that is, a personal identity (ego) separate from Source, is the fundamental illusion which creates problems for us in the third dimension. The ego helps us filter divinity into a form that we can integrate into the third dimension. So what exactly does that mean? It means that it helps us separate ourselves from Source. And yes, it seems counterintuitive. After all, aren't we trying to reconnect with Source?

The challenge is that as long as we remain in the third dimension, the ego will be a part of our being. If we had no ego, we would be overcome by the full energy of Spirit. We would be walking around like blabbering idiots, completely in bliss, unable to speak or function.

So although it would be great to be in bliss constantly with the full God force flowing through us without limits of any kind, it would be very difficult to think and function in our physical world unless we evolved to that high state a bit more gradually. Some humans have achieved this mastery and are able to successfully integrate this state of being into their human presence, but many of us are not quite there yet. Ego helps us manage our experiences in our dimension.

Another major concept related to the ego is the concept of individuation. Individuation is a function of the soul which helps us understand self-realization first (my will) and God-realization second (thy will, or God's will). This duality which we all experience is one way we learn service in the universe with the goal of becoming and being a coworker with God. [1]

On the other side of the spectrum from the ego is the spirit mind. The spirit mind's purpose is service. The spirit mind seeks to uplift humanity. The spirit mind tries to show the ego that we are all one. Although we need both the spirit mind and the ego to function on the physical plane, try not to let the functions of the ego mind block your true divinity and what comes through in your spirit mind.

YOUR TRUTH

There is no one in the world with your set of experiences, attitudes, beliefs, viewpoints, and karmic challenges. Nobody. So how can someone else know what should be true for you? When someone tells you their truth, do you accept it and make it your truth? Why or why not?

Truth for a person is the belief that a certain perception is accurate *for their reality*. If your reality is different or unique, *and it is*, then you can choose to accept or reject someone else's truth as your truth. Your truth is yours, and yours alone.

Know that the universe is a fluid place, and constantly changing. What is true one day may be more or less true the next day. Things change. You are changing. Consciousness changes. Just as you can change your thoughts and beliefs, you can change certain truths. It is part of our learning process.

Discernment is the third dimensional tool you have to ascertain and understand the truth of a given situation. Discernment is the act or process of exhibiting keen insight and good judgment. Use discernment to help analyze the world around you. With discernment, you can simply check into your heart to see how you feel about a situation. Then you can decide if it is your truth or not. Only you can decide if something is true for you. It can be important to understand and know your truth, as it forms a frame of reference from which you can view the world and grow personally.

SURRENDER AND TRUST

Depending on your situation and where you are in the world, it can often make sense to surrender to a situation. This can be a very enlightening decision to make. Perhaps an approach that you have taken in the past did not seem to work. At times like these, it's okay to surrender and trust in the outcome. You don't need to be in control of everything all the time. This is one way we grow personally. By surrendering, we allow the universe to bring us a solution, and make it right.

Trust is similar to allowing. When we trust, we know with a level of certainty that something will turn out okay. The more fully and completely you can trust, the better vibration you are projecting out into the universe, and the more perfect the result will be.

Some people have serious issues around trust. Perhaps something important to them was taken from them. Perhaps they learned distrust from parents. And so in looking for distrust in people and situations, they find it!

Some people really want to be "in control." They want to master the situation, and manage the events. Do you know someone who always wants to be in control of everything? This illusion of complete control works up to a point, but sooner or later the universe will confront you with something that is just beyond your ability to control.

That's when it's time to surrender to it. You may even know a person who is so driven and determined that they feel up to the challenge to take on the universe to gain control. Good luck! The universe is an opponent with no limits.

Others trust fully and completely, and surrender the situation to God, Spirit, and the universe for the most perfect resolution. Although they may look for clues and synchronicities from which to proceed, they have ultimately released the situation for the correct and proper outcome.

When we try to force our will to create a resolution that just isn't right, we run into trouble. It takes *so much more energy* to be distrusting, on your guard, and suspicious. It is draining. It is a lower expression of energy. It is counterproductive.

To be fully and completely trusting is a highly evolved state, knowing that the perfect outcome will present itself to you when you are ready. Strive to attain that level of trust and belief. It is a most worthy goal, and worth practicing every day.

> I NOW TRUST FULLY AND COMPLETELY IN SPIRIT TO BRING FORTH A DIVINE SOLUTION.

> I GIVE IT UP TO GOD.

MEDITATION AND GUIDANCE

Of all the things you can do to grow personally, meditation is probably the single most helpful thing you can do. The reason is that meditation allows you to get quiet, and to listen and communicate with your higher self. And remember, your higher self is smart! It is the sum of all your lifetimes: past, present, and future.

When you practice meditation, you increase your awareness and intuition. You are accessing parts of yourself that are peaceful and powerful, in the center of the storm. Don't be surprised if you develop some psychic abilities as a result of your meditation practice. It's fun!

> *"To learn to meditate is the biggest gift you can give to yourself in this life. Meditation will allow you to discover your true nature and find balance and roots to live well. Meditation leads towards awakening."*—Sogyal Rinpoche

Meditation allows you to come to quiet space, a space of oneness and knowing that contains all the knowledge that you could possibly ask for. Within that moment of time while meditating you are available and accessible to your unbounded potential, and you may ask to see what is before you.

You may sit in meditation and ask for guidance with your decisions. You can ask to be shown the potential for your reality if you choose the path to the right. You can also ask to be shown the various possibilities if you choose the path to the left. Ask to be shown, and then get quiet and see if you can ascertain or hear the answer. This is a great gift from Spirit.

Many people are not willing to look ahead, and ask for guidance. But it can be important when exercising your free will, and trying to make the best decisions you can. Guidance can come to you in many forms. Oftentimes answers will come to you during meditation. Sometimes answers come to you in gut feelings, intuition, urge or premonition. Be open to the possibilities. Listen to your impulses, inspiration, imagination and your desires. Allow for messages from your higher self.

GROWING BEYOND THE TRAPPINGS OF METAPHYSICS

In your own personal growth path, try not to get confused, stuck or detoured with the research and exploration of various subjects of metaphysics. These subjects include prophecies and predictions, earth changes, psychic phenomena, human origins, astrology, crop circles, tarot, sacred places, alien studies, lost civilizations, free energy, astral travel, and many more. Of course it can be great fun to explore and study some of these topics as part of your learning, growth, and awakening. And you should research what you like, and enjoy it fully. There are many great mysteries in the universe just waiting to be explored and understood.

But realize that these things are just pieces of the puzzle. They are not mandatory courses; they are elective courses. If they bring you closer to your truth, great. If not, try not to get stuck. *They are not "it."* It can be enjoyable to open up to various new realities. But realize that "the answer" is not inside a crop circle, tarot reading, alien artifact, or crystal skull. *The answer is inside you.*

THE ANSWER—WHAT "IT" IS

All of these metaphysical things and studies are just steps on the path. They are not the answer.

You are the answer! *Your divinity* is the answer. The answer is *you*, connecting to Spirit, and being one with All That Is. The answer is enlightenment, self-realization, God-realization, a permanent and effortless awareness of and union with the divine each moment. The answer is being here now, fully and in the moment. That's the goal. That's the answer. [2]

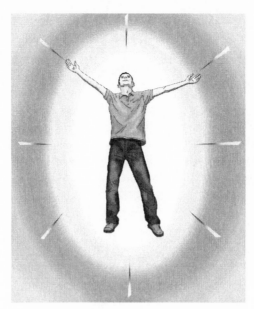

The Answer!

And probably the best way to get there, to get to that ultimate connection to Source and All That Is, is by expressing your most powerful emotion: *love*. Be love, and express love in all ways and all conditions. Love yourself, love others, and love Source. Express that love, unconditionally.

AFFIRMATIONS

I NOW ACCELERATE MY GROWTH PATH. I CHOOSE TO LEARN AND GROW QUICKLY NOW.

I NOW ASSUME MY ROLE AS CREATOR, AND FULLY EXPRESS THAT ASPECT OF MY BEING.

I NOW FULLY EMBRACE AND LIVE MY TRUE DIVINITY, CONNECTED TO SPIRIT, BEING ONE WITH ALL THAT IS.

QUESTIONS AND ANSWERS

Q. How do I know which lessons are most important to me as I go through my life?
A. Those things that come up in your own life that are giving you the most difficulty are the most important lessons for you. It can be compassion. It can be worthiness. It

can be love. It can be understanding. It can be judgment. It can be money. Often they are lessons of trust and belief. Challenges on the surface will give you clues to your deeper underlying life lessons.

Q. Do I have just one major life lesson, or a whole long list of them?

A. It depends on you. When you came here to incarnate as a soul, you chose to work on certain lessons. This is your life contract. One reason people incarnate on earth is that it is possible to learn multiple lessons in one lifetime. One reason for this is the physicality and free will concepts which together allow for quick results from choices made. Earth is a progressive school for the soul. Try to make the most of your time in this life.

CHAPTER SUMMARY

1) Human form is the "Crown of Creation," and fully capable of full God-self realization.

2) Personal growth is all about expanding your consciousness.

3) Earth is a fast track planet. This gives us multiple opportunities to learn and grow in an accelerated way.

4) Losing attachment to people and things helps us rise above issues which confront us, and raise our vibration.

5) When you are able to release a loved one back to the universe, you liberate yourself. Know that God is at work here, and that love is eternal.

6) Ego helps us filter divinity into a form we can integrate into the third dimension. Without the ego filtering divinity flowing through us we would be dysfunctional in the third dimension.

7) Truth for a person is the belief that a certain perception is accurate for their reality. Your truth is yours, and yours alone.

8) Discernment is the tool which helps you understand the truth of a given situation.

9) To be fully and completely trusting is a highly evolved state, knowing that the perfect outcome will present itself to you when you are ready.

10) Meditation is probably the single most helpful thing you can do to grow personally. This is because meditation helps you connect with your higher self. With this connection, divine guidance is available to you.

11) Try not to get seduced by various metaphysical studies. Although they can help lead you to the answer, they are not the answer.

12) The answer is you, connecting to Spirit, and being one with All That Is.

MANIFESTING WORKSHEET

Meditation is probably the single best way to grow personally, connect with your divinity, reconnect with Spirit, and stay wide awake. It is a wonderful thing to connect with and know your higher self, and realize that you are not alone in the world. In fact, you are far from being alone.

You have *so many* spirit guides, helpers, angels, and others who would assist you from the higher planes, that you would be shocked and amazed if you met them all! They are all there for you, with their specialties and strengths, to come into and go out of your life when needed, to help you, when called to do so. They sometimes try so hard to get through to you, when all it requires is for you to open the door just a crack.

By meditating, you open up your pathway of communications with your higher self and these guides, and are able to see more deeply and truthfully into your life. No longer will you need to make wrong turns, or travel down "dead end" streets. Your path will be much clearer, and your efforts will be more focused and enriched.

When you meditate, you align with and become your divine self. It connects you with who you really are, and the being that you will become. If you've never meditated before, start now. Get quiet, empty your mind, breathe deeply, and rekindle your relationship with your higher self. There is no perfect way to meditate. Just begin and allow yourself that quiet, peaceful fulfilling time.

REFERENCES

1. Ellen Mogensen, Heal Past Lives, (www.healpastlives.com)
2. Eric Klein, *Jewels on the Path*, (Medicine Bear Publishing, 1999) p. 70.

CHAPTER 21

Growing in Your Relationships

"Follow your bliss"—Joseph Campbell

RELATIONSHIPS AND PERSONAL GROWTH

Manifesting things for yourself is somewhat straightforward, since basically one person is involved, or affected. Manifesting relationships is completely different. Manifesting relationships involves at least two people, and sometimes three or more.

For example, suppose you intend to attract a new person into your life for a romantic relationship. However, one of the "ideal" people for you to have this relationship with is currently in another relationship. Perhaps that person has not yet completed their karma or learning lesson with this other person, and is not yet ready to move on (to you).

Some of the obvious possible outcomes to this scenario are that you wait for this person, or that someone else comes into your life instead at this time, or that this person comes into your life but as a friend, or that you never connect with this person in this lifetime. And there are many, many other possible outcomes too.

So, as you can see, it starts to get very complicated. No matter how much you may try to attract this person, if they are not "ready" the connection may not occur.

Relationships can sometimes be so complex, that it can sometimes be best to simply be clear with your intentions and affirmations, and let the universe sort it all out. The universe can see into *all the possibilities and potentialities,* and will do its best to make it the best for all concerned. Leave it up to the universe to handle the details. If you are "in the flow" and being open, you can let spirit "guide" you to the right place, at the right time, for the right reason, in order to perhaps meet the right person. And

198

that process of allowing the universe to sort it out is something you can sum up into one word: *trust.*

We often try to figure it all out, given our anxious, hard-working mental capacity. In romantic relationships, we think we can "make it happen" or "make that person want to be with me" or "find a way to get them to acknowledge me." Well, it doesn't always work that way. Obviously, you cannot make someone love you, or want to be with you. Sometimes the timing of it all just isn't right. Sometimes the universe may have other plans.

One thing you can do, however, is invoke the law of attraction, and just see what happens. One way to do this is to think of a romantic partner from the past that you loved deeply. Explore those feelings of love that you felt for that person. In doing so, you will project and vibrate out those strong energetic feelings, and possibly "pull" someone new toward you. Those powerful energetic feelings attract like a light bulb draws a moth in the darkest night. They are hard to ignore.

Alternatively, you can also create a vortex of attraction energy, with the hopes of attracting or pulling someone to you. This can also work well. Again, however, if the universe has alternative plans you must acknowledge that if you try too hard you will only "push" that person away from you.

LOSING "HOOKS"

Realize that as you grow and evolve personally, you will change. And as a result, the relationships you have with others will change too. As you evolve and attain higher levels of consciousness, you may even seem a bit cold or uncaring to people. Of course, nothing could be further from the truth. But what is happening is that your emotional "hooks" are no longer there. People can no longer manipulate you, "hook into" you, "guilt trip" you, or "push your buttons." You have graduated and risen above it.

This is a natural part of your personal evolutionary process, as you move from a karmic based way of relationship to a Spirit based way of relationship. [1] It can be a bit unsettling to those who love you to realize that you have changed, and that the "old ways" of relating to you, with all the karma, have somehow slipped away. However, realize that for the most part, these changes are all for the good.

LET YOUR LIGHT SHINE FORTH

"As we let our own light shine, we unconsciously give other people permission to do the same."—Marianne Williamson.

We are born naked, and as we grow, we are clothed. We put on shirts, pants, shoes and hats. And we also try on things like guilt, limiting beliefs, fears, and worries. Don't wait until the end of your life to shed these unwanted encumbrances.

You can shake off that heavy, rain-soaked dark cloak of limitation. Let your light inside shine forth brightly.

You can kick off those tight-fitting stylish shoes. Feel the ground again, beneath your feet. Feel what it's like to be *unbound*, again.

You can take off that hat. Let the light from above fill you up inside. It's okay. And just as the light fills you up, you can project up and out, in love.

Your skin, your bones, and your hair are all lovely and marvelous. But they are not you. You are not them. You are much, much more.

If you can allow yourself to stand "naked" before yourself and the world, you will be entirely liberated, within and without. You no longer need to wear your personal "shields," protecting your truth and love energy from others. You can stand tall, alive, and vibrant. Shed those layers of "clothing." Just step out of them. Shake them off. Let them go. Imagine your angels or guides helping you remove them, and all the limitations they represent. Step free. You will be lighter, freer, and happier.

LIBERATION

> I AM READY TO RECEIVE FULL LIGHT ACTIVATION. I AM FULLY OPEN.
> BRING ME FULL LIGHT ENERGY. GIVE ME THE MAXIMUM I CAN
> INTEGRATE AT THIS TIME.

All too often, we feel held back. We can feel held back by jobs, people, conditions, burdens, obligations, relationships, our physicality, our beliefs, our abilities.

It's time to liberate yourself. It's time to examine your world, piece by piece, to see what is or is not working for your highest good. Seek personal liberty. Become empowered. Be independent. Be strong. Bring healing light into your world. Be a guide for others. Lead the climb up the mountain. Hold the energy high for others.

Do you have *career* issues? Then manifest a change. It does not mean you have to quit your job. It could mean that your boss or coworker gets transferred to another office, or someone finally notices the great work you are doing.

Do you have *relationship* issues? Then manifest a solution. It could be something as simple as changing your perception of the situation. Or it could be as dramatic as making significant changes in your relationships. And that's okay too, if it's time for a change.

Do you have *abundance* issues? Then manifest some abundance in your life. Start the flow of energy moving again. Release feelings of worry and lack. Clear out the old, make room for the new. Affirm some new realities for yourself.

Do you have problems with *friendships?* Then manifest a change. What is it that your friends are mirroring back to you about yourself? Despair, worry, greed, selfishness? By changing yourself, you will automatically change your relationships with others. If you like, bring new friends into your life, friends with new ideas, fresh perspectives, and positive outlooks.

Do you have problems with *neighbors* or *roommates?* Manifest new opportunities, either for them, you, or both! For example, you can help plant a seed of new opportunities for them, so they relocate. You can manifest new opportunities for yourself that allow for changes in your situation. Affirm a change, then let the universe handle it. The universe has unlimited resources from which a solution can be found.

Do you have problems with *health?* Then shift it. Create a new and vibrant health consciousness for yourself, and see yourself changing and transforming into that new reality.

I AM WORTHY NOW, OF ALL THINGS, OPPORTUNITIES AND SITUATIONS.

When you liberate yourself from situations that are no longer supporting your highest growth, you are returning to your divine path, your right way, the perfect outpouring of your consciousness. If you feel uncomfortable in a current situation, listen to it! It is your body telling you that something is just not right. Don't ignore that message for too long. Make it right, and make it so.

SYNCHRONICITY

Wherever you go, if you look, you will see synchronicity. Synchronicity can be thought of as those chance encounters, chance events, and signs from Spirit that tell you that you are on the right path. Synchronicity is a gift to you. The problem is, it often remains unopened. In fact, you sometimes don't even realize that the gift has been handed to you.

Stay alert to those meaningful coincidences in life that cannot be easily explained. In doing so, you will become aware of divine interaction in your life. Stay receptive, and be ready to act when synchronicity becomes obvious to you. When you see it, have the courage to act on it. In the process of your increased awareness, you will find that you are connecting more with your higher self, and the messages it sends you.

> *"Laced throughout every day of your life, are hidden highways of opportunity, invisible crossroads of time, and avenues for great personal transformation that, if only traveled upon would reveal the extraordinary, the sublime, and the unexpected. Yet most slip by undetected, until there is first a childlike wonder at the ordinary, the routine, and the expected. Look for opportunities everywhere!"*
> —Mike Dooley, Totally Unique Thoughts [2]

Here's an example. Say you run into an old friend from high school that you haven't seen in several years. You say hello, speak briefly, and then go on your way. However, a week later, you run into that person *again*, by chance. This may be the universe telling you that you need to investigate this a bit further. Perhaps this person has a message for you, or you have a message for them. Perhaps there is someone they know who you need to meet. Perhaps you have some important information that they need to hear. Check it out, and see where it goes.

Another way synchronicity works is if a certain person, place or thing is mentioned to you in various ways by *two or more different people*. Alone, each message may be insignificant. However, if several people are telling you the same thing, it's time to listen! This is meaningful. Be aware.

Take notice of things occurring around you that are actually messages from the universe trying to gain your attention and awareness. If you want things in your life to occur with ease and grace, know that *if you notice and take action on the minor synchronicities first, you do not need to manifest big "wake up call" events later.*

- You don't have to manifest an auto accident before you get the message to slow down.
- You don't have to wait to get fired before you realize your job is not part of your joyful path.
- You don't have to wait to fail out of school before you realize that you are studying the wrong subject or field.
- You don't have to manifest a divorce before you realize your marriage needs work.
- You don't have to manifest a fire, hurricane, flood or tornado to fully appreciate your home, and the feeling of home and family.

- You don't have to manifest a heart attack before you realize that you are loved, and that you can love.
- You don't have to wait until your child runs away before you take a moment to tell them you love them.
- You don't have to wait until you are told you have a terminal illness to decide to live fully in each moment of every day.

In some cases, unfortunately, it is not until people "lose it all" before they receive and understand the message. It doesn't have to be that way. You do not have to manifest the lows in life to appreciate the highs. The choice of how to experience your learning is yours alone to make. You can grow just as easily through joy than through suffering.

CONSCIOUSLY CREATING YOUR DAYS

"Every day is a gift."

Using the knowledge that your consciousness and intention can be used to create and manifest your reality in the world, you can consciously create your day. You can focus on things you want to do, the way you want to be, and how things should go.

At the beginning of a day, consciously intend and affirm certain realities you wish to occur. Acknowledge various potentialities. Intend a particular outcome. Create your day.

As your day progresses, look for synchronicities. Look for the ways in which the universe works to bring you what you want. When you observe this happening, confirm it with yourself and express gratitude to the universe for providing it for you.

THE POWER OF WORDS

Words can be very powerful as you relate with others in your world. Be aware of how you interact with others. Do you speak words of inspiration and support of others, or do you criticize and condemn others?

When you come into situations and opportunities in other people's lives that may need help, know that sometimes just a kind word at the right time can make the difference. You have no idea that sometimes something said in passing can have far-reaching effects in a person's life, good or bad. Sometimes years later people will quote you on something you just said casually in passing, not hardly thinking about it!

Here's an example: I remember years ago when a new bookstore opened in my town. It proved to be a very popular store. I was thinking that it might be fun to get a part time job there, make a little money, and meet some fun people. When I mentioned my idea to a group of friends, my friend Rebecca, whose opinion I valued, casually dismissed the idea as being dumb. As a result of that one comment, my fun idea suddenly seemed stupid. I was crushed. I felt deflated. And I decided to pass on that opportunity. Has anything like that ever happened to you?

INSPIRING OTHERS

Here's a positive example which shows the power of a kind word expressed at the right time. A teenager named Jerry was afflicted with a birth defect; he had a bad leg and used a heavy awkward leg brace to help him walk. He always felt self-conscious and held back because of his obvious handicap.

A friend spoke encouraging words to Jerry at a critical time in his life. He told him that his bad leg should not hold him back. He told him that he should go to college and pursue a career. He gave him encouragement, when the outlook at the time perhaps looked a bit bleak. After a time, the friends drifted apart and they did not communicate regularly.

Well, fifty years later, unexpectedly, the friend received a letter from Jerry! Turns out Jerry attended college, studied engineering, married, had two children, had a fine career, and lived a full and satisfying life. In the letter he thanked his old friend, and expressed his appreciation for his support and inspiring words at a time in his life when it meant a great deal to him. And it meant so much to Jerry that he located his old friend fifty years later and sent him a warm-hearted letter of thanks.

What opportunities have passed you by, when you could have easily offered up an encouraging word to someone?

CALLING SOMEONE ON THEIR STUFF

As you become more aware of everything around you for what it truly is, you may need to "assist" others occasionally in other ways too. You may need to show compassion for another by being willing to do whatever is necessary to assist someone in taking their next higher step. That occasionally means kicking someone's feet out from under them; that occasionally means being a wake up-call; that occasionally means calling someone on their "stuff," and it often means loving them for their wholeness, their totality, the parts of them that are awake as well as the parts of them that are asleep. [3] Don't be afraid to call someone on their stuff. Sometimes that's what you've go to do.

As someone who is enlightened, you are responsible to tell it like it is, call it like you see it, and expose the truth of a certain situation. If it seems right to do so, speak up. Your gifts of awareness and enlightenment should be used to help your fellow man.

CONVERGING IN THE LIGHT

Your personal growth can be compared to climbing a mountain. At first it appears that there is only one path to the summit. But as you climb higher and rise above the tree line, you can see that there are many different paths (religions) that all lead to the summit. And really, no one path is better than any other, just different.

The truth is that all spiritual paths converge in the light, and all belief systems are left behind as you approach the summit. All limitations and thought forms break down as you get close to the summit. And that summit is the full universal life force realization, your direct experience of All That Is. [4]

AFFIRMATIONS

> I NOW SEE THE SYNCHRONICITIES IN LIFE THAT PRESENT THEMSELVES TO ME, AND ACT ON THESE MESSAGES FROM SPIRIT.

> I NOW ATTRACT TO ME PEOPLE WHO SUPPORT MY HIGHEST GOOD, PEOPLE WHO ARE KIND, FRIENDLY AND HELPFUL. I WORK WITH THEM IN CO-CREATIVE EFFORTS IN HARMONIOUS COCREATION.

> I AM A POWERFUL AND AWARE HUMAN BEING, ATTRACTING PEOPLE, SITUATIONS AND OPPORTUNITIES TO ME FOR MY HIGHEST GOOD.

QUESTIONS AND ANSWERS

Q. I am afraid that my relationships with friends and family will change if I grow and change too much. Should I be concerned?
A. Your relationships *will* change. Previous karmic challenges which "bound" you to others will slowly dissolve away. You will grow into a higher state of being. Overall, the changes in relationships that will occur are positive.

Q. My relatives think only lack and limitation. How do I get them to wake up?
A. You can make subtle suggestions and overtures of new ways to look at the world, and see if there is an interest. However, beyond that, it is up to them. This may or may not be your job to do.

Q. Aren't I overstepping my boundaries when I "call someone on their stuff?" Is it really my business?
A. Yes, it is your business. It up to you to bring the truth to light. After that, allow what may come of it.

CHAPTER SUMMARY

1) Personal relationships, when two or more are involved, get complicated quickly. Sometimes it is best to let the universe figure it out.

2) The universe can see into all the possibilities and potentialities in relationships, and will do it's best to work toward the ideal outcome for all concerned.

3) As you grow personally, the old ways of being will be no longer. People will no longer be able to "hook into" you, "guilt trip" you, or "push your buttons."

4) As you grow personally, you move from a karmic based way of relationship to a spirit based way of relationship.

5) Let your light shine forth, and stand "naked" before yourself and the world, unencumbered by limitation. You no longer need to hide your inner light.

6) Liberate yourself and break free of limiting patterns that no longer support your highest growth.

7) Stay alert to synchronicity, those meaningful coincidences in life that cannot be easily explained. In doing so, you become aware of divine intervention in your life.

8) You don't have to manifest traumatic events before you "get the message."

9) You can consciously create your day. Consciously intend and affirm certain realities you wish to occur, then look for ways in which the universe has brought you what you want.

10) Understand the power and responsibility of words. Sometimes something said in passing can have far-reaching effects in a person's life.

11) Make use of opportunities to encourage and inspire others. It is one of the best things you can do for your fellow man.

12) Being aware sometimes means calling people on their "stuff" and telling it like it is.

MANIFESTING WORKSHEET

Be a warrior of the light.
As you go through your day, do the following

- Find those situations where it would be wise to be honest and forthcoming, in which you say what needs to be said, and say it.
- Identify opportunities from which you can offer up an encouraging word to someone, and do it.
- Think about times in the past from which you wish you had intervened somehow. Make a vow to yourself that if a similar situation ever occurs in the future, you will act.

- Seek out people and circumstances from which your input and influence can have a positive effect, and act on it.
- Think about relationships you have with others that involve lots of "drama," misplaced energy, competition and strife. Transcend them into more spirit-based relationships where you can view things from a more detached, higher place.

At the end of today, write down three things you have done that helped you grow in your relationships and become a warrior of the light:

1) _____

2) _____

3) _____

REFERENCES

1. Tashira Tachi Ren, *What Is Lightbody*, (New Leaf Distributing Company, 1999), p. 51.
2. Mike Dooley, *Totally Unique Thoughts*, (www.tut.com)
3. Tashira Tachi Ren, *What Is Lightbody*, (New Leaf Distributing Company, 1999), p. 49.
4. Tashira Tachi Ren, *What Is Lightbody*, (New Leaf Distributing Company, 1999), p. 48.

CHAPTER 22

Raising Your Vibration, Sensitivity and Awareness

"Some things have to be believed to be seen."—Ralph Hodgson

THE IMPORTANCE OF RAISING YOUR VIBRATION

Your body is electrical in nature, and vibrates at a certain frequency. Not only that, but as we discussed earlier, your thoughts have certain vibrations too.

Examples of lower vibrations are when people are fearful, sad, despondent, angry, or lonely. When people vibrate at a higher level, they express things like joy, gratitude, forgiveness and love.

The higher the level to which you can raise your vibration, the more successful you will be in all your efforts, and especially efforts of creation and manifestation. To raise your vibration, do things that are creative, light-hearted, uplifting, helpful, calming, reflective, and positive.

As you grow and evolve into the higher vibrations, things will come much easier to you. Life will go more smoothly. You will be able to better see things for what they truly are. You will be able to make far better choices and decisions as you go through life.

The list below gives you some ideas on how to raise your vibration. Some of the common themes these things have are: they are fun, they help you focus, they involve love, they make you happy, and most importantly they help you live *in the moment*.

WAYS TO RAISE YOUR VIBRATION

1) meditate
2) write and send a thank-you note to someone

3) think about things and people in your life that you are thankful for
4) call or visit a good friend
5) take a walk
6) read the comics
7) do something nice for someone without telling them
8) read a book to a child
9) play with a dog or cat
10) stop and smell the flowers
11) read an uplifting book
12) listen to your favorite music
13) do a hobby
14) have tea or coffee with someone you haven't seen lately
15) do some gardening or landscaping
16) go to the park to play or fly a kite
17) count clouds in the sky, or stars in the heavens
18) read some old thank-you cards, birthday cards, or love letters
19) look at an old picture album that makes you happy
20) think about awards you have received, and other recognition for your efforts
21) go for a swim in a pool, lake or the ocean
22) walk barefoot along the beach, or through some soft green grass
23) bring something into the office for everyone (flowers, cookies, coffee)
24) collect some sea shells, pine cones, leaves, flowers
25) give a pat on the back to someone deserving
26) hug your spouse, partner, kids, parents, friends
27) spend an extra minute saying hello to a bank teller, coffee server, toll taker, fast food worker

THINGS THAT LOWER YOUR VIBRATION

The following are things that will usually lower your vibration. Try to *avoid* these if they are uncomfortable for you:

1) do not watch the nightly news with stories of murder, fire, war, and tragedy
2) do not hang out with negative, petty, depressing people
3) do not read sensational, trashy newspapers
4) do not argue with people, especially about trivial matters
5) do not watch television shows which highlight the despair of humanity
6) do not join a group discussion where only complaining takes place
7) do not focus on the follies or failures of others
8) do not gossip about others
9) do not read articles or watch shows that make you fearful or angry

GUARDING YOUR CONSCIOUSNESS

Raising your vibration means being aware of what you allow into your consciousness. Know that if you choose to watch a violent television show, or play a violent video game, you are allowing that experience into your consciousness. Is that what you really want?

Shows, games and competitions on television can be exciting and alluring, with sensational action, glamorous people, and enticing scenes. It all seems very lifelike. But by allowing these types of things into your life, you are allowing them into your consciousness. And you are shaped by what you see, know and feel, and choose to experience. So if you want a life filled with anger, violence, noise and action, this is fine. But if you want a peaceful harmonious life, it makes sense to guard your consciousness.

Examples of movies that have profoundly influenced many people who have seen them include the popular movies "Psycho" (1960) "Jaws" (1975) and the Blair Witch Project (1999). In "Psycho" (directed by Alfred Hitchcock) a famous scene in the movie depicts a woman being stabbed to death in the shower. In "Jaws" (directed by Steven Spielberg), we see people getting gobbled up by a huge man-eating shark, in a very realistic looking way. In the Blair Witch Project, three students are lost and terrorized in the woods.

If you have seen these movies, or others like them, you know that this visual imagery is so powerful that it can leave a lasting impression on your consciousness. Is that what you want? Is that really the way you want to be? Do you want to go through life afraid to take a shower, swim in the ocean, or walk through the woods?

Now think about movies that have lasting powerful *positive* impressions on you. Have you seen It's a Wonderful Life, Field of Dreams, Rocky, Rudy, E.T., Mr. Holland's Opus, Love Actually, or Heart and Souls? These kinds of movies uplift and inspire.

Because our news media and communications are seemingly everywhere, the world is a very small place. Realize that you do not need to know about every tragedy and every violent act in the world. It's okay to tune out to news. Why would you want to let someone "dictate" to you what is important to you? Why would you want to let someone tell you what they think is important for you to know? How do they know?

There are billions of people in the world. Things happen. Some of those billions of people are choosing singular and group manifestations that may seem tragic, but are being chosen by those involved for the greater good, or other reasons unknown to us. In many cases we have no idea why things happen in the world, and that's okay. God is working through all of our lives and situations. It's not that we don't care, because we do. It's about choosing what we want to focus our lives on, and being acutely aware of our consciousness.

HEALING ACROSS ALL TIME AND DIMENSIONS

Another way to raise your vibration is to consciously heal yourself in this lifetime. By healing yourself in this lifetime, you are actually also simultaneously healing yourself *across all time and dimensions.* Think of time as a circle, not a line. Things are not actually occurring in a sequential linear fashion as they appear to be, but all at the same time. So, by working through an issue you may have now, you also help heal it in your other lifetimes: past, present, and future.

For example, perhaps in this lifetime you are having problems with your throat. It has always been a source of difficulty for you. This may be because in a prior lifetime you were hanged, or drowned, or somehow silenced for speaking out.

Or perhaps in this lifetime you are experiencing a long-standing feud or conflict with a neighbor or co-worker. This may because in the past you had similar skirmishes with this person which were never resolved, so they carry over into this lifetime to be addressed.

Try to work through the issues in this lifetime which are giving you challenges. In doing so, you are in effect healing yourself in all times and dimensions. [1]

RECONNECTING WITH THE WORLD AROUND YOU

You can easily raise your vibration by reconnecting with nature, the sun, the moon, the trees, and flowers. As you reconnect you will remember this one simple truth: we are all connected, we are One. Not just with nature, but *everything* and *everyone*! And in knowing that, and by reconnecting at first with nature, you can then reconnect with one another.

And in doing so, realize that the connection is a universal one. The connection is very real, very strong, very powerful. By connecting to nature and to the universe you will see, know and feel that it is entirely unlimited in every way, and that it will gladly provide you with all that you want and desire many times over. It is simply a matter of aligning with it, and tapping into the source of All That Is, and making it yours, and you it.

JUDGMENT

Judgment can be defined as the *difference in the perception of the reality* of a situation. Thus, it is only the perception that can be problematic. The actual situation is unchanged, perhaps even static.

Coming to this understanding puts you at a much higher level of spiritual awareness and raises your vibration. If there is no right or wrong (just experience), there should be no judgment of it. If you come to your realization from a higher consciousness, you become much more tolerant and understanding of who another person is and why they are choosing to make the decisions they are making. Coming from a place of understanding also means that you may be able to see into the real truth of a situation, and what it is really about.

In fact, the judgment of others is actually really judgment of the self. When there is something that is distressing you, it is not because someone else did something to you, but because you are seeing something in yourself mirrored in the other person. Therefore what you are seeing is the imbalance within yourself.

When you understand that you cannot create someone else's reality and that you are not responsible for someone else's reality, the judgment, guilt, and blame begin to melt away. Coming from this heart center, rather than analysis and judgment, you realize that you have all the powers of the universe at your disposal. Because then everything is a gift, and a gift of love.

AFFIRMATIONS

> I NOW CHOOSE THOSE THINGS IN MY LIFE WHICH RAISE MY VIBRATION AND SUPPORT MY HIGHEST GROWTH.

> I NOW EVOLVE INTO A HIGHER PLACE OF BEING.

> I NOW BLESS THE DIFFICULT PARTS OF LIFE AND DIFFICULT EVENTS OF THE WORLD, AND RELEASE THEM TO THE UNIVERSE. I LEARN AND GROW.

> I NOW EMBRACE AND LIVE FULLY IN NATURE, MY ENVIRONMENT, AND MYSELF. I CHOOSE WHAT I WANT IN MY LIFE, AND I AM GRATEFUL FOR IT.

QUESTIONS AND ANSWERS

Q. Everyone around me has a low vibration. They watch violent TV shows, play video games, argue, yell, fight, etc. It drives me crazy, I can't stand it. Help!
A. This can be difficult. Try some affirmations and visioning to improve things. Ask for divine blessings for the situation. Visualize them developing other more peaceful interests. Try to help show them the reality of their choices. Best of all, keep your own personal vibration high, and it will help.

Q. I am interested in healing my past lives, and working through some issues that have carried into this lifetime which I need to get behind me and thus raise my vibration. How can I start doing it?

A. In times of meditation, ask to be shown and to understand your own personal past life information which may be negatively impacting your life today. Your higher self will help guide you with information that is most helpful to you at this time in your life. [2]

CHAPTER SUMMARY

1) If you can raise your vibration to a higher level, generally speaking things will come easier to you as you go through life.

2) You can consciously raise your vibration whenever you like by thinking positive things. Do things that are fun, make you happy, help you focus, express love, and help you live in the moment.

3) Guard your consciousness by not allowing violent, negative and depressing things into your life. You have a choice!

4) Our planet has billions of people on it; you do not need to know about every tragedy in the world.

5) The best way to assist your own growth and also help raise the vibration of the planet is by raising your vibration.

6) Raise your vibration by healing yourself in this lifetime. By doing so, you simultaneously heal yourself across all time, lifetimes, and dimensions.

7) Get out into nature to find peaceful solitude, raise your vibration and reconnect with Source.

8) Judgment is the difference in the perception of the reality of a situation. Since there is no right or wrong (just experience), there should be no judgment of it.

MANIFESTING WORKSHEET

To raise your vibration and be fully and completely at peace with yourself, work through some of these exercises:

1) Slow down from your active day. Take time out for yourself.

2) Build a personal altar in your home, and use it. It can be non-denominational. It simply needs only to be inspiring to you personally.

3) Breathe deeply and calm yourself from the chatter and "monkey mind" and anxious overactive mental state. Slow down, and live in the present moment.

4) Go out into nature, and commune with nature. See Spirit in nature.

5) Think about times when you did something nice for someone, then love yourself for doing it.

6) Release yourself from being overly concerned with tragic events in the world. Send healing love to these situations, and then release them.

Write five things below that you will do for yourself to raise your vibration:

1) _____
2) _____
3) _____
4) _____
5) _____

REFERENCES

1. Ellen Mogensen, Heal Past Lives, (www.healpastlives.com)
2. Ellen Mogensen, Heal Past Lives, (www.healpastlives.com)

CHAPTER 23

The New Age

"All the forces in the world are not so powerful
as an idea whose time has come"—Victor Hugo

THE GREAT SHIFT IN CONSCIOUSNESS

As we explore new powers of manifestation and creation, we begin to realize that it is not just us that is changing, our world is changing too. Science is continuing to make remarkable advances, communication methods are rapidly advancing, the world is becoming smaller, and many of the world's nations are seemingly becoming more compassionate to one another.

In fact, we are all experiencing the beginning of a great shift in consciousness. We are collectively raising our global consciousness, whereby the entire earth plane and its inhabitants are undergoing a fundamental shift in dimensional awareness. The entire planet, and every living person and thing on it is moving into a *new age*.

The new higher dimensional phases of human evolution will be based on sharing, goodwill, trust, cooperation, community and love. This new era of civilization will be achieved by a widespread awareness of the underlying unity of all people. It will be glorious, and far superior to our current third dimensional world of competition, aggressiveness, mistrust, greed and fear.

Once critical mass is reached, and enough people have discovered their divinity, the human race will experience a period of intense introspection. The planetary transformation will result in a totally spiritual culture that will raise human beings to higher and higher vibrations and dimensions. Some people call the new age the Christ Consciousness, Buddha Consciousness, God Consciousness, or the Divine. It can also be called the Love vibration. It is being in a state of knowingness. It is being fully at peace with oneself. In a physical sense, the planet will rise from the third dimension to the fifth dimension.

There will be a new age, but there will be no new age religion. It is not needed. Things like sin and salvation and other polarized limiting third dimensional constructs will slowly melt away from our world. People will come to realize that spiritual growth is the real goal. There will be no judgment of others. Many great and wise entities from all over the universe have incarnated into humanity at this time in our evolution in order to help mankind with this transformation. Do not fear!

On a personal level, you change the world when you bring spiritual change to yourself. This occurs automatically as you constantly share who you are and all that you have become with those around you. You don't even have to utter a single word. Just by being who you are, you change your environment and the world around you.

> I NOW BEGIN A WHOLE NEW PART OF MY LIFE FILLED WITH MAGICAL MANIFESTATIONS, ASTOUNDING MIRACLES, AMAZING SYNCHRONICITIES, AND WONDROUS EASE AND GRACE. I AM A SHINING EXAMPLE OF CO-CREATION AND MAGNIFICENCE IN ACTION AND BEING.

A NEW WAY OF BEING

We are changing, adapting, and evolving into a new paradigm of being. Our bodies are actually being physically "rewired" in a way. And although this change is evolutionary rather than revolutionary, it is happening quickly.

In our new paradigm, those who remain afraid to sail to the "edge of the world" and explore new ways of being will find it increasingly difficult to function in the world. Those who continue to pursue the "old ways" will find that with each passing week, month, and year, these methods are less and less effective.

In this new paradigm, your purpose is to develop and use your gifts of intentionality, to be a creator. Realize that this skill, when mastered, will open many doorways to you, and contribute a great deal to your personal growth.

In the fifth dimension, our bodies become more etheric (lighter, more spirit-like), time slips away, and the veil of illusion is lifted. We will see things not as they appear to be, but the way they truly are.

EARTH CHANGES AND END TIMES

Naturally, there is a little bit of fear of the unknown that comes with a change such as this. We may first pass through some various physical or dimensional shifts (sometimes called the "End Times") as we approach and arrive at the new age. Realize however that the End Times need not be catastrophic as described in the book of the Bible called Revelations.

The term End Times simply means that it will be the end of the world *as we know it.* And the way we know it includes time, space, density, competition, limitation, struggle, strife, greed and fear. Life as we know it will change, because we are moving from the third dimension into the fifth dimension. We will embark on a new part of our human evolution which will include much higher levels of understanding and compassion.

Humanity as a species will collectively decide if the transition from our current third dimensional reality into a fifth dimensional new age is a relatively smooth transition, or a more challenging one. Predictions have been made for both kinds of outcomes. Collectively, we will all ultimately determine the manner of the global transformation.

FOLLOW YOUR JOY

We came into this life with a special plan or purpose, and that plan is to help elevate humanity and life on earth through our own unique service. It is our responsibility to be successful in carrying out our plan and to infuse our service with our own special God-given talent. Find out what that talent is, and start expressing it. It will likely give you much joy as you express your divine nature.

In the third dimension, the beliefs that have been common include that one must "work hard to succeed." As the new age approaches, our beliefs will change. We will move into a place in which it will be important to "find your passion" and explore it. You have free will, and you are free to express your divinity in any way you choose. And the best path to take is one that takes you on your true path.

> I NOW CHOOSE AN ACCELERATED GROWTH PATH. I NOW LEARN AND
> EVOLVE QUICKLY. I NOW EXPERIENCE PEOPLE, SITUATIONS AND
> OPPORTUNITIES TO GROW AMAZINGLY QUICKLY, WITH EASE AND GRACE.
> I NOW FOLLOW MY JOY, AND FOLLOW MY BLISS.

The "old ways" of being spiritual included being selfless, sacrificing, saintly, obedient, unquestioning, and modest. But that's the way it was, *hundreds* of years ago. Our new reality involves following your passion, manifesting magic, seeing synchronicities, dreaming big, doing what feels right, and making it all a fun, joyous expression of your true nature and divinity. There's no reason not to.

A TIME FOR COMPASSION

This is also a time to be kind and show compassion for your fellow human beings. With things changing so much in us and around us, it is only natural that some people manage the changes better than others.

When you run into people on the street that you know, you may be asked, "What are you doing? You look so wonderful." Let them know that you are looking at life in a whole new way, and that you are consciously creating your life around you. Tell them how you are accessing new energies available on the planet. Offer support, compassion, and more information if asked for it. [1]

> I NOW MANIFEST MIRACLES AND SYNCHRONICITIES WITH EASE. I MANIFEST MULTIDIMENSIONALLY, ON ALL LEVELS, IN ALL WAYS, FOR THE GOOD OF ALL.

AN IDENTIFICATION WITH ALL BEINGS

As you grow personally and develop your capacity for intuition, you come to feel and know the absolute universality of life. There is no sense of separateness from what is seen. There is no difficulty or delay in conscious understanding of the world around you.

At its highest point intuition becomes universal love. It is essentially *an identification with all beings.* Unconditional love makes it impossible to regard another with criticism. Instead, true compassion is the most common feeling. That divine seed of light is expressed from within.

When we stop thinking of ourselves as separate from one another, and when we move our ego out of the way, we can then recognize the dreams and hopes of others as being not greatly different from our own. Thus, we shift our energetic focus from the overactive solar plexus center of personal desire to the heart center of inclusive awareness and love. This reinforces the group consciousness and universal love energy.

THE NEXT STEP IN HUMAN EVOLUTION

In our lifetimes, we have experienced the maximum separation from Source. Like a big rubber band, we have stretched as far from Source energy as possible. Because of this, our consciousness sees itself as a being completely separate from Source, and we get separated from our true abilities as a divine being. It is part of this process from which we express our individuality.

We have witnessed first-hand the issues (conflict, greed, limitation, etc.) that arise when we are separated from Source. In addition to these limitations of being separate, it takes a huge amount of energy to hold that rubber band so stretched out, so distant, so separate, with so much illusion.

We have now reached and passed the maximum point, and are returning to Source. And just like the rubber band that snaps back fast, our return to Source is occurring *quickly*.

As we return to Source, we are now experiencing new discoveries, theories, realities and possibilities concerning chakras, DNA, and quantum physics. We continue to learn more about things like sacred geometry, the merkabah, other dimensions, and more as these too are beginning to come into our awareness. We are now entering the next big step in human evolution. We live in exciting times.

THE ADAM KADMON MAN

Know that we are quickly evolving into not only a new state of consciousness, but also a new kind of being, the Adam Kadmon man. The name Adam Kadmon literally means "man of all knowledge." The Adam Kadmon is a hu-man who has integrated their light body into their physical form.

The Adamic seed and DNA components which are part of our humanity will activate and, as part of our evolutionary development, make the Adam Kadmon man our new reality. (source: *The Keys of Enoch*) As this occurs, humanity will become fully-functioning, fully-conscious, and will operate at very high levels.

The Adam Kadmon Man is the result of integrating
the etheric light body into the physical human form.

The human qualities of free will and emotions may present a challenge for humans during this evolutionary process. Nonetheless, as an Adam Kadmon man, you will be able to assimilate your entire physical form into a multidimensional interdimensional status. You will be in the now. Linear time will cease to exist. You will become a highly evolved human, fully connected to Source, in a highly enlightened state of being.

KEEP THE FLAME BURNING BRIGHTLY

For those who have achieved a level of mastery of themselves, there comes a special responsibility. And that responsibility is to *keep the flame of truth burning brightly.* What exactly does that mean?

It means blazing the trail if none have gone before. It means offering a kind word of assurance when someone is struggling. It means being honest and true to yourself and others when things may be unclear. It means calling someone on their "stuff." It means pursuing the truth. It means keeping your heart open wide.

You have *no idea* how many people you affect every day as you go through life. You have *no idea* the waves you set in motion with your actions. Make every moment count. Make every personal interchange precious. Be a warrior of the light, use your sword of truth, and *keep the flame of truth burning brightly.*

Keep the Flame of Truth Burning Brightly.

A Lightworker's Poem

Keep the flame burning brightly, for all to see
Let it shine always, for you and me
Keep the flame burning brightly, and show what can be
Past, present and future, through eternity

MANIFESTING MAGNIFICENCE

MY HEART SINGS WITH JOY, AS I HAVE PUT SPIRIT IN THE DRIVER'S SEAT.

Using the tools and methods discussed in this book, you can create and live your life the way you choose to. You can accomplish and be anything you want.

You will know when you are on the right path, and doing your life's work, because it will feel great. You will feel alive, vibrant, and you will eagerly start your day.

And in doing what you love to do, whatever it may be, you will be helping others. You will be connecting to Spirit, and you will be expressing your divinity. And although it may not seem like you are serving mankind in your daily work, you are.

Ask yourself, if you could do anything, be anybody, travel anywhere, have any career, what would it be? If money didn't really matter anymore, what would you spend your time doing?

Think hard about this concept. Now that you know you *can* create the perfect life you choose to live, there is absolutely *nothing* holding you back, unless you put it there. And now you know how to change it.

Ask yourself, "What is the most important thing I could accomplish in my life?" Ask yourself, "What is the most valuable thing I could possibly do for myself, for my family, for my community, for humanity?" Ask yourself, "What would be my most joyful expression of my life?"

As you answer these questions, realize that these answers are very likely your journey, your path, your unique expression of soul, your life plan, your contract with yourself. It is what you are meant to do. It is why you incarnated in human form at this time. It is why you are here.

And if you are not doing it now, that's okay. But realize that you may want to work in that direction, to start moving toward that path, to start evolving into that reality, to start taking steps, large or small, in that divine direction. And in doing so, your connection to Source will be strong, you will be divinely inspired, you will be consciously creating, you will be living the life you choose to live, you will be positively affecting those around you, and you will be *Manifesting Magnificence*.

AFFIRMATIONS

I NOW MOVE TO MY DIVINE SPIRIT WORK.

I NOW EVOLVE INTO A HIGHER STATE OF BEING.

I AM A HUMAN FULL OF LOVE, LIVING, BEING, AND LOVING.

I AM A DIVINE SPARK IN THE EYE OF GOD.

I AM DIVINE LOVE.

CHAPTER SUMMARY

1) Mankind continues to evolve, and we are all moving into a new age of expanded consciousness. The entire planet, and every living person and thing on it, is moving into a new age.

2) Like a rubber band that has stretched to the maximum point, we are now returning to Source quickly.

3) The new age will be achieved by a widespread awareness of the underlying unity of all people.

4) The new age allows for increased levels of understanding, communication, manifestation, group consciousness, and love.

5) The new age will usher in a totally spiritual culture and will raise humanity to higher dimensions.

6) The new age is a change or graduation from the third dimension to the fifth dimension.

7) You change the world when you bring spiritual change to yourself.

8) We are now opening up to completely new possibilities of existence. As a result, we are all evolving mentally, physically, consciously, and spiritually.

9) The "end times" describes the point at which we transition into the new age.

10) It will become increasingly important to find your passion and explore it.

11) Make an effort to show compassion to your fellow humans during the shift into the new age. Some will find the shift more challenging than others, and they may need help from you.

12) As the new age approaches, the universal community of all life becomes clear. You will feel a strong identification with all beings.

13) We are evolving into a new kind of human being, the Adam Kadmon man.

14) Keep the flame of truth burning brightly.

REFERENCES

1. Eric Klein, *Jewels On The Path*, (Medicine Bear Publishing, 1999), p. 105.

List of All Affirmations

Chapter 1—Understanding Manifestation

I now open my heart and mind to all the possibilities in the universe. I am now open to seeing the universe in a whole new way.

I now release all fears, doubts and limitations. I now remain open to all possibilities. I trust in the divine to help me see all the opportunities available to me.

I now open to a whole new way to view the world. I now bring in new information and awareness to my being, and I now relate to the world in an exciting new way.

Higher levels of wisdom, knowledge and understanding now come to me. I now integrate this new information into my being for my highest good.

I now look to the unlimited sources of the universe to provide for me in great supply. I do not depend on persons or conditions for my abundance. The universe is unlimited, and is my source of abundance and creation.

I am now committed to my highest purpose. It is my first priority. I make a pledge to honor myself and my work, now and always.

I now grow in body, mind and spirit. I now open up to an expanded way of knowing, loving and being.

My teachers, guides, and spiritual masters are now with me. With their guidance, I now proceed with my next level of learning.

Chapter 2—Developing Your Personal Power

I NOW CHOOSE AN ACCELERATED GROWTH PATH, AND GROW QUICKLY AND CORRECTLY IN ACCORDANCE WITH MY LIFE PLAN. I AM NOW READY FOR MY NEXT LEVEL OF AWAKENING, LEARNING AND GROWTH.

I NOW LOOK TO THE UNLIMITED SOURCES OF THE UNIVERSE TO PROVIDE FOR ME IN GREAT SUPPLY. I DO NOT DEPEND ON PERSONS OR CONDITIONS FOR MY ABUNDANCE. THE UNIVERSE IS UNLIMITED, AND IS MY SOURCE OF ABUNDANCE AND CREATION.

I AM NOW COMMITTED TO MY HIGHEST PURPOSE. IT IS MY FIRST PRIORITY. I MAKE A PLEDGE TO HONOR MYSELF AND MY WORK, NOW AND ALWAYS.

I NOW GROW IN BODY, MIND AND SPIRIT. I NOW OPEN UP TO AN EXPANDED WAY OF KNOWING, LOVING AND BEING.

MY TEACHERS, GUIDES, AND SPIRITUAL MASTERS ARE NOW WITH ME. WITH THEIR GUIDANCE, I NOW PROCEED WITH MY NEXT LEVEL OF LEARNING.

I NOW CHOOSE AN ACCELERATED GROWTH PATH, AND GROW QUICKLY AND CORRECTLY IN ACCORDANCE WITH MY LIFE PLAN. I AM NOW READY FOR MY NEXT LEVEL OF AWAKENING, LEARNING AND GROWTH.

Chapter 3—Personal Responsibility

I NOW RECLAIM MY LIFE, MY DIRECTION, MY PATH, AND MY GOALS. SPIRIT NOW GUIDES ME AS I LEARN AND GROW.

I NOW STEP FORWARD BOLDLY. I NOW REASSUME MY ROLE AS CREATOR.

I NOW RISE ABOVE LOWER CHALLENGES. I NOW FORGIVE THAT WHICH NEEDS FORGIVENESS. I NOW ALLOW WHAT MAY TRANSPIRE TO OCCUR FOR THE HIGHEST GOOD OF ALL. I NOW RELEASE THIS SITUATION TO THE DIVINE WILL OF THE UNIVERSAL SPIRIT.

I NOW RELEASE AND AM RELEASED FROM EVERYTHING AND EVERYBODY THAT ARE NO LONGER PART OF THE DIVINE PLAN FOR MY LIFE. EVERYTHING AND EVERYBODY THAT ARE NO LONGER PART OF THE DIVINE PLAN FOR MY LIFE NOW RELEASE ME. 1

I NOW TAKE FULL RESPONSIBILITY FOR MY CURRENT POSITION IN LIFE AND WHERE I AM IN THE WORLD TODAY.

THE FORGIVING LOVE OF SPIRIT NOW SETS ME FREE FROM MY PAST, AND MISTAKES I HAVE MADE IN THE PAST. I FACE THE FUTURE WISE, FREE, UNBOUND AND UNAFRAID.

I NOW TAKE FULL RESPONSIBILITY FOR WHO I AM AND MY RELATIONSHIPS WITH OTHERS IN MY LIFE. I NOW UNDERSTAND AND ACKNOWLEDGE THE DIVINE WORKING WITHIN ME AND THROUGH ME.

I NOW FULLY ACKNOWLEDGE THE DIVINITY IN ME, AS I AM GUIDED IN THE CORRECT WAY.

Chapter 4—Making Way For the New

I NOW RELEASE BACK TO THE UNIVERSE ALL THINGS, OBJECTS, AND CONDITIONS THAT ARE NO LONGER PART OF THE DIVINE PLAN FOR MY LIFE. I NOW RELEASE FULLY AND COMPLETELY, AND EXPRESS GRATITUDE FOR THE SERVICE THESE THINGS HAVE RENDERED ME UP TO NOW.

I NOW FULLY RELEASE ALL THAT IS NO LONGER PART OF MY DIVINE PLAN BACK TO THE PERFECT OUTPOURING OF THE UNIVERSE.

I NOW LET GO OF THOSE THINGS, CONDITIONS AND RELATIONSHIPS WHICH NO LONGER SUPPORT MY HIGHEST GROWTH. YOU ARE NOW RELEASED. I NOW ESTABLISH DIVINE ORDER IN MY LIFE AND IN MY WORLD.

I LET GO AND TRUST.

Chapter 5—Forgiveness

MAY THE DIVINE LOVE IN ME MEET THE DIVINE LOVE IN YOU FOR A BETTER UNDERSTANDING.

ALL THAT HAS OFFENDED ME, I FORGIVE. WITHIN AND WITHOUT, I FORGIVE. THINGS PAST, THINGS PRESENT, THINGS FUTURE, I FORGIVE. I FORGIVE EVERYTHING AND EVERYBODY WHO CAN POSSIBLY NEED FORGIVENESS IN MY PAST AND PRESENT. I POSITIVELY FORGIVE EVERYONE. I AM FREE, AND ALL OTHERS ARE FREE, TOO. ALL THINGS ARE CLEARED UP BETWEEN US, NOW AND FOREVER. 2

THE DIVINE LOVE OF SPIRIT NOW FREES ME FROM ATTACHMENT, RESENTMENT, AND CONDITIONS WHICH HOLD ME BACK AND ARE NO LONGER PART OF THE DIVINE PLAN FOR MY LIFE.

I NOW FORGIVE AND RELEASE EVERYTHING AND EVERYBODY OF THE PAST AND PRESENT THAT IS NO LONGER PART OF THE DIVINE PLAN FOR MY LIFE. I LOVE YOU, AND RELEASE YOU.

DIVINE LOVE AND FORGIVENESS NOW RADIATE OUT FROM MY BEING TO THOSE I RESOLVE WITH NOW. I LOVE YOU AND I FORGIVE YOU.

I FORGIVE EVERYONE AND EVERYTHING THAT CAN POSSIBLY NEED FORGIVENESS IN MY LIFE NOW.

I FORGIVE MYSELF FOR NOT BEING EVERYTHING I THINK I SHOULD BE.

_____(NAME OF PERSON TO FORGIVE), I NOW FORGIVE YOU. I NOW RELEASE YOU FROM THIS DIFFICULT SITUATION BACK TO THE UNIVERSE. I NOW LET GO AND RELEASE THIS SITUATION TO A HIGHER POWER. THINGS ARE FREED UP BETWEEN US, NOW AND FOREVER.

Chapter 6—Universal Laws and Truths

THE INFINITE INTELLIGENCE NOW WORKS THROUGH ME TO IMPROVE ALL ASPECTS OF MY LIFE.

SPIRIT NOW GUIDES ME AS I OPERATE IN MY WORLD.

I NOW APPLY THE WISDOM OF THE AGES INTO MY LIFE FOR MY BENEFIT AND GREATER UNDERSTANDING.

I AM NOW GUIDED TO THE ESSENTIAL TRUTH OF SITUATIONS, AND UNDERSTAND HOW THEY WORK IN MY WORLD. I SEE EVERYTHING CLEARLY NOW, FOR WHAT IT TRULY IS.

Chapter 7—Science and Quantum Physics

I NOW AWAKEN TO AN ENTIRELY NEW DIMENSIONAL AWARENESS, FILLED WITH ASTOUNDING NEW REALITIES AND OPPORTUNITIES.

I NOW GROW INTO A WHOLE NEW STATE OF BEING, ACCESSING DIMENSIONS MULTIDIMENSIONALLY, AND RELATING TO MY WORLD IN A WHOLE NEW SUPERIOR WAY.

I NOW GROW AND CHANGE IN ALL WAYS ON ALL LEVELS FOR MY GREATER GOOD. I NOW DEVELOP AND EMBRACE THESE NEW CAPABILITIES AND GROW IN MY ABILITITIES OF WHAT IT MEANS TO BE HUMAN.

I NOW CALL UPON THE WISDOM OF THE AGES AND DIVINE GUIDANCE TO ASSIST ME AS I CREATE MY WORLD AROUND ME.

Chapter 8—Intention

I NOW MANIFEST MAGNIFICENTLY. I DISSOLVE ALL LIMITING CONDITIONS AND BELIEFS, AND CREATE WITH EASE.

IF I AM NOT CURRENTLY ON MY DIVINE SPIRIT PATH, PLEASE SHOW ME WHAT IT IS. HELP ME TO KNOW IT, TO RECOGNIZE IT, AND TO DO IT.

I NOW CLEARLY INTEND THE BEST FOR MYSELF AND OTHERS, AND MY LIFE IMPROVES DRAMATICALLY AS A RESULT.

THE DIVINE LOVE OF SPIRIT NOW ILLUMINATES MY PATH, AND MY INTENTION IS DIVINELY GUIDED.

I NOW INTEND THE HIGHEST EXPRESSION OF MY BEING, THE MOST MAGNIFICENT EXPRESSION OF MY SOUL FORCE, AND THE CLEAREST MOST DIVINE MANIFESTATION OF MY LIFE PATH.

I NOW CO-CREATE WITH SPIRIT.

Chapter 9—Affirmations

MY HEART SINGS WITH JOY, AS I NOW MOVE INTO A WHOLE NEW WAY OF BEING. I NOW CONSCIOUSLY CREATE MY LIFE MOMENT BY MOMENT, AND I AM GRATEFUL FOR THE DIVINE RESTORATION OF MY AFFAIRS. I NOW CONSCIOUSLY MANIFEST IN MY LIFE.

I NOW MANIFEST A WONDERFUL NEW PERSONALLY FULFILLING CAREER OPPORTUNITY WHICH BRINGS ME MUCH JOY AND ABUNDANCE. I MANIFEST THIS IN HARMONIOUS RELATIONSHIP WITH MY FAMILY, AND IN HARMONIOUS BALANCE WITH MY LIFE PLAN. THIS OR SOMETHING BETTER COMES TO ME NOW, AND I REMAIN ETERNALLY GRATEFUL.

I NOW ASK FOR COMPLETE UNDERSTANDING AND SUPPORT OF MY JOURNEY ON THE SPIRITUAL PATH BY THOSE WHO KNOW ME AND LOVE ME.

I NOW FORGIVE EVERYONE WHO CAN POSSIBLY NEED FORGIVENESS IN MY LIFE NOW. EVERYONE NOW FORGIVE ME.

I NOW AFFIRM MY GOOD, AND IT COMES TO ME IN THE PERFECT WAY, AT THE PERFECT TIME, FOR MY HIGHEST GOOD.

I AM NOW BALANCED AND IN HARMONY WITH THE UNIVERSE. THINGS COME TO ME EASILY NOW.

I NOW CREATE IN HARMONIOUS BALANCE WITH MY HIGHER SELF AND MY LIFE PLAN.

I NOW CALL IN MY TEACHERS, GUIDES, MASTERS AND ANGELS. I NOW EMBARK ON MY HIGHEST SPIRIT WORK, AND NOW ACCEPT AND APPRECIATE DIVINE SUPPORT AND GUIDANCE.

THE LOVING SPIRIT OF GOD NOW WORKS THROUGH ME TO BRING LOVE AND LIGHT TO ALL.

I AM GUIDED TO THE BEST COURSES, TEACHERS AND LEARNING OPPORTUNITIES FOR MY HIGHEST GROWTH, AND I NOW THRIVE AND EXCEL IN THIS ENVIRONMENT WHERE I AM LEARNING ON MANY LEVELS.

I NOW SEE AND ENVISION AN ENTIRELY NEW REALITY FOR MYSELF, FILLED WITH DIVINE LOVE.

THE LOVING SPIRIT NOW GUIDES ME WITH DREAMS AND VISIONS TO MY HIGHEST SPIRIT PATH, AND I REMAIN OPEN TO THESE MESSAGES. I NOW SEE INTO THE POSSIBILITIES AND DOORWAYS OF OPPORTUNITIES WHICH OPEN UP TO ME.

Chapter 10—Visioning

I NOW ENVISION AND EXPERIENCE A NEW PEACEFUL LOVING REALITY FOR MYSELF, FILLED WITH POSITIVE PEOPLE, MEANINGFUL LEARNING, AND LOVING RELATIONSHIPS.

I AM NOW A SWIRLING VORTEX OF ATTRACTION ENERGY, AND ATTRACT TO ME ONLY THAT WHICH IS FOR MY HIGHEST GOOD.

Chapter 11—The Flow of Energy

I NOW RELEASE TO THE UNIVERSE THOSE THINGS AND PEOPLE IN MY LIFE WHICH NO LONGER SERVE MY HIGHEST GOOD. I NOW BRING NEW PEOPLE AND SITUATIONS INTO MY LIFE. I AM NOW WITH THE RIGHT PEOPLE IN THE RIGHT WAY, AND IT FEELS GREAT!

I TRUST IN THE UNIVERSE TO PROVIDE APPROPRIATELY FOR ME NOW, IN A DIVINE WAY, FOR MY HIGHEST GOOD.

I NOW SURRENDER THE DETAILS OF THIS SITUATION TO SPIRIT. I NOW RELEASE AND TRUST IN THE UNIVERSE TO BRING THE PERFECT RESOLUTION, AT THE RIGHT TIME, IN THE RIGHT WAY.

I TRUST IT WILL BE SO. AND SO IT SHALL BE. AND SO IT IS!

I NOW ACCEPT MY UNCLAIMED GOOD. I NOW BRING TO ME AND MANIFEST THAT WHICH HAS BEEN HELD BACK. I NOW MANIFEST GLORIOUSLY IN MY LIFE NOW, AS I AM WORTHY AND DESERVING OF ALL THE ABUNDANCE THAT SPIRIT HAS FOR ME NOW.

I NOW THANK THE UNIVERSAL SPIRIT FOR SHOWING ME THE DIVINE WAY OF ALL THAT IS.

I NOW RELEASE ALL LIMITING BELIEFS FROM MY BEING. I NOW RECEIVE ALL THE UNIVERSE HAS FOR ME, APPROPRIATELY. ALL MY ACCUMULATED GOOD NOW COMES FORTH TO ME AND SHOWERS ME AS RICH BLESSINGS, AND I AM GRATEFUL.

I NOW RELEASE THE OLD, AND BRING NEW INTO MY LIFE.

I NOW TRUST IN THE UNIVERSE TO GUIDE ME IN ALL WAYS THAT ARE FOR MY HIGHEST GOOD.

I NOW MOVE TOWARD MY HIGHEST SPIRIT WORK, AND MY HEART SINGS WITH JOY. THOSE THINGS AND SITUATIONS THAT ARE NO LONGER FOR MY HIGHEST GOOD NOW SLIP AWAY AND OUT OF MY LIFE WITH EASE AND GRACE.

I NOW LET GO AND TRUST.

I NOW RELEASE ALL FEARS AND LIMITATIONS FROM MY BEING. I AM CONFIDENT IN MIND, BODY AND AFFAIRS. ALL THINGS COME EASILY TO ME NOW.

Chapter 12—Free Will

I NOW CHOOSE AND RISE UP TO THE HIGHEST AND MOST MAGNIFICENT EXPRESSION OF MY BEING. I SHED AND RID MYSELF OF LOWER LIMITING BELIEFS. I SEE THE WAY CLEARLY NOW, AND FOLLOW MY BLISS AND TRUE PATH.

I NOW PROCLAIM AND EXERCISE MY FREE WILL, AND INTEND AND AFFIRM ONLY THE HIGHEST PATH FOR ME.

IF A HIGHER PATH IS AVAILABLE TO ME NOW, I NOW SEE IT CLEARLY.

Chapter 13—Group Manifestation

I CHOOSE TO CONNECT NOW WITH MY HIGHEST SPIRIT GUIDES, TEACHERS AND MASTERS. I NOW MANIFEST GREATLY IN ACCORDANCE WITH MY DIVINE WILL AND THE PERFECT EXPRESSION OF MY BEING.

I NOW CONNECT WITH THOSE WHO CHOOSE TO CO-CREATE WITH ME AND WORK WITH ME TO ACHIEVE OUR COLLECTIVE GOALS AND GROUP VISION.

I AM NOW IN RELATIONSHIP WITH THE UNIVERSE, CREATING AND MANIFESTING WITH THE UNIVERSE AND UNIVERSAL ENERGY.

PLEASE DRAW TO ME THE PEOPLE WHO BELONG IN MY LIFE NOW, WHO WILL CO-CREATE WITH ME NOW IN A SYNERGISTIC CO-CREATIVE EFFORT. I NOW TAKE THE NEXT STEP. UNITE ME WITH THESE PEOPLE NOW.

GUIDE OUR GROUP AS WE WORK TOGETHER AS ONE AND CREATE WITH EASE AND GRACE.

BRING TO OUR GROUP THE GUIDES, MENTORS, LEADERS, FACILITATORS AND OTHERS WHO WOULD PARTICIPATE IN OUR MISSION, CREATING TOGETHER WITH US FOR THE GREATER GOOD.

I NOW ALIGN WITH MY GROUP, AND WE ACCOMPLISH GREAT THINGS TOGETHER.

I NOW FULLY EXPRESS MY PASSION AND ENTHUSIASM FOR MY MISSION.

Chapter 14—Workplace Manifestation

I NOW ALIGN WITH OTHERS IN MY GROUP FOR THE BEST POSSIBLE SYNERGY AND THE GREATER GOOD. WE NOW ACCOMPLISH GREAT THINGS TOGETHER AS ONE.

I NOW EMPOWER THOSE I WORK WITH TO BE AT THEIR BEST, AND THEY EMPOWER ME IN RETURN. I ACKNOWLEDGE THE DIVINITY IN EVERYONE I WORK WITH.

I AM WORTHY. NO ONE HAS A RIGHT TO FORCE THEIR FREE WILL ON ME. I AM A VALUED, WORTHY, LOVING, COMPASSIONATE PERSON.

Chapter 15—Prosperity and Abundance

I AM WEALTHY IN MIND, BODY AND AFFAIRS. I EXPRESS DIVINE ABUNDANCE IN MY LIFE NOW. I RICHLY DESERVE AND ALLOW ALL THAT THE WORLD HAS FOR ME NOW.

I NOW EXPRESS COMPLETE LOVING GRATITUDE FOR ALL I AM, ALL I HAVE, ALL I KNOW, ALL I FEEL, ALL I UNDERSTAND, AND ALL I LOVE.

I NOW AFFIRM ABUNDANCE. I NOW BRING IN MY UNCLAIMED GOOD. I GLADLY ACCEPT AND RECEIVE ALL THE ABUNDANCE WHICH FLOWS TO ME NOW. I AM RICH IN ABUNDANCE NOW.

I NOW ATTRACT CONTINUED AND EXPANDING PROSPERITY AND ABUNDANCE TO ME, KNOWING THAT THERE IS AN UNLIMITED SUPPLY IN THE UNIVERSE AVAILABLE TO ME NOW.

I REMAIN ETERNALLY GRATEFUL FOR ALL THE LOVE AND ABUNDANCE IN MY LIFE NOW, AS IT POURS FORTH TO ME IN GREAT SUPPLY.

IN EVERY DAY IN EVERY WAY I ATTRACT ABUNDANCE AND PROSPERITY TO ME.

Chapter 16—Health

ALL THE CELLS OF MY BODY ARE BATHED DAILY WITH THE HEALING WHITE LIGHT ENERGY OF SPIRIT. I GET BETTER AND STRONGER EVERY DAY.

I NOW HEAL MYSELF IN ALL WAYS AND ON ALL LEVELS.

I AM WHOLE AND HEALTHY IN MIND, BODY AND AFFAIRS. I WELCOME EACH NEW DAY WITH GRATITUDE AND THANKFULNESS.

I NOW MANIFEST VIBRANT HEALTH AND LIFE FORCE ENERGY THROUGHOUT MY BEING. I NOW FULLY RELEASE ALL PHYSICAL, MENTAL AND EMOTIONAL PATTERNS AND ENERGIES THAT ARE NO LONGER CONTRIBUTING TO MY GOOD.

VIBRANT HEALTH AND BOUNDLESS ENERGY NOW FLOW THROUGH ME AS I CONNECT WITH THE HEALING POWER OF UNIVERSAL LIFE FORCE ENERGY.

EVERY DAY, IN EVERY WAY, I'M GETTING BETTER AND BETTER.

I NOW LOVE OPENLY AND COMPLETELY, AND RECEIVE LOVE OPENLY AND COMPLETELY.

I AM NOW HEALED ON ALL LEVELS IN ALL WAYS.

I AM NOW IN PERFECT HEALTH, ACHIEVING LEVELS OF HEALTH AND WELLNESS THAT AMAZE ME.

I AM WELL, I AM WHOLE, I AM STRONG, I AM HEALTHY.

I HAVE ALL THE ENERGY I NEED TO ACCOMPLISH MY GOALS AND TO FULFILL MY DESIRES.

GOD'S LOVE HEALS ME AND MAKES ME WHOLE.

I AM FULL OF VITALITY AND ENERGY. I AM VIBRANT AND ALIVE, AND LOOK FORWARD TO NEW OPPORTUNITIES IN MY LIFE.

Chapter 17—Gratitude

I NOW EXPRESS COMPLETE GRATITUDE FOR ALL THE WONDERFUL PEOPLE, MEANINGFUL RELATIONSHIPS, LEARNING SITUATIONS, WONDROUS OPPORTUNITIES, AND UNCONDITIONAL LOVE IN MY LIFE. THANK YOU, THANK YOU, THANK YOU.

THIS IS A TIME OF GREAT BLESSINGS. ABUNDANCE AND PROSPERITY FLOWS TO ME NOW IN A NEVERENDING WAVE. I REMAIN ETERNALLY GRATEFUL. THANK YOU, THANK YOU, THANK YOU.

I AM TRULY GRATEFUL FOR ALL THAT HAS OCCURRED IN MY LIFE AND THE LOVE, LEARNING, GROWTH AND INSIGHT IT HAS PROVIDED ME WITH. I AM ETERNALLY GRATEFUL. THANK YOU, THANK YOU, THANK YOU.

I REMAIN GRATEFUL TO THE UNIVERSAL SPIRIT FOR THE ALIGNMENT AND RESTORATION OF MY DIVINE SPIRIT PATH.

THANK YOU GOD.

I AM GRATEFUL FOR THE GIFTS I RECEIVE EACH MOMENT OF EVERY DAY. I AM THANKFUL FOR ALL THAT I AM RECEIVING.

I REMAIN ETERNALLY GRATEFUL FOR EVERYONE AND EVERYTHING IN MY LIFE NOW. THANK YOU, THANK YOU, THANK YOU.

Chapter 18—Love

I NOW OPEN MY HEART CHAKRA WIDE. I AM FULL OF UNLIMITED LOVE. I NOW LOVE UNCONDITIONALLY, OPENLY, AND COMPLETELY, IN BLISS. LOVE FLOWS THROUGH ME NOW, IN A NEVERENDING WAVE.

I LOVE MYSELF, HONESTLY, OPENLY, UNCONDITIONALLY, JUST THE WAY I AM.

I FORGIVE MYSELF FOR NOT BEING EVERYTHING I THINK I SHOULD BE. I NOW FULLY ACCEPT AND LOVE MYSELF THE WAY I AM.

I BATHE IN THE UNCONDITIONAL LOVE OF SPIRIT, AND IT RADIATES FROM ME AT ALL TIMES.

I NOW LOVE ETERNALLY, ENDLESSLY, AND WITHOUT LIMITS. MY BOUNDLESS LOVE TRANSCENDS LIFETIMES AND DIMENSIONS. MY LOVE GROWS EVERMORE, WITH EACH PASSING MOMENT OF MY LIFE.

I NOW OPEN MY HEART WIDE, AND LOVE OTHERS COMPLETELY AND UNCONDITIONALLY, KNOWING THAT LOVE HEALS ALL.

I EXPRESS MY LOVE FREELY, KNOWING THAT AS I GIVE LOVE, I AM INSTANTLY SUPPLIED WITH MORE.

I FEEL UNLIMITED UNCONDITIONAL UNIVERSAL LOVE POUR FORTH FROM MY HIGHER SELF, ANGELS, AND SPIRIT GUIDES TO ME, AND I SHARE THAT LOVE WITH ALL THOSE AROUND ME.

LOVE NOW ENCOMPASSES MY BEING FULLY AND COMPLETELY. LOVE WORKS THROUGH ME AND POSITIVELY AFFECTS ALL ASPECTS OF MY LIFE.

I AM A VESSEL IN ALIGNMENT WITH SOURCE. I AM A HUMAN FULL OF LOVE. LOVE POURS FORTH FROM MY BEING, NOW AND EVERMORE.

I AM A RADIATING CENTER OF DIVINE LOVE. I NOW EXPRESS LOVE TO ALL THOSE I MEET. I RADIATE LOVE TO ALL PERSONS, PLACES AND THINGS. DIVINE LOVE IS WORKING THROUGH ME NOW.

I LOVE MYSELF COMPLETELY, AND I GIVE AND RECEIVE LOVE EASILY AND JOYFULLY.

I AM LOVE.

Chapter 19—Enlightenment

I AM ETERNALLY GRATEFUL FOR BEING SHOWN THE WONDERS OF LIFE, LOVE AND SPIRIT. I NOW LIVE FULLY IN THE MOMENT. I AM FULL OF UNCONDITIONAL LOVE FOR MANKIND.

I NOW ACHIEVE A STATE OF MASTERY AND ENLIGHTENMENT, AND POSITIVELY SHIFT THE WORLD AROUND ME.

I NOW EXPRESS GRATITUDE FOR ALL DIVINE EXPRESSIONS OF MY LIFE. I AM COMPLETELY GRATEFUL FOR ALL THINGS THAT HAVE TRANSPIRED IN MY LIFE, AND ALL THE DIVINE LOVE, GUIDANCE AND SUPPORT I AM RECEIVING.

I NOW APPROACH LIFE IN AN ENLIGHTENED WAY, AND SEE WITH CLARITY.

I LIVE FULLY IN THE PRESENT, FULLY IN THE NOW, FULLY IN MY TRUE POWER.

Chapter 20—Personal Growth

I NOW RELEASE ALL FEELINGS OF ATTACHMENT AND LOSS. I NOW RELEASE THIS SITUATION TO THE HEALING LOVE OF SPIRIT. I GIVE THANKS FOR THE DIVINE RESTORATION OF MY AFFAIRS AT THIS TIME.

I LET GO AND TRUST. ALL IS OCCURING IN DIVINE PERFECTION.

I NOW TRUST FULLY AND COMPLETELY IN SPIRIT TO BRING FORTH A DIVINE SOLUTION.

I GIVE IT UP TO GOD.

I NOW ACCELERATE MY GROWTH PATH. I CHOOSE TO LEARN AND GROW QUICKLY NOW.

I NOW ASSUME MY ROLE AS CREATOR, AND FULLY EXPRESS THAT ASPECT OF MY BEING.

I NOW FULLY EMBRACE AND LIVE MY TRUE DIVINITY, CONNECTED TO SPIRIT, BEING ONE WITH ALL THAT IS.

Chapter 21—Growing in Your Relationships

I AM READY TO RECEIVE FULL LIGHT ACTIVATION. I AM FULLY OPEN. BRING ME FULL LIGHT ENERGY. GIVE ME THE MAXIMUM I CAN INTEGRATE AT THIS TIME.

I AM WORTHY NOW, OF ALL THINGS, OPPORTUNITIES AND SITUATIONS.

I NOW SEE THE SYNCHRONICITIES IN LIFE THAT PRESENT THEMSELVES TO ME, AND ACT ON THESE MESSAGES FROM SPIRIT.

I NOW ATTRACT TO ME PEOPLE WHO SUPPORT MY HIGHEST GOOD, PEOPLE WHO ARE KIND, FRIENDLY AND HELPFUL. I WORK WITH THEM IN CO-CREATIVE EFFORTS IN HARMONIOUS COCREATION.

I AM A POWERFUL AND AWARE HUMAN BEING, ATTRACTING PEOPLE, SITUATIONS AND OPPORTUNITIES TO ME FOR MY HIGHEST GOOD.

Chapter 22—Raising Your Vibration, Sensitivity and Awareness

I NOW CHOOSE THOSE THINGS IN MY LIFE WHICH RAISE MY VIBRATION AND SUPPORT MY HIGHEST GROWTH.

I NOW EVOLVE INTO A HIGHER PLACE OF BEING.

I NOW BLESS THE DIFFICULT PARTS OF LIFE AND DIFFICULT EVENTS OF THE WORLD, AND RELEASE THEM TO THE UNIVERSE. I LEARN AND GROW.

I NOW EMBRACE AND LIVE FULLY IN NATURE, MY ENVIRONMENT, AND MYSELF. I CHOOSE WHAT I WANT IN MY LIFE, AND I AM GRATEFUL FOR IT.

Chapter 23—The New Age

I NOW BEGIN A WHOLE NEW PART OF MY LIFE FILLED WITH MAGICAL MANIFESTATIONS, ASTOUNDING MIRACLES, AMAZING SYNCHRONICITIES, AND WONDROUS EASE AND GRACE. I AM A SHINING EXAMPLE OF CO-CREATION AND MAGNIFICENCE IN ACTION AND BEING.

I NOW CHOOSE AN ACCELERATED GROWTH PATH. I NOW LEARN AND EVOLVE QUICKLY. I NOW EXPERIENCE PEOPLE, SITUATIONS AND OPPORTUNITIES TO GROW AMAZINGLY QUICKLY, WITH EASE AND GRACE. I NOW FOLLOW MY JOY, AND FOLLOW MY BLISS.

I NOW MANIFEST MIRACLES AND SYNCHRONICITIES WITH EASE. I MANIFEST MULTIDIMENSIONALLY, ON ALL LEVELS, IN ALL WAYS, FOR THE GOOD OF ALL.

MY HEART SINGS WITH JOY, AS I HAVE PUT SPIRIT IN THE DRIVER'S SEAT.

I NOW MOVE TO MY DIVINE SPIRIT WORK.

I NOW EVOLVE INTO A HIGHER STATE OF BEING.

I AM A HUMAN FULL OF LOVE, LIVING, BEING, AND LOVING.

I AM A DIVINE SPARK IN THE EYE OF GOD.

I AM DIVINE LOVE.

RECOMMENDED READING

You Can Heal Your Life by Louise L. Hay, Hay House

Creating Money: Keys to Abundance by Sanaya Roman and Duane Packer, H.J. Kramer, Inc.

Bridges to Reality by Arnold M. Patent, Celebration Publishing

You Can Have It All by Arnold M. Patent, Celebration Publishing

Ask and It Is Given: Learning to Manifest Your Desires by Esther and Jerry Hicks, Hay House

Creating True Prosperity by Shakti Gawain, Nataraj Publishing

Open Your Mind To Prosperity by Catherine Ponder, DeVorss & Company

Personal Power Through Awareness by Sanaya Roman, H.J. Kramer, Inc.

Wealth Beyond Reason by Bob Doyle, Boundless Living Publishing

Seth Speaks by Jane Roberts, Bantam Books

Notes From The Universe by Mike Dooley, Totally Unique Thoughts

TERMS DEFINED

Abundance—The conscious awareness that sufficient sources and resources exist.

Adam Kadmon Man—The next form of human which we are evolving to. A higher dimensional human who integrates and merges the light body into physical form.

Affirmation—A verbal or written statement of intention

Ascension—Personal spiritual dimensional transformation

ATP (Adenosine Triphosphate)—A coenzyme and one of the most important compounds in the metabolism of all organisms, ATP serves as the major energy source within the cell to drive a number of biological processes such as photosynthesis, muscle contraction, and the synthesis of proteins. ATP serves as the immediate source of energy for the mechanical work performed by muscle.

Axiotonal—Electrical lines of light and meridians which connect the physical human body to the human light body

Cellular consciousness—The conscious awareness that memories that are held within the cells of the physical body.

Chakra—A series of centers of spiritual energy in the human body.

Collective consciousness—The combined awareness of two or more beings.

Consciousness—A defined state of awareness.

Co-creation—The act or state of creating a life journey in partnership with the Creator's energy. On the Earth plane each human co-creates as part of the Creator experiencing Itself.

Conscious creation—The act of knowingly manifesting by controlling your thoughts and thought processes.

Christ Consciousness—The divine energy of Spirit expressed and experienced as a conscious feeling and state of being.

Divine Oneness—the concept that we live in a world where everything is connected to everything else. Everything we do, say, think and believe affects others and the universe around us.

Discernment—The act or process of exhibiting keen insight and good judgment about something that is not easily known or understood.

DNA (Deoxyribonucleic Acid)—the molecule that carries genetic information in all living systems

Ego—A collection of beliefs in limitations (fears) that allows for the perceived illusion of separation from the Creator. Also known as the "veil" or "veils." For each human incarnation the essential self creates an ego so that the human aspect may participate in an evolutionary journey on the Earth plane.

Etheric (ethers, ethereal, etheric fabric)—A reference to the living spirit force that permeates and surrounds all beings. Light, spirit-like in form, without real physical form.

Higher Self—A Spirit-like part of you that is highly evolved. Also called the God-self, oversoul, inner-being, inner-self, or expanded self. It is the sum of all your lifetimes, past, present, and future.

Incarnate—To be born into a physical body, to be human.

Junk DNA—DNA that does not code for proteins or their regulation but constitutes approximately 95 percent of the human genome.

Karma—A deed or action that has consequences, the effects of a person's actions, a natural, impersonal law of moral cause and effect.

Law of Attraction—A universal law which states that you attract energetically into your life whatever energy you radiate or emanate. This law describes the experience of drawing to you the people, situations, and life lessons that you are choosing to experience.

Life contract (life plan)—Your agreement with yourself about what you would attempt to complete in this lifetime, and the life lessons you would learn in doing so.

Lightworker—A person whose awareness focuses on helping to shift the consciousness of the planet positively

Material plane—The third dimension, our physical realm. A place in which human beings can evolve through a journey of experiences.

Merkabah (also spelled Merkaba)—The divine light vehicle used by the Masters to connect with and reach those in tune with the higher realms. The Mer-Ka-Ba is the vehicle of Light mentioned in the Bible by Ezekiel. The Spirit / Body surrounded by counter-rotating fields of Light, (wheels within wheels), spirals of energy as in DNA, which transports Spirit / Body from one dimension to another.

Mitochondria—A spherical or elongated organelle in the cytoplasm of nearly all eukaryotic cells, containing genetic material and many enzymes important for cell metabolism, including those responsible for the conversion of food to usable energy.

Multidimensional—Of, relating to, or having several dimensions.

New Age—A predicted time into which mankind's consciousness evolves dimensionally.

Newtonian Physics (classical physics)—The science dealing with the description of the positions of objects in space under the action of forces as a function of time. In 1687, Isaac Newton published his *Principia*, which presents the basic laws of motion, the law of gravitation, the theory of tides, and the theory of the solar system.

Passion—The core energy by which you feel the presence of your own Creator light. Passion is the realization that you are a limitless being of light and is the force that allows your life journey to continually evolve.

Quantum physics, quantum mechanics—Quantum mechanics is the study of mechanical systems whose dimensions are close to or below the atomic scale, such as molecules, atoms, electrons, protons and other subatomic particles. Quantum theory generalizes classical mechanics and provides accurate descriptions for many previously unexplained phenomena.

Reincarnation—The belief that a person's soul returns to earth multiple times in different human bodies in order to learn and grow, so that life-skills may be gained, karma can be cleansed, and the God within can be discovered. Through good works in each life or through enlightenment, the soul purifies his spirit and attains unity with "God," which is everything that exists.

Sacred geometry—a mathematical order to the intrinsic nature of the universe. A belief system attributing a religious or cultural value to many of the fundamental forms of space and time. The religious and spiritual use of geometry and ratio, such as in the Golden Ratio, the star tedrahedron as applied to crop circles, the great pyramid, and Stonehenge

Scalar wave antennae—A type of human energetic antennae comprised of chakras number 8-12 which are located in and above the head, which access and are receptive to higher dimensional vibrations.

Sixth sense—Intuition and "knowing." Humans are not limited to the five senses; all have access to the sixth sense.

Third dimension—A physical, material dimension of reality, such as the Earth plane. This dimension is based upon a duality system of yin and yang, in which everything appears to have an opposite.

Veil of illusion—A figurative screen which separates the third dimension from the higher dimensional planes.

Vibration—The frequency or frequencies of oscillation of all sound and light. Everything in creation is a vibrating pattern of energy. All matter, thoughts and emotions are energies vibrating at particular frequencies. Each sound, thing, and even thought has its own vibrational frequency, unique unto itself.